162-0

A METS PERFECT SEASON

HOWIE KARPIN

TRIUMPH
BOOKS

Library of Congress Cataloging-in-Publication Data

Karpin, Howie, 1954-
  162-0 : a Mets perfect season / Howie Karpin.
    p. cm.
  ISBN 978-1-60078-532-0
  1. New York Mets (Baseball team)-History. I. Title. II. Title: One hundred sixty two to zero.
  GV875.N45K37 2011
  796.357'64097471-dc22

                          2010043595

This book is available in quantity at special discounts for your group or organization. For further information, contact:

Triumph Books
542 South Dearborn Street
Suite 750
Chicago, Illinois 60605
(312) 939–3330
Fax (312) 663–3557
www.triumphbooks.com

Printed in U.S.A.

ISBN: 978-1-60078-532-0

Editorial and page production by Red Line Editorial

Photos courtesy of AP Images unless indicated otherwise

THIS BOOK IS DEDICATED TO THE MEMORY OF
BILL SHANNON.

CONTENTS

FOREWORD

Just the thought of going through an undefeated baseball season boggles the mind because the chances of finishing with a record of 162–0 are infinitesimal.

The Mets established a club record in 1986, when the eventual World Champions won 108 regular-season games.

That falls 54 games short of an undefeated season, yet that's considered one of the best single-season win totals in baseball history.

The nature of the game—the grind of a 162-game season—does not lend itself to team perfection as it does in the National Football League or college football.

There have been undefeated teams in both pro and college football, but not in baseball. Nor is it likely to ever happen. But within the boundaries of this book, it does happen to the Mets.

In nearly 50 years of existence, the New York Mets have provided many memorable regular-season moments.

The Mets are reknowned for their remarkable run to the World Championship in 1969, when they were 100–1 longshots going into the season. It's the regular season that the fans thoroughly enjoyed, as they "lived" and never really "died" as the Mets became the talk of the town.

In the final six weeks of the 1973 season, the Mets made a miraculous run to the National League's East Division title and came up one game short of a second World Series title.

The 1986 World Championship season's bookmark moment came in Game 6 of the World Series against the Boston Red Sox. The Mets rose like a phoenix when they were down to their last out and rallied to win a game that ended with Bill Buckner's infamous error at first base. That year, the Mets rolled through the National League's regular season, providing the franchise with a plethora of memorable games.

Baseball's regular season is like no other.

There's the grind of playing nearly every day over six months. Some games, you just don't have it. No matter how hard you push yourself, no matter if you execute every baseball skill correctly, you can still come up on the short end.

You can't run out the clock in baseball, but you can run out of time. In this instance, time is the calendar.

The 162-game schedule pans out over a period of 180 days, from April to October.

As the games dwindle down to a precious few, you're racing the calendar.

In this book, time is no problem.

The history of the Mets was thoroughly researched to put together a mythical, undefeated season.

Of course, even in real life, you need the players to be successful, so throughout the course of the book, you'll be reminded of those who helped set the course of franchise history.

Marquee names like Tom Seaver, Jerry Koosman, Cleon Jones, Tommie Agee, Bud Harrelson, Tug McGraw, Donn Clendenon, Rusty Staub, Darryl Strawberry, Dwight Gooden, Keith Hernandez, Ron Darling, Gary Carter, Mookie Wilson, Len Dykstra, Al Leiter, John Franco, Mike Piazza and Jose Reyes are all prominently mentioned.

We can't forget the "lesser known" Mets who made huge contributions.

Those who come to mind include Jerry Grote, Ed Kranepool, Al Weis, Ron Swoboda, Wayne Garrett, Ed Charles, John Milner, Lee Mazzilli, Ray Knight, Wally Backman, Tim Teufel, Sid Fernandez, Jesse Orosco, Robin Ventura, John Olerud and Edgardo Alfonzo.

Some of the all-time greats have spent some time in a Mets uniform, including Willie Mays, Warren Spahn, Richie Ashburn, Nolan Ryan, Rickey Henderson and Pedro Martinez.

Lest we forget some of the managers including Gil Hodges, Yogi Berra, Dave Johnson, Bobby Valentine and Willie Randolph.

Maybe I get a mention as well.

As you go through the season, enjoy the memories of some great Met games.

—David Wright

INTRODUCTION

Baseball has always been a passion in my life. I wasn't blessed with the talent to be an active participant on the field or in the front office, but I've been fortunate to be around the game since 1980.

While I religiously follow today's baseball, I've always enjoyed looking back at baseball's past. Browsing the old box scores or reading some of the newspaper accounts from past games was a labor of love as I was putting this book together.

I've covered the New York Mets as a reporter for the past 30 years and for the past 12, I have been an official scorer who has worked games at Shea Stadium, and presently, Citi Field.

In 2011, the Mets will be participating in their 50th year of existence as a member of the National League. They've provided not only their loyal fans, but baseball fans everywhere, with a rich history of memorable games and events.

Many all-time great players have worn the Mets uniform. While there are those who were great while wearing the white jersey with the blue pinstripes and 'METS' in script across the chest on an upward slant, some players had a singular moment in the sun and they get to share the marquee.

From the very first season in 1962 to the miraculous championship year of 1969, to a second world title in 1986, right up until a new era at Citi Field, the Mets have put together a glorious history in their own right.

There are many famous moments from the first 49 years that are spotlighted within these pages, but the less memorable moments get their due as well. This book highlights all those moments and more. I hope that you enjoy the read as much as I enjoyed putting it together.

MARCH/APRIL

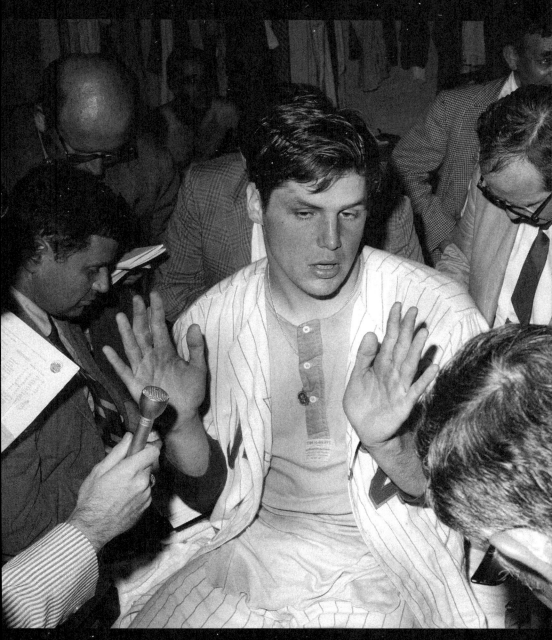

No Mets pitcher has ever thrown a no-hitter, but Tom Seaver came close. Seaver talks to reporters in the locker room after he threw a one-hitter against the Chicago Cubs in 1969.

Agbayani's Pinch Grand Slam Ends it Tokyo

Benny Agbayani's pinch-hit grand slam in the top of the 11th inning gave the Mets a 5–1 victory over the Chicago Cubs in a regular-season game that was played at the Tokyo Dome in Japan.

Some 55,000 fans were on hand to watch the Mets stage a two-out rally in the 11th that led to the deciding blow off Cubs pitcher Danny Young, who was making his major league debut.

Todd Zeile started the rally with a two-out single. Walks to Rey Ordonez and Melvin Mora followed. Agbayani then drove one over the 406-foot sign in center field to snap a 1–1 tie and earn him the replica of a shogun helmet, which is a tradition in Japan that goes to the star of the game.

The Mets took a 1–0 lead in the top of the fifth inning (the Mets were the designated road team) off Cubs starter Kyle Farnsworth. Zeile and Ordonez led off with back-to-back walks. Mets pitcher Rick Reed sacrificed the runners to second and third base. Rickey Henderson's sacrifice fly then drove in the first run.

> ## At a Glance
> **WP:** Cook (1–0)
>
> **HR:** Agbayani (1)
>
> **Key stat:** Reed 8 IP, 1 unearned run

The Cubs answered with an unearned run in the fifth off Reed and the game remained 1–1 until the 11th.

Afterward, the humble Agbayani downplayed his heroics.

"It's only one game," he said. "It's not like I did it for 50 games."

Castillo Comes Through in the Clutch

Mets backup catcher Alberto Castillo was sitting around for nearly four-and-a-half hours when he finally got the call.

Castillo delivered a pinch-hit, walk-off RBI single with two out in the bottom of the 14th inning to give the Mets a thrilling 1–0 win over the Philadelphia Phillies at Shea Stadium before a crowd of 49,142.

Castillo was the only position player left on the bench, so manager Bobby Valentine used him to bat for pitcher Turk Wendell.

With runners on first and third base and two outs in the 14th, Phillies reliever Ricky Bottalico threw a 3–2 fastball and Castillo delivered the game-winning single to right to score Brian McRae from second base.

Afterward, Castillo said getting the count full worked in his favor.

"He (Bottalico) paid for it," Castillo said. "I think he was getting too tired."

Both starting pitchers were brilliant. Curt Schilling threw eight scoreless innings while striking out nine for the Phillies. Right-hander Bobby Jones put up six scoreless innings on his pitching line.

The Phillies had a major threat in the top of the eighth. With runners on first and third against Mets reliever Greg McMichael, Mike Lieberthal lined out to third. Valentine replaced McMichael with lefty Dennis Cook, who got out of it when he struck out Rico Brogna, a former Met.

Castillo was not known for his hitting, but he stood out on this day.

"I believe I can be a good hitter," he said, "but sometimes I try to do too much."

This time, it was just enough.

At a Glance

WP: Wendell (1–0)

Key stat: Six Mets pitchers combine for 14 scoreless innings

New Faces Don't Shine, But They Bring a Win

The Mets debuted four new players but it was the incumbents who did the damage. Left-handed pitcher Al Leiter allowed just an unearned run in six innings of work and Edgardo Alfonzo had three hits in a 6–2 win over the Pittsburgh Pirates at Shea Stadium.

A crowd of 53,734 watched first baseman Mo Vaughn and second baseman Roberto Alomar make their debuts with the Mets. Left fielder Roger Cedeno and right fielder Jeromy Burnitz were back for their second tour. Cedeno played for the Mets in 1999 and Burnitz in 1993–94. The foursome was a combined 2-for-17 with three RBIs.

Vaughn was 0-for-5 for the first time to begin a season since 2000.

"As long as you win the game, that's the bottom line," the 6-foot-1, 225-pound Vaughn said.

> ## At a Glance
> **WP:** Leiter (1–0)
> **HR:** Payton (1)
> **Key stat:** Alfonzo 3-for-4

The Mets didn't exactly pound the Pirates. Six of their nine hits were of the "bloop" variety, but it was enough to get the job done.

The Mets scored three runs in the second inning off starter Ron Villone on three "soft" hits, a walk and a hit batsman.

Mets center fielder Jay Payton took the Pirates' lefty deep in the fourth inning with a solo shot for a 4–1 lead.

David Weathers and Armando Benitez gave the Mets three scoreless innings in relief of Leiter, who was pleased to get off on the right foot.

"All the expectation and anticipation for this year is very high," Leiter said, "not only for all the fans but for all the guys in the clubhouse."

Mets Make It a Whitewash in Miami

The Mets pounded out 17 hits en route to a 13–0 thrashing of the Marlins at Dolphin Stadium before a crowd of 13,720.

David Wright and Ryan Church each had a home run and three hits while Carlos Beltran had three doubles, although one should have been ruled a home run.

David Wright, right, and Ryan Church, left, combined for two home runs and six hits in a 13–0 win over the Florida Marlins on April 2, 2008.

The television replay rule was not yet in effect so Beltran's blast was never reviewed. However, the second-base umpire who was closest to the play, Rick Reed, thought it was a home run. (The other three umpires eventually overruled Reed.)

"That's why I believe in the replay," Beltran said. "You could have at least one a game for each team. Right now, it didn't mean anything because we were ahead by five runs. But what if we were losing by two runs or one run? That can cost a game."

(Major League Baseball instituted the "instant replay rule" on Aug. 28, 2008.)

Oliver Perez gave the Mets six scoreless innings for the win.

"I'd like to bottle that and put it away," Mets manager Willie Randolph said. "(Perez) was awesome tonight. He was in a zone and threw his off speed pitches where he wanted. All his pitches looked crisp. He stayed in his rhythm and didn't freelance like he can do."

The Mets took a 3–0 lead in the second inning on an RBI from Carlos Delgado, followed by a two-run homer by Church.

Wright's three-run homer was the big blow in a five-run sixth inning that blew the game wide open.

"I feel good at the plate and you've got to take advantage of it when you feel that way," Wright said. "This can be a fickle game."

At a Glance

WP: Perez (1–0)

HR: Church (1), Wright (1)

Key stat: Wright 3-for-5, 3 RBIs; Beltran 3 doubles

3B David Wright

David Wright has been the Mets' starting third baseman since he made his major league debut on July 21, 2004.

Wright is a five-time All-Star, two-time Gold Glove winner and a two-time National League Silver Slugger award winner.

The Norfolk, Va., native is one of 34 players who have joined the "30-30" club (30 home runs and 30 stolen bases in the same season).

Wright accomplished the feat during the 2007 season, when he hit 30 home runs and had 34 stolen bases.

The 28-year-old third baseman tied Mike Piazza's club mark of 124 RBIs during the 2008 season and he became the club's all-time leader in doubles when he passed Ed Kranepool's total of 225 early in the 2010 season.

On April 13, 2009, Wright had the first Mets hit at Citi Field—a first-inning double—and he hit the first Mets home run in the fifth inning— a three-run shot off the Padres' Walter Silva.

Ventura's Homer Ends Hex at 'the Ted'

Robin Ventura's second two-run home run of the game in the top of the 10th inning lifted the Mets past the Atlanta Braves 6–4 before a crowd of 42,117 at Turner Field.

The Mets came into the game having lost 18 of 21 at "the Ted."

With two outs in the 10th, Ventura took Kerry Ligtenberg's fastball and deposited it into the bleachers in right field for a two-run lead. Tsuyoshi Shinjo, who was on first base with his first major league hit, scored ahead of Ventura. (Shinjo made his major league debut as a pinch runner in the eighth inning when he ran for Benny Agbayani.)

It was a battle of southpaws as Al Leiter took the mound for the Mets against Tom Glavine. Leiter tossed seven solid innings, allowing two runs on six hits. After the game, Leiter reflected on the Mets' inability to consistently win games at Turner Field.

"You don't want to fall into, 'How are they going to win this?'" Leiter said. "We've had some pretty wacky ways of losing here."

Ventura's two-run homer in the eighth (also with Shinjo on first) off Braves reliever John Rocker snapped a 2-2 tie.

Atlanta tied the game 4–4 in the bottom of the eighth on a Rafael Furcal RBI double and an RBI single from "noted Met killer" Brian Jordan.

"A lot of things are going to happen in a Mets and Braves game," Mets third baseman Edgardo Alfonzo said. "They're going to be tight games, they're going to be close games. That's why you have to prepare for that. That's the way it's been the last couple of years. It's been exciting."

The Mets took a 2–0 lead in the first inning off the future Met on a two-run homer by Mike

Mets	AB	R	H	RBI
Agbayani lf	1	0	0	0
Shinjo pr-lf	1	2	1	0
Alfonzo 2b	5	1	1	0
Ventura 3b	5	2	2	4
Piazza c	5	1	1	2
Zeile 3b	3	0	1	0
Payton cf	3	0	1	0
Hamilton rf	3	0	0	0
Perez rf	1	0	0	0
Ordonez ss	3	0	0	0
Leiter p	3	0	0	0
Franco p	0	0	0	0
Wendell p	0	0	0	0
Cook p	0	0	0	0
Harris ph	1	0	0	0
Benitez p	0	0	0	0
Totals	34	6	7	6

Braves	AB	R	H	RBI
Furcal ss	5	2	2	1
Veras 2b	4	0	0	0
A Jones cf	5	0	1	0
C Jones 3b	4	0	2	1
Jordan rf	4	0	1	1
Lopez c	4	1	1	1
Surhoff lf	4	0	1	0
Helms 1b	3	0	0	0
Rocker p	0	0	0	0
Abbott ph	1	0	0	0
Ligtenberg p	0	0	0	0
Glavine p	2	0	0	0
Martinez 1b	2	1	1	0
Totals	38	4	9	4

NYM	2	0	0	0	0	0	2	0	2	-	6	7	0
ATL	1	0	0	0	0	1	2	0	0	-	4	9	0

Mets	IP	H	R	ER	BB	SO
Leiter	7	6	2	2	0	6
Franco	0	2	2	2	0	0
Wendell	1	1	0	0	0	0
Cook W (1-0)	1	0	0	0	0	1
Benitez S (1)	1	0	0	0	0	0
Totals	10	9	4	4	0	7

Braves	IP	H	R	ER	BB	SO
Glavine	7.1	3	3	3	6	2
Rocker	1.2	2	1	1	0	2
Ligtenberg L (0-1)	1	2	2	2	0	1
Totals	10	7	6	6	6	5

DP—New York; Atlanta 2. 2B—New York Alfonzo; Atlanta Surhoff, Furcal. HR—New York Ventura 2 (1,2), Piazza (1); Atlanta Lopez (1). HBP—Atlanta Veras. LOB—New York 4; Atlanta 5. SB—Atlanta C Jones. Attendance: 42,117.

2B Edgardo Alfonzo

Edgardo Alfonzo was one of the Mets' best hitters during the late 1990s and into the early 2000s.

The native of Venezuela played eight seasons with the Mets and ranks in the club's all-time top 10 lists in 15 offensive categories.

Alfonzo set a club record when he went 6-for-6 against the Astros in Houston (see Aug. 30, 1999).

During the 2000 National League Championship Series against St. Louis, Alfonzo batted .444 with eight hits and four RBIs.

In the 1999 National League division series vs. Arizona, Alfonzo hit two home runs in Game 1, including a grand slam, and drove in a club-record-tying five runs.

The versatile Alfonzo played third and second base during his Mets tenure. He is the Mets' all-time leader in several postseason categories, including games played, hits, doubles, RBIs and runs scored.

Piazza. Atlanta got one back in the first and then tied the game in the seventh on a solo home run by Javy Lopez.

In a mild surprise, Ventura batted third against the left-hander Glavine, ahead of Piazza. Ventura had batted third only five times the previous season.

"Robin's batting third to get Glavine out of his rhythm before he gets to Mike," Mets manager Bobby Valentine said.

Shinjo not only recorded his first big-league hit, he made a nice catch on a Dave Martinez liner to left field to send the game into extra innings.

Coming into the game, the Mets' numbers at Turner Field were staggering. Since the Braves began play at their new ballpark in 1997, the Mets were 6–21, including 0–6 in 1998.

An extra-inning win at Turner Field was a good start toward turning things around in Atlanta.

"They're a good team and they know we're a good team," Valentine said. "We're starting to mold the character of this team again."

Kent Takes Advantage of Windy Wrigley

All you had to say about this one was: "The wind was blowing out at Wrigley."

The Mets beat the Cubs 12–8 thanks to Jeff Kent's four-hit day, but it was also a game in which Dwight Gooden gave up seven runs (five earned) on 11 hits in 5 ²/₃ innings, yet got a win. The 1985 National League Cy Young Award winner also made it a memorable day for one Tuffy Rhodes, a career minor leaguer who hit three home runs off Gooden.

At a Glance

WP: Gooden (1–0)

HR: Vizcaino (1), Hundley (1), Kent (1)

Key stat: Kent 4-for-5, HR, 2 RBIs

A crowd of 38,413 that included first lady Hillary Clinton watched the teams put up 20 runs on 30 hits against eight different pitchers.

Rhodes came up in the sixth inning against Mets left-hander Eric Hillman with a chance at a fourth consecutive home run, but he walked. The Cubs center fielder and leadoff batter completed his career day with a single off Mets closer John Franco in the ninth.

"We made him a legend," Mets manager Dallas Green said.

With the game tied at two in the fourth inning, the Mets scored four times to take a lead they would never relinquish.

Kent led off the inning with a home run off Cubs starter Mike Morgan. Ryan Thompson doubled in two more and Jose Vizcaino completed the scoring with a sacrifice fly that gave the Mets a 6–2 lead.

Rhodes' third home run in the fifth inning helped narrow the gap, but Hillman, Mike Maddux and Franco combined for 3 ¹/₃ effective innings out of the bullpen to nail down the win.

Seaver's Second Stint Starts Strong

Hall of Fame pitcher Tom Seaver made this walk many times before, but as he left the bullpen in right field to begin his second tour of duty with the Mets, a crowd of 51,054 came to its feet for a memorable standing ovation.

After a five-and-a-half year stint with the Cincinnati Reds, Seaver tossed six shutout innings in his first game back to lead the Mets to a 2-0 win over the Philadelphia Phillies and Steve Carlton at Shea Stadium.

On June 15, 1977, the popular right-hander was dealt to the Reds in exchange for Pat Zachry, second baseman Doug Flynn and outfielders Steve Henderson and Dan Norman.

Earlier that year, Seaver criticized Mets chairman of the board, M. Donald Grant, for not trying to improve the team. *New York Daily News* columnist Dick Young wrote a piece that said Seaver was jealous of former Mets pitcher Nolan Ryan and the amount of money he was making with the California Angels, while invoking the names of both spouses.

"That Young column was the straw that broke the back," Seaver said to Bill Madden of the *Daily News* in an interview nearly 30 years later. So "The Franchise" was gone, but in December 1982, the Reds traded Seaver back to the Mets for pitcher Charlie Puleo, outfielder Lloyd McClendon and a third player.

There was a heightened sense of excitement that day at Shea and the matchup of the two future Hall of Famers did not dissapoint. Carlton matched Seaver zero for zero for six innings, but the left-hander faltered in the seventh as the Mets broke through.

At a Glance

WP: Sisk (1–0)

Key stat: Seaver and Sisk combine for shutout

Mike Howard's RBI single scored the first run and the second run came courtesy of a Brian Giles sacrifice fly.

Seaver did not qualify for the win, but it didn't matter. It was a successful return to the place where he made his name as a three-time Cy Young Award winner.

"It was a very emotional day," the Mets' first Hall of Famer said. "It was great to be back, but so emotional I still felt it for two innings."

Rookie Doug Sisk (who had less than nine innings of big-league experience) relieved Seaver to toss three adventurous, but scoreless, innings for his first win in the majors.

After the game, Phillies second baseman and future Hall of Famer Joe Morgan offered this view of the veteran right-hander.

"He's (Seaver) smarter," Morgan said. "He knew everybody was coming back from spring training, anxious and jumping, he fed us a lot of slower speeds, and guys kept swinging at bad pitches."

Seaver's first inning was right out of a movie as he faced two future Hall of Famers (and one who arguably should be in). "Tom Terrific" struck out the leadoff batter, Pete Rose, but walked Morgan, who moved to second on Seaver's throwing error. Seaver came back to retire Gary Matthews on a 4–3 ground-out and then got future Hall of Famer Mike Schmidt to fly out to left.

In the seventh, Dave Kingman, who struck out in his other three at-bats, singled to left. George Foster followed with a single to right to put runners at first and second with nobody out. The game turned with the next batter.

Hubie Brooks was instructed to sacrifice, but he put down such a good bunt toward third that he was able to reach safely to load the bases.

"He was supposed to sacrifice," Mets manager George Bamberger said, "but he made a perfect bunt."

Brooks admitted he wasn't looking for a hit.

"I wasn't trying to be cute and beat it out," he said. "I just wanted one good pitch, and got it. Once I hit the ball, I didn't even know where it went."

Howard didn't waste any time as he drove the first pitch from Carlton into left field to score Kingman. Giles lined to Rose and Foster was able to tag and score the second run.

When it was over, Seaver's line was "Tom Terrific": six innings pitched, three hits, no runs, one walk and five strikeouts.

Rose, who struck out twice, marveled at his ex-teammate's performance.

"I don't remember the last time I struck out twice in a game," Rose said. "I only missed two pitches all spring."

Doc's Debut Good Enough for a Win

Ever since Dwight Eugene "Doc" Gooden was the fifth overall selection of the 1982 draft, the Mets anxiously awaited his entrance into the major leagues.

It didn't take long as Gooden spent two seasons in the minors, where he led the Class A Carolina League in wins, strikeouts and ERA while playing for the Lynchburg Mets in 1983. Doc had 300 strikeouts in 191 innings and won 19 games, which reaffirmed manager Dave Johnson's conviction that the 19-year-old right-hander was ready for the majors.

Gooden's first major league game was a success as he tossed five innings of one-run ball to earn the victory in the Mets' 3–2 win over the Astros before 18,925 at the Houston Astrodome.

"He's got the most live arm I've seen in a long time," said Astros first baseman and future Met Ray Knight. "His fastball explodes just like Nolan Ryan's."

The Mets were going to be cautious with Gooden, who became the third-youngest pitcher in franchise history. (Jerry Hinsley in 1964 and Jim Bethke in 1965 were a few months younger.)

"We had him at 81 pitches and that's enough," Johnson said. "Win or lose, it's positive, and that's what we wanted."

All along, the plan was for Doc to pitch in the environmentally controlled Astrodome.

> ### At a Glance
>
> **WP:** Gooden (1–0)
>
> **HR:** Strawberry (2)
>
> **Key stat:** Gooden allows one run in five innings

"The Astrodome is awesome," Gooden said before the game. "I never saw anything like it."

Gooden took to the Astrodome mound right away as he set down the first three hitters, including his first big-league strikeout of the third Astros hitter, Dickie Thon.

The young right-hander gave up his first hit to Alan Ashby in the third inning and his first run in the fifth on a RBI single by Bill Doran.

The Mets scored a run in the second inning on Darryl Strawberry's home run (a 400-foot blast to center field) off Astros starter Bob Knepper. They added two more runs in the fifth inning on Mookie Wilson's two-run double.

The Astros narrowed the gap and completed the scoring with a run off Mets reliever Dick Tidrow in the sixth. Knight's RBI single scored one run, but on the same play, Mets left fielder George Foster threw out Jose Cruz at the plate to cut down the potential tying run.

After Tidrow, the Mets bullpen nailed down the victory.

Doug Sisk tossed a scoreless seventh inning while Jesse Orosco pitched scoreless ball over the final two for the save.

Gooden's first pitching line: five innings pitched, one run, three hits, two walks and five strikeouts.

"I'm satisfied," Gooden said after the game. "Five is good enough. Now, I hope to build it up."

Knepper had always given the Mets trouble but they touched up the left-hander for seven hits and three runs in five innings of work.

Gooden would go on to capture the 1984 National League Rookie of the Year Award while setting a new rookie record for strikeouts. Doc ended up fanning 276 hitters to shatter Cleveland Indians rookie pitcher Herb Score's previous mark of 245 set in 1955. (See: 9/12/1984)

April 7, 1970

Mets Win Opening Game of the Season for the First Time

It would take nine years and one remarkable World Championship before the Mets would win the first game of a season.

Donn Clendenon's pinch-hit, two-run single in the top of the eleventh inning gave the Mets a 5–3 win over the Pirates at Forbes Field before a crowd of 34,249.

Mike Jorgensen led off the 11th with a single. An error by Pirates catcher Jerry May put runners on first and second base with no one out. After a sacrifice bunt moved up the runners, Mets manager Gil Hodges sent up Clendenon to bat for Ken Boswell, who was originally sent up to hit for pitcher Ron Taylor.

The Mets' first baseman drove reliever Joe Gibbon's first pitch into center field for two runs and a 5–3 lead.

Ron Taylor got the win with two scoreless innings in relief while Tug McGraw retired the Pirates in the bottom of the eleventh for the save.

Kranepool's Crush Lifts Mets in a Pinch

The Mets were down to their final out when manager Joe Torre looked down the bench and eyed a familiar number.

Ed Kranepool slammed a ninth-inning, walk-off, two-run homer off Stan Bahnsen to give the Mets a thrilling 6–5 win over the Expos before a crowd of 7,259 at Shea Stadium.

"He's the best left-handed pinch-hitter I've ever seen," Torre said. "He'd been in the locker room swinging a bat because it was warm in there. So I looked at him and he took off his baseball cap, reached for his helmet and walked up to the plate."

The Mets trailed 5–2 in the eighth inning when Lee Mazzilli hit a two-run homer off Expos starter Rudy May to narrow the gap to one run.

Bahnsen replaced May with one out and one on in the bottom of the ninth and got Tim Foli to fly out to left for the second out.

Kranepool drove Bahnsen's second pitch high over the wall in right field and the Mets had an exciting come-from-behind win.

The Mets' No. 7 certainly made his 70th career pinch-hit count.

"The pressure is always on the hitter," Kranepool said. "You also can't be selective because if you wait for your best pitch, you might miss it, anyway. So you have to be aggressive."

Pitcher Mardie Cornejo, who was making his major league debut, was the winner in relief.

At a Glance

WP: Cornejo (1–0)

HR: S.Henderson (1), Mazzilli (1), Kranepool (1)

Key stat: Cornejo 2 IP, 2 hits

Carter's First Game as a Met One to Remember

They couldn't have written a better script in Hollywood for Gary Carter's first game in a Mets uniform.

The Mets acquired Carter from Montreal in December of 1984 as part of a five-player blockbuster trade. The Expos got third baseman Hubie Brooks, catcher Mike Fitzgerald, outfielder Herm Winningham and promising pitcher Floyd Youmans.

It was labeled the "biggest trade in Mets history" since 1977, when they sent superstar pitcher Tom Seaver to the Reds. This time, they received the superstar and it paid immediate dividends.

A Shea Stadium crowd of 46,781 that included Vice President George H.W. Bush for half of the game saw Carter slam a one-out, walk-off home run in the bottom of the 10th off former Met Neil Allen to give the Mets a thrilling 6–5 win over the St. Louis Cardinals.

"It was a storybook ending all right," Mets manager Dave Johnson said afterward.

The game-time temperature was 42 degrees, but the game was hotly contested throughout.

At a Glance

WP: Gorman (1–0)

HR: Carter (1), Foster (1)

Key stat: Carter hits game-winning homer

After Bush threw the ceremonial first pitch to Carter, Mets starting pitcher Dwight Gooden, who would go on to win the 1985 National League Cy Young Award, retired the Cardinals in order in the first inning. The Mets' offense then did its part, scoring twice in the bottom half of the inning. Keith Hernandez's RBI single and a bases-loaded walk to Howard Johnson gave the Mets a 2–0 lead.

It wasn't all good for Carter in his initial game in Queens. In his first Mets' at-bat in the first inning, he was plunked on the elbow by a Joaquin Andujar fastball.

"It scared me at first," Carter said, "I had no feeling in my arm."

Carter stayed in the game and committed a passed ball in the third inning that enabled the Cards to tie the game 2–2.

"I just flat out missed the ball," the future Hall of Famer said afterward.

April 9, 1985
Mets 6, Cardinals 5 (10 innings)

In his second at-bat, Carter took a called third strike and then, in the fourth, he bounced into a force-out. Finally, in the sixth inning, the 6-foot-2 catcher lined a hit into center field and slid hard into second base for a double. When he got up, Carter pumped his fist in an emotional show of relief.

The Cardinals got even in the ninth inning, when Mets reliever Doug Sisk walked Jack Clark on a 3–1 pitch with the bases loaded.

The Mets had the bases loaded and two outs in the bottom of the ninth against Allen, but Mookie Wilson flied out to center to end the threat.

Left-hander Tom Gorman, who got the win, sat the Cards down in order in the top of the 10th. The Mets had Keith Hernandez, Carter and John Christensen (in for Darryl Strawberry, who was injured earlier in the game) ready to bat in the bottom half.

After Hernandez struck out to start the inning, Carter took a breaking ball from Allen for a strike. Carter looked for a second curveball and guessed right as he hit what Allen would later call a "good pitch" over the wall in left field and into the bullpen for a dramatic victory.

"There aren't enough words to describe what I feel," Carter said after the game. "What a beginning. Passed ball. Strikeout. Andujar steals a base. But the result at the end was outstanding."

After the game, Hernandez, the unofficial captain of this team, put the win in its proper perspective.

"It's just one game," Hernandez said, "but you get a good feeling."

Despite the early April cold weather, Gooden gave up three earned runs in six innings and was in line for the win.

"It was tough gripping the ball," Gooden said, "so I threw more breaking balls than usual. I threw extra pitches in the bullpen before the start of the game and I took extra warm-ups on the mound to stay warm."

Following the game, Carter was asked about dealing with the pressure that results from increased expectations.

"Pressure comes from within," he said. "Everybody's picked us to win. I just want to help them get there."

Grote's Heroics Too Late for a Win for Seaver

Jerry Grote led off the bottom of the 11th inning with a walk-off home run to give the Mets a 1–0 win over the Cincinnati Reds before 22,005 at Shea Stadium.

Mets starting pitcher Tom Seaver was brilliant as he tossed nine scoreless innings, giving up five hits while striking out 10.

"I had my best fastball since the middle of last summer," said Tom Terrific. "I kept telling myself it would be there one day. Today it was."

Jerry Grote's home run in the bottom of the 11th inning gave the Mets a 1–0 win over the Reds on April 11, 1971. Grote, a member of the Mets for parts of 12 seasons, was also known for his defensive play as a catcher.

April 11, 1971
Mets 1, Reds 0 (11 innings)

Reds pitchers combined to walk 12 batters, but the Mets couldn't capitalize on numerous chances. Cincy starting pitcher Greg Garrett walked seven in 5 $^2/_3$ innings while reliever Clay Carroll walked three in three innings.

The Mets stranded 13 runners through 10 innings, including leaving the bases loaded in the fifth and sixth innings.

In the 11th, Grote went to the plate against Reds losing pitcher Wayne Granger "looking for a first pitch fastball."

The fiery backstop got a fastball and drove it over the auxiliary scoreboard in left field for the only run of the game.

"It's got to be the first ball I ever hit out of the infield off the guy (Granger)," Grote said.

At a Glance

WP: McGraw (1–0)

HR: Grote (1)

Key stat: Seaver 9 IP, 5 hits, 10 Ks

April 11, 1962

First Game in Mets History

Tuesday, April 10, 1962, was the day that the Mets were scheduled to play their inaugural game in St. Louis. In what may have been an omen, the game was rained out and pushed back to Wednesday, April 11, as the Cardinals welcomed the club into the National League with an 11–4 thrashing before 16,147 at Busch Stadium.

The first game in team history provided a number of "firsts."

The Mets' first batter was center fielder and future Hall of Famer Richie Ashburn, who flied out to center.

Right fielder Gus Bell got the Mets' first hit, a single with one out in the second inning. Third baseman Charlie Neal's RBI single drove home Ashburn with the Mets' first run, while first baseman Gil Hodges hit the Mets' first home run off Cardinals right-hander Larry Jackson in the fourth inning.

On the "other side of the coin," Roger Craig was the Mets' first losing pitcher, but he recorded the first strikeout by a Mets pitcher when he fanned Cardinals catcher Gene Oliver in the third inning.

Prospect Leary Makes Quick Exit in Debut

It was billed as Tim Leary's major league debut, but the New York bullpen stole the show with seven solid innings as the Mets edged the Chicago Cubs 2-1 at Wrigley Field.

Leary, the Mets' first draft choice in 1979, started strong with a 1–2–3 first inning that included two strikeouts. It was after the second inning when the former UCLA product felt his arm tighten and had to be removed from the game.

"He felt some stiffness in the elbow during the second inning," Mets manager Joe Torre said. "He wanted to keep pitching, but we felt it best to take him out."

Mets lefty Pete Falcone replaced Leary and tossed five scoreless innings.

A crowd of 7,475 fans braved a game time temperature of 47 degrees to watch the teams remain scoreless through seven innings.

At a Glance

WP: Allen (1–0)

Key stat: Brooks 3-for-4

Dave Kingman's RBI single in the eighth inning snapped the scoreless tie, but the Cubs tied the game in their half on a bases-loaded walk to former Met Steve Henderson.

Hubie Brooks tripled off Cubs pitcher Rawly Eastwick to start the ninth and scored on Mike Cubbage's sacrifice fly.

Mets closer Neil Allen, who was already in the game, pitched a scoreless ninth to earn the win.

Leary's career never lived up to its promise. The Santa Monica, Calif., native played for six more teams in a 13-year career and won a total of 78 games.

Strawberry's Blast Makes a Winner of McDowell

Darryl Strawberry's walk-off home run to lead off the ninth inning propelled the Mets to a 2–1 win over the Cincinnati Reds at Shea Stadium.

A crowd of 26,212 saw Strawberry drive a 1–1 pitch from future teammate and losing pitcher John Franco over the wall in right field and into the bullpen.

"I'm thinking he's going to keep it down," said Strawberry, "but it came right over the plate."

Mets rookie reliever Roger McDowell pitched two innings to earn the win.

The Mets trailed 1–0 in the sixth, but a three-base error from Reds center fielder Eric Davis (on a ball he lost in the sun) led to Keith Hernandez's sacrifice fly and a tie game.

"I saw the ball leave the bat," Davis said, "then I lost it in the sun, and didn't see it until it got to my face."

Mets starting pitcher Ed Lynch tossed seven solid innings in place of Sid Fernandez, who was sent back to the minors.

At a Glance

WP: McDowell (2–0)

HR: Strawberry (1)

Key stat: Lynch 7 IP, 1 run

April 13, 1967

Seaver's Major League Debut Features No Decision

Tom Seaver made his major league debut but did not figure in the decision as the Mets beat the Pittsburgh Pirates 3–2 in front of an announced crowd of 5,005 at Shea Stadium.

Seaver gave up two runs on six hits in 5 ⅓ innings. He walked four and struck out eight in his initial big-league start and appearance.

Triple Play Sets Stage for Big Homer by Klaus

At a Glance

WP: Bethke (1–0)

HR: Klaus (1)

Key stat: Kranepool 3-for-4, 3 RBI

The Mets turned a triple play and beat the Houston Astros 5–4 in 10 innings on Bobby Klaus' walk-off home run.

Leading off the inning, Klaus victimized losing pitcher Claude Raymond with his fifth major league home run and first as a Met.

A paid crowd of 7,894 at Shea Stadium braved an intermittent rain to witness the third triple play in Mets history, but the first one that came in a win.

In the top of the second, Houston had runners at first and third with no one out. Jimmy Wynn hit a deep fly ball to right field, where Johnny Lewis caught it for the first out. Walt Bond tagged from third and tried to score, but Lewis made a one-hop throw to Mets catcher Chris Cannizzaro, who tagged the Astros' first-baseman.

Houston's Bob Aspromonte was looking to take second base if the throw went home, but Mets first baseman Ed Kranepool properly faked cutting off the throw. That gave Cannizzaro time to throw down to shortstop Roy McMillan, who was covering second, to complete the triple play.

April 15, 1968

Mets and Astros Play 24 Innings

The longest night game in major league history finally ended in the bottom of the 24th inning on an error as the Astros got by the Mets 1–0 before a crowd of 14,219 at the Houston Astrodome.

With one out and the bases loaded, Mets shortstop Al Weis allowed Bob Aspromonte's grounder to go between his legs to score Norm Miller from third base with the only run of the marathon game.

A total of 13 pitchers (eight by the Mets) were used.

'Tom Terrific' Keeps Chalking Up the Ks

Tom Seaver was in total command as he struck out 14 Pirates en route to a three-hit shutout of Pittsburgh and a 1-0 win before a crowd of 18,491 at Shea Stadium.

Seaver lived up to his moniker of "Tom Terrific" as he did not walk a batter (he went to a 3–2 count on only four hitters), struck out at least one Pirate hitter in every inning and threw 115 pitches, 81 for strikes.

With one out in the fourth, Donn Clendenon hit a solo home run off losing pitcher Dock Ellis. That proved to be the only run that Seaver would need.

"I didn't think I had good stuff after warming up in the bullpen," Seaver said.

Bucs third baseman Richie Hebner, a future Met, was one of six hitters who got the ball out of the infield and he disagreed.

> ## At a Glance
> **WP:** Seaver (2–0)
> **HR:** Clendenon (1)
> **Key stat:** Seaver CG, 3 hits, 14 Ks

"It's (Seaver's) the best fastball I've seen in three years in the big leagues," Hebner said.

Clendenon burned his old team by turning on an inside fastball from Ellis into the bullpen in left field.

Besides the 14 strikeouts, Seaver recorded six outs on the ground, three on pop-ups, three on fly outs and one line out.

The future Hall of Fame right-hander had plenty of gas left in the tank as he struck out two in the ninth, including future Hall of Famer Roberto Clemente for a third time to end the game.

Mets manager Gil Hodges needed only one word to sum up Seaver's day.

"Magnificent," he said.

Marathon Game Ends in 20th with Pelfrey Closing

"It was the most unbelievable game I've ever been a part of," Mets right fielder Jeff Francoeur said. "How we won, I have no clue."

He was referring to one of the most bizarre games in Mets history that finally ended with starting pitcher Mike Pelfrey closing out an historic 2–1 win at Busch Stadium before a crowd of 43,709.

The game was scoreless through 18 innings but in the top of the 19th, the Mets broke through to take a 1–0 lead. With one out and the bases loaded, Francoeur's sacrifice fly scored Jose Reyes from third base with the first run.

The Cards answered in their half of the 19th off Mets closer Frankie Rodriguez. With Albert Pujols at second and two outs, Yadier Molina (who has burned the Mets before) singled to right to drive in Pujols and tie the game.

Even though the Cards tied the game, the Mets got a huge break. Ryan Ludwick led off with a single but he was thrown out trying to steal second with Pujols at the plate. It's conceivable that the Cards would've won the game, had Ludwick not been thrown out.

The Mets regained the lead in the top of the 20th against outfielder and losing pitcher Joe Mather.

Angel Pagan began the rally with a single. Mike Jacobs singled Pagan to third and Pagan scored on Jose Reyes' sacrifice fly.

"That's the happiest 0-for-7 I've ever had in my life," Reyes said. "I played good defense, got the RBI, and we won the game. And finally, it's over."

With Rodriguez, the Mets closer, having already been used, Mets manager Jerry Manuel was stuck for someone to finish this game. Pelfrey volunteered and got the job done by tossing a scoreless inning for his first big-league save.

"Pelfrey asked to pitch. He stepped up and said, 'Hey I can do this,'" Manuel said.

The marathon was the fourth in franchise history of 20 innings or more, but it was the first time the Mets won.

"For a 0–0 game, this one was kinda fun because it moved rather quickly," said veteran Mets broadcaster Howie Rose.

At a Glance

WP: Rodriguez (1–0)

Key stat: Pagan 3-for-6, scores game-winning run

Mets 2, Cardinals 1 (20 innings)

A total of 19 pitchers (including two Cardinal position players) were used in the game that lasted 6 hours and 53 minutes.

The Cards left the bases loaded in the 10th, 12th and 14th innings and left a total of 22 runners on base.

St. Louis was 1-for-18 with runners in scoring position, while the Mets were 0-for-7.

"Our guys were fighting all day to stay in the game," a drained Manuel said afterward. "We weren't getting it done offensively but we were fighting."

The teams continued to have trouble scoring in extra innings and both were running out of players.

"After awhile, it became apparent (Cardinals manager Tony) La Russa had just about 'given up,'" Rose said.

In the bottom of the 14th, La Russa allowed pitcher Blake Hawksworth to bat with two outs and the bases loaded, even though he had a position player available in backup catcher Bryan Anderson. La Russa used Anderson as pinch-hitter for Hawksworth in the 16th.

Mather became the first Cardinals position player to render a pitching decision since May 1988.

Infielder Felipe Lopez also pitched a scoreless inning, while pitcher Kyle Lohse played three innings in left field and had two putouts.

Mets starting pitchers John Maine (pinch runner) and Jon Niese (pinch-hitter) were also substituted into the game.

The numbers within the box score were mind-boggling. A total of 652 pitches were thrown in the game, 399 for strikes. There were 19 walks and 35 strikeouts.

Individually, Jason Bay and Francoeur also went 0-for-7 for the Mets.

"That game messed up Jeff Francoeur for six weeks," Rose said.

Pagan was 3-for-6 but the rest of the Mets were a combined 6-for-55. Pujols was 2-for-5 and was walked four times while Lopez was 1-for-8.

"This was crazy," Pelfrey said. "I've been involved in some wild games but this was really something. I thought it was never going to end."

"I've never played 20 innings before in my life," Reyes said. "That was a crazy game. Crazy game."

Ryan's Coming Out Party Ends with Record 15 Ks

You could make the argument that this was "the breakout" game for future Hall of Fame pitcher Nolan Ryan.

Picked by the Mets in the 12th round of the 1965 draft, Ryan dominated the Philadelphia Phillies in a 7–0 rout at Shea Stadium.

Ryan gave up a leadoff single to Phils second baseman Denny Doyle in the top of the first but that was their only hit of the game. From there, the Texas native mowed down the Phils with 15 strikeouts to tie the overall franchise record and set the club mark for a nine-inning game. (Jerry Koosman struck out 15 in a 10-inning game; see: May 28, 1970.)

After Doyle reached in the first, the Phils had eight other runners (six walks, two Mets errors) reach base, but could not bust through against the 23-year-old fireballing right-hander.

Ryan fanned the side in the first, third and sixth innings. He had 11 strikeouts after five and 15 through eight, but he didn't fan a batter in the ninth, so his bid to tie or break the record of 19 came up short. Cardinals pitcher and future Hall of Famer Steve Carlton fanned 19 Mets in a 4–3 defeat on Sept. 15, 1969.

The Mets took a 3–0 lead in the first off losing pitcher and future Hall of Famer Jim Bunning. Tommie Agee, Bud Harrelson and Joe Foy led off with singles to produce one run, while a pair of Phillies errors led to two more.

Ken Boswell homered into the lower deck in right field for a 5-0 lead in the sixth inning off Phillies right-handed reliever Barry Lersch, who had tried out for the United States Olympic swimming team as a diver in 1964.

Ryan received a standing ovation from the 23,500 on hand at Shea when he came to the plate in the bottom of the eighth and promptly singled. He then scored on Agee's two-run, 420-foot bomb to center off Lowell Palmer to close out the scoring.

Phillies	AB	R	H	RBI
Doyle 2b	3	0	1	0
Money 3b	2	0	0	0
Briggs lf	4	0	0	0
Johnson 1b	4	0	0	0
McCarver c	3	0	0	0
Compton c	0	0	0	0
Hisle cf	4	0	0	0
Stone rf	4	0	0	0
Bowa ss	3	0	0	0
Bunning p	0	0	0	0
Lersch p	1	0	0	0
Hutto ph	1	0	0	0
Palmer p	0	0	0	0
Totals	29	0	1	0

Mets	AB	R	H	RBI
Agee cf	4	2	2	2
Harrelson ss	4	1	1	0
Foy 3b	5	2	2	1
Jones lf	4	0	1	0
Shamsky 1b	3	0	1	1
Swoboda rf	3	0	0	0
Boswell 2b	3	1	1	1
Grote c	4	0	0	0
Ryan p	4	1	1	0
Totals	34	7	9	5

											R	H	E
PHI	0	0	0	0	0	0	0	0	0	-	0	1	3
NYM	3	0	1	0	0	1	0	2	X	-	7	9	2

Phillies	IP	H	R	ER	BB	SO
Bunning L (0-2)	2	6	4	2	1	1
Lersch	4	1	1	1	3	1
Palmer	2	2	2	2	0	2
Totals	8	9	7	5	4	4

Mets	IP	H	R	ER	BB	SO
Ryan W (1-0)	9	1	0	0	6	15
Totals	9	1	0	0	6	15

E—Philadelphia Stone 2, McCarver; New York Harrelson, Foy. DP—New York. 2B—New York Shamsky. HR—New York Agee (1), Boswell (1). HBP—New York Shamsky. LOB—Philadelphia 8; New York 8. SB—New York Agee. Attendance: 23,500.

Ryan joined left-hander Al Jackson, righty Jack Hamilton and future Hall of Famer Tom Seaver as the fourth Met to toss a complete game, one-hitter.

Less than 20 months later, Nolan Ryan would be a major part of, arguably, the worst trade in club history.

On Dec. 10, 1971, Ryan, along with right-handed pitcher Don Rose, outfielder Leroy Stanton and catcher Frank Estrada were sent to the California Angels in exchange for shortstop Jim Fregosi.

Mets manager Gil Hodges may have been a prophet when, on the day the deal was made, he said, "You always hate to give up on an arm like Ryan's, he could put things together overnight."

Ryan went on to a 27-year career in which he won 324 games and set the career record with 5,714 strikeouts.

In a two-year span, Fregosi played in 146 games as a Met and batted .233 with five home runs and 43 RBIs. On July 11, 1973, Fregosi's contract was sold to the Texas Rangers.

Al Jackson Goes the Distance in Mets' First Win at Shea

Al Jackson went the distance on a complete game, six-hit shutout to lead the Mets to a 6–0 victory over the Pittsburgh Pirates and their first-ever win at Shea Stadium before 30,185 fans.

The southpaw from Waco, Texas, held the Bucs down through the first six innings but ran into trouble in the seventh. Back to back singles by Donn Clendenon (a future Met) and Bob Bailey put the Pirates in business with two on and one out. Jackson got out of the inning when he induced future Hall of Famer Bill Mazeroski to ground into an inning-ending double play.

The Mets scored four times in the fourth inning, thanks to a pair of two-run singles from third baseman Rod Kanehl and second baseman Ron Hunt. Interestingly, Mets manager Casey Stengel flip-flopped the two, after starting Hunt at third base in previous games.

Kanehl said he didn't know about the switch until right before the game.

At a Glance

WP: Jackson (1–1)

Key stat: Jackson CG 6-hitter, 6 Ks; five Mets had two hits apiece

---

"I was standing around talking about stealing signs from second base, this was before the game and Casey came over," Kanehl said. "(Casey) said, 'You better forget that, kid, you're playing third.' That's the first I knew about it."

Kanehl and Hunt were two of five Mets who had two-hit games, but the story was Jackson, who admitted after the game that he didn't have his best stuff.

"Little Al" Jackson was selected by the Mets from the Pittsburgh Pirates in the 1961 expansion draft that stocked the rosters of the two new teams (the other was the Houston Colt .45s) that entered the National League in 1962.

The 5-foot-10 southpaw pitched for the Mets for the first four seasons of their existence. Following the 1965 season, Jackson was traded along with infielder Charley Smith to the Cardinals for third baseman Ken Boyer.

Jackson came back to Flushing when he was traded back from the Cardinals after the 1967 season to complete an earlier deal between the clubs. In June 1969, Jackson's career with the Mets ended when he was sold to the Cincinnati Reds. Jackson, who was a two-time 20-game loser, had a career record of 43–80 with the Mets.

Spahn Chalks Up 2,500th 'K' Against Dodgers

Future Hall of Fame southpaw Warren Spahn tossed a complete game in helping the Mets beat the Dodgers 3–2 at Dodger Stadium.

A crowd of 36,161 was on hand to see the 43-year-old Spahn—who would eventually become the winningest left-handed pitcher in baseball history—shut down the hometown Dodgers with eight scoreless innings.

Leading 3–0 in the ninth inning, Spahn gave up a leadoff single to Wes Parker. An error by Mets first baseman Ed Kranepool put two on with no outs. RBI singles from Tommy Davis and John Roseboro followed to cut the lead to 3–2. At that point, Mets manager Casey Stengel made his way to the mound with every intention of lifting his veteran starter.

Spahn somehow convinced Stengel to keep him in, and Spahn used more than 20 years of big-league experience to "milk" that one-run lead and wiggle out of a first-and-third, no-out jam.

Spahn struck out Jim Lefebvre for the first out and the 2,500th "K" of his illustrious career. Spahn induced the next batter, Ron Fairly, to hit a comebacker to the mound. The lefty fielded the ball and trapped Davis off third base for the second out.

John Kennedy was the Dodgers' last hope. The count went to 2–2 and then Spahn got his 2,501st strikeout when the third baseman went down swinging.

At a Glance

WP: Spahn (1–0)

Key stat: Spahn CG, 1 earned run

Claude Osteen, a 24-year-old lefty, started for the Dodgers and was just as stingy as Spahn through seven innings, but the Mets finally broke through in the eighth. Roy McMillan's squeeze bunt scored pinch runner Johnny Lewis with the first run.

Lewis singled in two more in the ninth to provide Spahn with a three-run cushion.

Did You Ever See Such Hittin' by Hickman?

Mets center fielder Jim Hickman homered in both games as the Mets swept a doubleheader from the Milwaukee Braves, 8–5 and 9–2, before a crowd of 26,775 at the Polo Grounds.

In the opener, Hickman's eighth-inning grand slam capped a five-run rally that lifted the Mets to the 8–5 victory.

Trailing 5–3, Ed Kranepool tripled to lead off the eighth inning while Mets catcher Choo Choo Coleman followed with a walk. Charlie Neal doubled in a run to make it 5–4. With one out, Tim Harkness was intentionally walked to load the bases.

Hickman stepped to the plate and lined a ball over the short wall in left field for the third grand slam in team history and an 8–5 lead.

Mets pitcher Roger Craig faced some trouble in the ninth. With one out, Milwaukee brought the tying run to the plate, but Craig finished it when he got Frank Bolling to hit into a 5–4–3, game-ending double play.

The nightcap pitted the Mets' Galen Cisco against a two-time 20-game winner in the Braves' Lew Burdette. The Mets trailed 2–0 as they batted in the sixth inning, but a couple of familiar names produced three runs and a 3–2 lead.

With runners on second and third and one out, Duke Snider lined a two-run double to left field to tie the game. Following a walk to Frank Thomas, Kranepool took the cue and singled to left to score Snider with the go-ahead run.

The Mets blew the game open by scoring five runs in the eighth, keyed by Hickman's second home run of the day, a two-run shot.

Braves	AB	R	H	RBI
Cline rf	4	0	1	0
Bolling 2b	5	1	1	0
H Aaron rf	4	1	2	1
Mathews 3b	4	1	2	0
Larker 1b	2	1	1	1
T Aaron ph-1b	1	0	0	0
Maye lf	4	0	0	0
Gabrielson lf	0	0	0	0
Torre c	4	1	1	1
McMillan ss	1	0	0	0
Cloninger p	0	0	0	0
Lemaster p	1	0	0	0
Jones ph	1	0	0	0
Piche p	1	0	0	0
Raymond p	0	0	0	0
Dillard ph	1	0	0	0
Totals	**33**	**5**	**8**	**3**

Mets	AB	R	H	RBI
Hickman cf	3	1	1	5
Hunt 2b	2	0	0	0
Snider rf	5	0	0	0
Thomas lf	5	1	2	0
Craig p	0	0	0	0
Kranepool 1b	3	2	2	0
Hodges 1b	0	0	0	0
Coleman c	3	1	0	0
Neal 3b-ss	4	2	2	3
Moran ss	2	0	0	0
Schreiber ph-3b	1	0	0	0
Hook p	1	0	0	0
Throneberry ph	1	0	0	0
MacKenzie p	0	0	0	0
Harkness ph	0	0	0	0
Kanehl pr-lf	0	1	0	0
Totals	**30**	**8**	**7**	**8**

```
MIL  1 0 0 0 0 4 0 0 0 - 5 8 2
NYM  0 3 0 0 0 0 0 5 X - 8 7 1
```

Braves	IP	H	R	ER	BB	SO
Cloninger	1.2	3	3	3	3	0
Lemaster	2.1	0	0	0	0	2
Piche	3	2	2	2	3	2
Raymond L (2-1)	1	2	3	3	1	0
Totals	**8**	**7**	**8**	**8**	**7**	**4**

Mets	IP	H	R	ER	BB	SO
Hook	6	7	5	5	3	5
MacKenzie W (2-0)	2	1	0	0	0	3
Craig S (1)	1	0	0	0	2	0
Totals	**9**	**8**	**5**	**5**	**5**	**8**

E—Milwaukee Larker, Mathews; New York Coleman. DP—New York 2. 2B—New York Neal. 3B—New York Kranepool. HR—Milwaukee H Aaron (3); New York Hickman (2). SH—New York Kranepool. SF—New York Hickman. HBP—New York Hunt. LOB—Milwaukee 6; New York 8.

Mets 8, Braves 5 (Game 1); Mets 9, Braves 2 (Game 2)

Cisco got the win with six innings of two-run ball. Burdette was lit up for seven earned runs on 11 hits in 7 $\frac{1}{3}$ innings.

Mets pitcher Ken McKenzie, who got the win in the opener, picked up the save after he finished the game with three scoreless innings.

After the game, Mets manager Casey Stengel was giddy about the two wins.

"We finally look like we did in spring training," said the "Ol' Perfessor."

In typical "Stengel-ese," Casey praised Hickman's day when he added, "Did you ever see such hittin' and that guy sure hit us one and then when he hit the center field fence, did you ever see such hittin' and then he hit the other homer."

Hickman played five years for the Mets before being dealt to the Los Angeles Dodgers in November 1966. The native Tennesseean is best known for having the game-winning, RBI single in the bottom of the 12th inning of the 1970 All-Star Game that led to the famous collision at home plate between the Pete Rose and Indians catcher Ray Fosse.

Did You Know?

Moises Alou holds the record for the longest hitting streak in franchise history. From Aug. 23-Sept. 26, 2007, Alou hit in 30 straight games. During the streak, Alou hit .403 (48-for-119).

Seaver Ties Record with 19 Strikeouts

It was a pitching performance that ranks with not only the best in the history of the New York Mets, but in baseball history as well.

Tom Seaver tied a major league record by striking out 19 Padres, including a record-setting final 10 batters in a two-hit, 2–1 win over the San Diego Padres before a crowd of 14,197 at Shea Stadium.

It was a bright, sunny day at Shea and as the game wore on, the shadows made it more difficult for the hitters. Combine that with Seaver's brilliance and it was the formula for a classic.

Dave Campbell had one of the two hits off Seaver but he also struck out once. During a recent interview, Campbell (who works as an analyst for ESPN Radio) said that during Seaver's game-ending run, the Padres actually touched the ball only once.

"We had one foul ball," Campbell said. "Cito Gaston (in the ninth inning) hit a little dribbler towards the dugout."

Seaver broke the previous club record of 15 strikeouts by Nolan Ryan and Jerry Koosman in an extra-inning game.

> ## At a Glance
>
> **WP:** Seaver (3–0)
>
> **Key stat:** Seaver complete game, 19 strikeouts

"I had great stuff and location," Seaver said during a recent interview. "Shadows and other stuff helped."

It was surprising that San Diego even got two hits off "The Franchise." It was even more surprising that they got a run. Al Ferrara, who would become a footnote of history later on, led off the second inning with a solo home run off Seaver that tied the game at one.

The Mets had taken a 1–0 lead in the first inning on an RBI double by Ken Boswell.

"Actually he (Seaver) wasn't that strong in the early innings," Mets catcher Jerry Grote said. "He just kept building up as the game went on. The cool weather helped and by the end of the game, he was stronger than ever."

In the third inning, Tommie Agee singled and Bud Harrelson ripped a triple into the corner in right field to score the go-ahead run.

From there it was Seaver's show.

With two outs and a runner on first base in the fourth inning, Campbell singled for San Diego's final hit. Seaver worked out of the jam by getting Jerry Morales to look at a called third strike.

Two more strikeouts in the fifth inning gave Seaver a total of nine.

With two outs in the sixth inning, Seaver struck out Ferrara to begin his remarkable string of 10 straight.

Nate Colbert struck out swinging to start the seventh. A called third strike got Campbell looking and Morales was caught looking once again to end the inning.

"He was throwing 96 (mph), but of course there were no radar guns back then," Campbell said.

Three more strikeouts in the eighth gave Seaver a total of 16 and the club record.

"Everybody congratulated me when I got No. 16 in the eighth inning," Seaver said. "I just told them let's get some more runs. All I could think of was Carlton had struck out 19 of us and still lost." (see: Sept. 15, 1969)

In the ninth, the 25-year-old Seaver blew three fastballs past Van Kelly and Cito Gaston was caught looking for strikeout No. 18.

Ferrara was the final batter and the home run he hit in the second was certainly on Seaver's mind.

"I was still worried I'd make a mistake and Ferrara might hit it out," Seaver said, "but when I got two strikes on him, I thought I might never get this close again so I might as well go for it."

Seaver threw two sliders and two fastballs and fanned Ferrara to cap a performance for the ages.

Grote set a record for catchers with 20 putouts, breaking the previous mark of 19, which was shared by the Dodgers' John Roseboro and the Tigers' Bill Freehan.

Before the game, Seaver accepted his 1969 National League Cy Young Award and then went out and used a potpourri of his stuff to put his name in the record books.

The future Hall of Famer threw 136 pitches in this classic. Reportedly, there were 81 fastballs, 34 sliders, 19 curveballs and two change-ups.

Padres rookie right-hander Mike Corkins was doing his best to keep San Diego in the game as he gave up two runs on four hits in seven innings pitched.

Mets Win Their First Game Behind Hook

After it was over, the first winning pitcher in the history of the New York Mets was watching his teammates popping champagne to celebrate their first win.

Jay Hook went the distance and the Mets put up a "W" for the first time in their history as they "whupped" the Pittsburgh Pirates 9-1 at Forbes Field.

A reported crowd of 24,560 watched the Mets take a 6–0 lead after two innings. Five of those runs came against Pirates starter and loser Tom Sturdivant, who lasted one inning and faced three batters.

The Mets scored twice in the first inning on a pair of sacrifice flies from Gus Bell and Frank Thomas.

Hook's two-run single in the second keyed a four-run inning as the Mets batted around for the first time in franchise history. The historic rally made it more comfortable for the right-handed Hook, who sat down the first six Pirate hitters and retired the Bucs 1–2–3 in three of the first four innings.

Elio Chacon's RBI single gave the Mets a 7–0 lead in the sixth. The Bucs got their only run of the game in the sixth on a RBI ground-out.

Hook proceeded to set down the next seven hitters before Bob Skinner singled.

Dick Stuart and future Hall of Famer Roberto Clemente followed with force-outs and the Mets could exhale with their initial victory.

The Mets pounded out 14 hits in the Monday night game. Leadoff batter Felix Mantilla and Chacon both had three hits with two runs scored.

Chacon and Bobby "B.J." Smith had two RBIs apiece. Former Brooklyn Dodger great Gil Hodges did not start, but got in the game and contributed to the hit parade with two singles.

According to the game story in the *The New*

Mets	AB	R	H	RBI
Mantilla 3b	3	2	3	1
Chacon ss	4	2	3	2
Bell rf	3	0	1	1
Smith rf	1	0	1	2
Thomas lf	3	0	1	1
DeMerit lf	0	0	0	0
Bouchee 1b	2	0	0	0
Hodges 1b	3	0	2	0
Neal 2b	5	1	2	0
Hickman cf	4	1	0	0
Cannizzaro c	3	1	0	0
Hook p	4	2	1	2
Totals	35	9	14	9

Pirates	AB	R	H	RBI
Virdon cf	4	0	0	0
Groat ss	4	0	1	0
Skinner lf	4	0	1	0
Stuart 1b	4	0	0	0
Clemente rf	4	0	0	0
Burgess c	0	0	0	0
McFarlane c	2	0	0	0
Hoak 3b	2	0	1	0
Mazeroski 2b	3	0	0	0
Sturdivant p	0	0	0	0
Olivo p	1	0	1	0
Schofield ph	1	1	1	0
Lamabe p	0	0	0	0
Logan ph	1	0	0	0
Haddix p	0	0	0	0
Totals	31	1	5	1

											R	H	E
NYM	2	4	0	0	0	1	0	2	0	-	9	14	0
PIT	0	0	0	0	0	1	0	0	0	-	1	5	3

Mets	IP	H	R	ER	BB	SO
Hook W (1-0)	9	5	1	1	1	2
Totals	9	5	1	1	1	2

Pirates	IP	H	R	ER	BB	SO
Sturdivant L (1-1)	1	3	5	5	2	0
Olivo	5	7	2	1	1	2
Lamabe	2	3	2	2	1	3
Haddix	1	1	0	0	0	2
Totals	9	14	9	8	4	7

E—Pittsburgh Skinner, Groat, Stuart. DP—New York; Pittsburgh. 2B—New York Neal, Thomas, Mantilla; Pittsburgh Olivo. 3B—New York Smith. SH—New York Mantilla. SF—New York Thomas, Mantilla, Bell. LOB—New York 7; Pittsburgh 4. Attendance: 16,676.

April 23, 1962
Mets 9, Pirates 1

York Times, "And as the runs crossed the plate in the first and second, there was the old man running up and down the Met dugout waving his arms like a traffic cop. In the dressing room, the Mets weren't raucous but they made as much noise as some Yankee teams on the days they clinched pennants."

Hook gave up one run on five hits, while walking one and striking out two.

Mets manager Casey Stengel had his first win. As he congratulated Hook, Casey said, "I might have to pitch him for the next ninety-nine games."

The *New York Times* had an article about how the fans back in New York were reacting to the first-ever win.

Robert Lipsyte wrote, "If the city has not completely opened its heart to the new National League baseball team, it has not at least closed its mind. Although there was no dancing in the streets, there was a general feeling of relief in Times Square last night."

Did You Know?

The club record for most hits in consecutive, official at-bats is nine, set by Jose Vizcaino in 1996. Vizcaino began the streak on April 23 with a double. In his next plate appearance, Vizcaino did not record an at-bat as he sacrificed. After that, it was two singles, a double, two more singles, another double, a single and a triple. In the ninth inning of the game against the Cardinals on April 25, Vizcaino's streak ended when he struck out.

HoJo Shows His Bat Works off the Bench

Howard Johnson tied the game with a two-run homer in the ninth and George Foster's RBI single in the 10th powered the Mets past the Cardinals 5–4 at Busch Stadium before 33,597 fans.

"HoJo" rocketed a 2–2 pitch from Cardinals losing pitcher Todd Worrell deep into the seats in right field to tie the game 4–4.

Worrell walked Wally Backman to start the 10th. With two outs, Backman scored from second on Foster's hit.

Foster made an error that allowed the Cards to take a 4–2 lead in the eighth, but he more than atoned for his mistake.

"I can't do anything about the error," Foster said. "When I go up after that, it's my turn at bat. And we're not going to give them the game."

Johnson was benched in favor of Ray Knight because HoJo had not been hitting. He entered the game as a pinch-hitter in the seventh inning and stayed in the game at shortstop.

At a Glance

WP: McDowell (2–0)

HR: Strawberry (1), Johnson (1)

Key stat: Foster 3-for-5

After the game, Johnson admitted that the benching didn't sit well with him.

"I was dissapointed not to start, but I could see the handwriting on the wall. Ray Knight's hitting good and you've got to go with him," Johnson said.

Darryl Strawberry hit a solo home run in the second inning off St. Louis starting pitcher Bob Forsch. The round-tripper gave "Straw" four hits in eight at-bats against the righty. All four hits were home runs.

Seaver Warms Up to Wrigley with Four-Hitter

Tom Seaver overcame the elements, and an untimely error, to pitch a 10-inning, complete game four-hitter as the Mets beat the Chicago Cubs 2–1 at a chilly Wrigley Field.

A sparse crowd of 1,077 braved a cold wind and temperatures in the 40s to watch Seaver hold the Cubs to an unearned run on just four hits.

Seaver was one out away from a complete game shutout, but an error by the usually reliable shortstop Bud Harrelson allowed the tying run to score. With Don Kessinger at second base and two outs, Ron Santo hit a grounder that went under Harrelson's glove.

Seaver got Lee Thomas to fly out to left to end the inning, but the damage was done with an unearned run.

The future Hall of Fame pitcher led off the 10th with a single to right and moved to second on Cleon Jones' sacrifice bunt.

A wild pitch by Cubs losing pitcher Bill Hands moved Seaver to third with one out.

Mets left fielder Tommie Reynolds struck out and third baseman Ken Boyer was walked intentionally to set up first and third.

Cubs manger Leo Durocher went to Bob Hendley, a left-hander, to face left-handed hitting Al Luplow.

Mets manager Wes Westrum decided to let Luplow hit and it paid off as he delivered an RBI single to right-center field to score Seaver with the go-ahead run.

> ### At a Glance
> **WP:** Seaver (2–0)
>
> **Key stat:** Seaver 10 IP, 4 hits, 1 unearned run

Hernandez: 'Maybe I Should Get Divorced Every Day'

"Maybe I should get divorced every day. I'd be broke, but I'd also be in the Hall of Fame."

That was Keith Hernandez speaking with reporters following his career-high seven RBIs that led the Mets to a 13–4 thrashing of the Braves at Atlanta-Fulton County Stadium.

Before the game, the Mets' captain received the word that his divorce became final. The first baseman hit two home runs, including his seventh career

Keith Hernandez, right, shown prior to the 1984 All-Star Game with teammates, from left, Darryl Strawberry, Dwight Gooden, and Jesse Orosco, reached the 1,000-RBI mark on April 28, 1985, against the Atlanta Braves.

grand slam. Hernandez also achieved a personal milestone as he reached 1,000 RBIs for his career.

Coming into the game, Hernandez was in a slump. But he snapped an 0-for-13 skid with a two-run homer off future Met Tom Glavine that tied the game 4–4.

"I'm happy just to contribute for once," Hernandez said. "You never know about these things. You get in a hot streak and it's effortless. You get in a slump and it's like you are picking the bat up for the first time."

The Mets broke the game wide open by scoring seven times in the eighth inning, keyed by a Hernandez slam.

With one out and the bases full, Hernandez went deep against former Met pitcher Charlie Puleo.

Dwight Gooden went the distance, allowing three earned runs on 10 hits.

"I didn't have my best stuff," Gooden said, "but it's strange, I can remember only one game against the Braves where I didn't have trouble."

In addition to Hernandez's milestone evening, 10,405 fans saw two Mets reach milestones. Shortstop Kevin Elster set a career high with four hits and manager Dave Johnson recorded his 400th career victory.

At a Glance

WP: Gooden (5–0)

HR: Carter (7), Hernandez 2 (1,2)

1B Keith Hernandez

The fortunes of the New York Mets changed dramatically for the better on June 15, 1983. That was the day the Mets sent pitchers Neil Allen and Rick Ownbey to the St. Louis Cardinals in exchange for first baseman Keith Hernandez.

The San Francisco native was a "general" in the infield and is widely considered one of the best defensive first baseman of all time.

Hernandez won 11 straight Gold Gloves from 1978–1988 and was the co-National League Most Valuable Player in 1979, when he shared the award with the Pirates' Willie Stargell.

The 1984 season was Hernandez's best as a Met. He batted .311 with 15 home runs, 94 RBIs, 97 walks and had an on-base percentage of .409.

Keith Hernandez was inducted into the Mets' Hall of Fame in 1997.

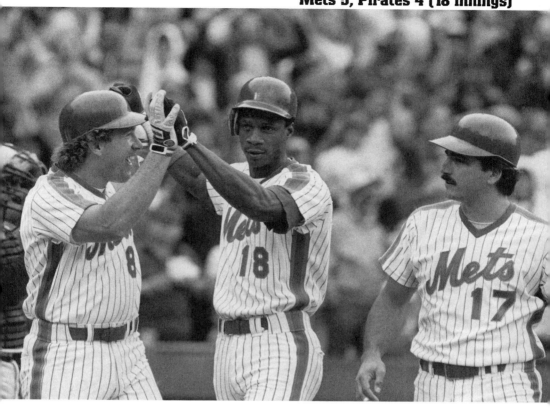

Super Sundae Even Better When Mets Win in 18

Five hours and 21 minutes after the first pitch was thrown, pinch runner Mookie Wilson stepped on the plate, courtesy of an error, to give the Mets a wild 5–4, 18-inning win over the Pittsburgh Pirates at Shea Stadium.

The game was a virtual "potpourri" of baseball. From Darryl Strawberry's first career grand slam to 10 ²/₃ innings of no-hit ball from Pirates pitchers, to an unusual balk call, the fans got their money's worth.

Pirates losing pitcher Lee Tunnell walked Gary Carter to start the 18th. Wilson ran for Carter, who caught all 18 innings.

After Darryl Strawberry (18) smacked his first career grand slam on April 28, 1985, against the Pittsburgh Pirates, Gary Carter, left, greeted him at home plate along with Keith Hernandez.

April 28, 1985
Mets 5, Pirates 4 (18 innings)

Strawberry's single put runners at first and third with no outs. Clint Hurdle, who had already thrown out the potential winning run at the plate in the 10th, hit a hard grounder toward first base. The ball went through Jason Thompson's legs for an error as Wilson scored the winning run.

"It's always special when you win in extra innings," Mets manager Dave Johnson said.

Johnson's managerial skills were on full display as he rotated Rusty Staub and Hurdle between left and right field, depending on who was hitting for the Pirates.

Staub saved a run in the top of the 18th when he ran down pinch-hitter (and pitcher) Rick Rhoden's fly ball down the line in right field with a runner on first and two outs.

"That was as fast as I could run," the 41-year old veteran Staub said.

The Pirates had the bases loaded with no outs in the ninth inning but could not score. The inning ended when Rafael Belliard tried to score on a pitch in the dirt, but Carter tossed a back-handed flip to pitcher Jesse Orosco, who was covering home and tagged Belliard to end the threat.

April 28, 1972

Agee Slam Beats Dodgers

A crowd of 51,210 packed Dodger Stadium to see Tommie Agee's eighth-inning grand slam power the Mets to a 6–1 win over the Los Angeles Dodgers.

The Mets snapped a 1–1 tie on Ken Boswell's RBI single in the eighth inning and had the bases loaded when Dodgers manager Walter Alston replaced starter Bill Singer with left-hander Jim Brewer, a screwball pitcher who had good success against right-handed batters.

Agee swung through two screwballs to get down in the count, but he found the 0–2 pitch to his liking. He drove it deep into the left-field seats, way beyond the 370-foot mark.

Both teams traded runs in the second inning. The Mets got their run on an RBI single by Ed Kranepool while the Dodgers scored courtesy of Bill Russell's RBI single.

The Mets had the same situation in the 12th inning, but a 6–2–3 double play killed the inning and the game continued.

Strawberry's slam in the first off Pirates starter Mike Bielecki was the last hit the Mets would get until the 12th inning, when Rafael Santana singled.

Roger McDowell made his first major league start and held the Pirates to one run until the sixth inning, when he gave up back-to-back doubles to Bill Madlock and Thompson that cut the lead to 4–2.

Reliever Calvin Schiraldi later gave up a game-tying two-run homer to Pirates catcher Tony Pena, but that was all Pittsburgh would score for the rest of the game.

Joe Sambito, Doug Sisk, Orosco and Tom Gorman pitched scoreless ball for the remaining 12 innings.

The left-handed Gorman went the final seven innings to earn the win.

The Mets played the game under protest after first-base umpire Harry Wendelstedt called a balk on first baseman Keith Hernandez in the ninth. Hernandez broke toward home in a bunt situation, then went back to first to field a pickoff throw from Sisk.

"I never heard of that rule," Hernandez said.

"There isn't one," Johnson added.

It was "Super Sundae" at Shea on this Sunday afternoon. Fans got a free chocolate sundae.

Pirates	AB	R	H	RBI
Orsulak cf	6	0	1	0
Ray 2b	8	0	2	0
Madlock 3b	8	1	2	0
Thompson 1b	6	1	2	1
Hendrick rf	8	1	2	1
Pena c	6	1	2	2
Kemp lf	4	0	2	0
Robinson p	0	0	0	0
Candelaria p	0	0	0	0
Lezcano ph	1	0	0	0
Guante p	1	0	0	0
McWilliams ph	1	0	0	0
Tunnell p	1	0	1	0
Belliard ss	4	0	2	0
Almon ph-ss-lf	4	0	1	0
Bielecki p	1	0	0	0
Mazzilli ph	0	0	0	0
Holland p	0	0	0	0
Morrison ph	1	0	0	0
Scurry p	0	0	0	0
Frobel lf	3	0	1	0
Rhoden ph	1	0	0	0
Dybzinski ss	0	0	0	0
Totals	**64**	**4**	**18**	**4**

Mets	AB	R	H	RBI
Backman 2b	5	0	1	0
Johnson 3b	2	1	1	0
Knight ph-3b	6	0	0	0
Hernandez 1b	4	1	0	0
Carter c	6	1	0	0
Wilson pr	0	1	0	0
Strawberry cf	6	1	2	4
Heep lf	3	0	0	0
Chapman ph	1	0	0	0
Hurdle lf-rf	4	0	0	1
Christensen rf	5	0	0	0
Gorman p	2	0	0	0
Santana ss	7	0	1	0
McDowell p	2	0	0	0
Schiraldi p	0	0	0	0
Sambito p	0	0	0	0
Gardenhire ph	1	0	0	0
Sisk p	0	0	0	0
Orosco p	1	0	0	0
Staub rf-lf	3	0	1	0
Totals	**58**	**5**	**6**	**5**

PIT 0 1 0 0 0 3 0 0 0 0 0 0 0 0 0 0 0 0 - 4 18 3
NYM 4 0 0 0 0 0 0 0 0 0 0 0 0 0 0 0 0 1 - 5 6 1

Pirates	IP	H	R	ER	BB	SO
Bielecki	4	2	4	4	4	0
Holland	1	0	0	0	1	1
Scurry	2	0	0	0	1	2
Robinson	0.2	0	0	0	2	0
Candelaria	1.1	0	0	0	0	0
Guante	5	3	0	0	2	5
Tunnell L (0-2)	3	1	1	1	1	3
Totals	**17**	**6**	**5**	**5**	**11**	**11**

Mets	IP	H	R	ER	BB	SO
McDowell	5.1	6	3	3	1	2
Schiraldi	0.2	3	1	1	0	1
Sambito	1	1	0	0	0	0
Sisk	1	1	0	0	4	0
Orosco	3	2	0	0	1	2
Gorman W (2-1)	7	5	0	0	1	5
Totals	**18**	**18**	**4**	**4**	**7**	**10**

E—Pittsburgh Belliard, Pena, Thompson; New York Santana. DP—Pittsburgh 2; New York 3. 2B—Pittsburgh Hendrick, Thompson; New York Staub. HR—Pittsburgh Hendrick (1); New York Strawberry (6). SH—Pittsburgh Orsulak. LOB—Pittsburgh 14; New York 13. Attendance: 36,423.

Craig's Win over Dodgers Not a Sign of Things to Come

Roger Craig went the distance on a seven-hitter as the Mets held off the Dodgers 4–2 at the Polo Grounds.

Craig was pleased to have beaten his old team for the first time, but little did he know that he would go on to lose his next 18 decisions.

A balk in the second inning by the right-hander allowed Ron Fairly to score from third base to give the Dodgers a 2–1 lead. From there, Craig settled down to keep the deficit at one.

The Mets scored three times in the seventh to grab a 4–2 lead.

Dodgers' starter Bob Miller, a 1962 Met, gave up a leadoff double to Ed Kranepool. After Charlie Neal's single put runners on the corners, Kranepool scored on a wild pitch by Miller. The Mets scored the go-ahead run when Dodgers reliever Ed Roebuck committed a balk to allow Neal to score from third and Jim Hickman singled home the third and final run of the inning.

In their first season (1962), the Mets dropped 16 of 18 games to the Dodgers, so this win was a little sweeter for the 23,494 fans at the Polo Grounds. One delirious fan took this opportunity to drop a sign down from the upper deck that read, "O'Malley Go Home," in reference to Dodgers owner Walter O'Malley, who was portrayed as the "villain" who moved the club to Los Angeles.

At a Glance
WP: Craig (2–2)
Key stat: Craig CG 7-hitter, 2 runs

Craig would not win another decision until Aug. 9, when he went the distance against the Cubs to improve his record to 3–20.

MAY

First baseman Ed Kranepool spent his entire 18-year career with the Mets. He ranks first in team history with 5,436 at-bats and 1,418 hits.

Teufel Makes Mets a Winner with Walk-Off Homer in a Pinch

Tim Teufel's walk-off, pinch-hit home run in the ninth inning gave the Mets a 7–6 victory over the Montreal Expos before 28,808 at Shea Stadium.

Teufel, a right-handed hitter who was batting for Wally Backman, lined a 2–1 pitch from Montreal lefty Bob McClure over the fence in left field to end a game that featured six home runs in all.

Darryl Strawberry's two-run homer in the first inning got the power show going.

Former Met Mike Fitzgerald hit a solo shot off Mets starter Ron Darling to cut the lead to 2–1.

Mets catcher Barry Lyons connected off Expos starter Bryn Smith in the second for a 3–1 lead, but Montreal grabbed a 4–3 advantage in the third against Darling. After back-to-back singles began the inning, Tom Foley gave the Expos the lead with a three-run homer.

The Mets came back with three runs in their half of the third. Darling drove in one run with a double and Len Dykstra's RBI single made it 6–4.

The Expos tied it in the seventh. Montreal pinch-hitter Wallace Johnson slammed a one-out home run off Darling and Tim Wallach's RBI double to left knotted the game at six.

Mets closer Jesse Orosco had to wiggle out of trouble in the ninth to set up Teufel's heroics. Montreal had runners on second and third with one out but Orosco struck out Andres Gallaraga for the second out. After an intentional walk to Wallach, Orosco caught Fitzgerald looking for the final out.

At a Glance

WP: Orosco (1–1)

HR: Strawberry (6), Lyons (2), Teufel (1)

Key stat: Strawberry 2-for-4, 2 RBIs

Sullivan an Unlikely Hero in Forgettable 1967 Season

Backup catcher John Peter Sullivan played one season with the Mets, but he had his "moment in the sun" in this game.

Sullivan's walk-off single in the 12th inning led the Mets to a thrilling 3–2, come-from-behind win over the San Francisco Giants before a crowd of 17,402 at Shea Stadium.

San Francisco pushed a run across in the top of the 12th inning to take a 2–1 lead. Jack Fisher went 11 $^2/_3$ innings before Willie Mays' single gave the Giants the lead and chased Fisher. Left-hander Don Shaw relieved Fisher and ended the inning by retiring future Hall of Famer Willie McCovey on a ground-out.

In the home half of the 12th, Al Luplow singled and scored on a one-out triple by Ed Kranepool. Cleon Jones ran for Kranepool and scored on Sullivan's hit to make a loser of Giants reliever Lindy McDaniel.

San Francisco starter and future Hall of Famer Gaylord Perry gave up a run on six hits in 11 innings of work.

At a Glance

WP: Shaw (1–1)

HR: Kranepool (2)

Key stat: Kranepool 3-for-5, 2 RBIs; Mets hit into triple play

Sullivan played five years in the majors. After his playing career, the Mets backstop spent 15 years as a coach for the Kansas City Royals, Atlanta Braves and Toronto Blue Jays. During his one-year stint in Queens, the Somerville, N.J., native hit .218 with no home runs and six RBIs.

In the second inning, Mets third baseman Ken Boyer hit into a 1–6–3 triple play. With runners on first and second, Boyer lined a ball back to the mound, where Perry grabbed it for the first out. Shortstop Hal Lanier covered second and took the throw from Perry for the second out, and relayed to McCovey at first to complete the triple play.

A Marquee Moment for Hamilton with 1-Hitter

Right-hander Jack Hamilton made 14 starts in a Mets uniform, but none better than the complete game one-hitter he tossed in an 8–0 win over the St. Louis Cardinals at Busch Stadium.

Hamilton allowed only two base runners in pitching the second one-hitter in team history.

With two outs in the bottom of the third inning and the Mets holding a 5–0 lead, Cardinals losing pitcher and future Met Ray Sadecki put down a bunt single for the Cardinals' only hit of the game. Future Hall of Famer Lou Brock followed with a walk, but Hamilton struck out Alex Johnson to end the inning.

At a Glance

WP: Hamilton (3–1)

HR: Swoboda (1), Bressoud (1)

Key stat: Hamilton CG 1-hitter

The Mets' offense backed Hamilton's gem with some early run support. Ed Bressoud started the game with a single to left. Jim Hickman drew a two-out walk and Ron Swoboda clubbed a 1–1 pitch from Sadecki into the bleachers in left field.

The Mets added two more in the second on RBI singles by Bressoud and Ken Boyer for a 5–0 lead.

A sparse crowd of 7,924 watched the Mets make their final appearance at the 46-year-old Busch Stadium a memorable one. On May 12, 1966, the Cardinals christened Busch Stadium II.

The Cardinals hit two fair balls to the outfield against Hamilton. Brock fouled out to Swoboda in left field in the sixth, while six Cards struck out against the 27-year old right-hander.

Ron Swoboda's three-run home run in the first inning put the Mets on their way to an 8–0 win over the Cardinals on May 4, 1966.

Strawberry Hitless in Debut, but Gets Fans Talking

In a game in which the Mets ushered in the "new" in rookie outfielder Darryl Strawberry, veteran outfielder George Foster's walk-off, three-run homer in the bottom of the 13th inning led the Mets to a 7–4 win over the Cincinnati Reds at Shea Stadium.

Strawberry, the 21-year-old phenom, made his major league debut and was 0-for-4, but the feeling around Shea Stadium was that a new era in Mets history had begun.

The expectations were so high for the young outfielder that some reporters were comparing his debut to that of Hall of Famer Willie Mays back in 1951.

"I'm not familiar with the things Willie has done," Strawberry said before the game.

The 6-foot-6, 190-pounder opened some eyes in batting practice, and had the photographers clicking non-stop with some long drives that carried into the stands at Shea.

Strawberry hit third in the lineup and in his first big-league at-bat, he struck out against one of the NL's best pitchers, Mario Soto.

"Soto is very impressive and I had a tough night at the plate," Strawberry said, "but I'll face him another day and will be looking for revenge."

> ### At a Glance
>
> **WP:** Orosco (1–0)
>
> **HR:** Foster (4), Kingman (5), Heep (3), Brooks (4)
>
> **Key stat:** Orosco three scoreless innings in relief

Strawberry would strike out three times in the game, but in the 13th, he walked against losing pitcher Bill Scherrer, stole second and scored the winning run on Foster's homer.

In the 11th, the crowd of 15,916 nearly had the thrill of a lifetime. Strawberry faced reliever Tom Hume and narrowly missed hitting the game-winning home run, as the ball was just foul.

"I didn't contribute with the bat, but I hope I helped the club anyway," Strawberry said. "I was pleased with the fans' reaction. They've waited a long time to see me."

Strawberry, who was chosen as the first overall pick in the 1980 draft, was hitting .333 in 16 games with three home runs and 13 RBIs in 17 games for Tidewater, the Mets' AAA affiliate. In 1982, the Los Angeles native led the Class AA Texas League with 34 home runs.

The Mets trailed 3–1 with two outs in the ninth inning when Dave Kingman tied the game with a two-run homer off Soto.

Kingman, whose home run was the 2,000[th] regular-season blast in Mets history, had to leave the game after that at-bat because of a strained calf muscle.

The Reds took a 4–3 lead in the 10th inning on an RBI double by Eddie Milner (who was former Met John Milner's cousin), but the Mets tied the game once again on a two-out home run by Hubie Brooks.

With the fanfare for Strawberry's debut dominating the headlines, it should be noted that Tom Seaver was outstanding to keep the Mets in the game.

"The Franchise" gave up three runs in eight innings with seven strikeouts to keep the Mets within striking distance.

Foster's blow against Reds pitcher Frank Pastore burned his old team, but he refused to revel in the glory.

"It was special because it won the game, and not because it was against the Reds," Foster said.

Strawberry led the team with a .306 average and four home runs in spring training, but there was some hesitation on the part of management to promote their young star so soon.

General manager Frank Cashen said, "Under ideal circumstances, we still prefer he stay down."

Ever since he was drafted, Strawberry had a spotlight on him. Cashen said, "When he (Strawberry) was in Kingsport, Tennessee, his first year, people from all around were flying in to see him. I don't remember anyone coming up to the majors with this kind of attention."

Before the game, Cashen offered some "fatherly" advice to his young slugger, about all the attention he would be receiving.

"That's why I talked to him in a brief, but intense conversation," Cashen said. "I told him not to go shouldering the burden. The danger is that Darryl will think he has to do it."

Strawberry would go on to play eight years with the Mets before signing with the Los Angeles Dodgers as a free agent following the 1990 season.

During his Mets tenure, Strawberry hit 252 home runs to become the club's all-time leader. He has a franchise-best 733 RBIs and 662 runs scored, in addition to being the team's all-time leader in extra-base hits with 469.

Southpaw Koosman Adds Another to His Long List of Wins

Left-hander Jerry Koosman dominated the San Francisco Giants to the tune of a three-hit shutout as the Mets scored a 6–0 victory before a crowd of 5,245 at Candlestick Park.

Koosman walked two and struck out seven, including future Hall of Famer Willie McCovey for the final out of his 26th career shutout and last as a New York Met.

The 34-year-old took the mound with a 1–0 lead thanks to Dave Kingman's sacrifice fly in the top of the first.

The Giants did not get their first hit until Derrel Thomas singled to lead off the fourth. A one-out single by Bill Madlock in the seventh and a Tim Foli (who played parts of four seasons with the Mets) leadoff double in the eighth were the only other hits.

Mets manager Joe Frazier shook up the lineup by moving second baseman Lenny Randle to leadoff and dropping center fielder Lee Mazzilli to seventh. The move paid immediate dividends as Randle went 3-for-5 with a RBI, two runs scored and a stolen base to spark the offense.

The Mets broke the game open in the fourth inning with three runs, two that came courtesy of a two-run single by Koosman.

> ### At a Glance
>
> **WP:** Koosman (2–3)
>
> **Key stat:** Koosman CG 3-hitter; Randle 3-for-5. RBI

After a stellar 12-year career during which he became the Mets' all-time winningest left-hander, Koosman was traded to the Minnesota Twins following the 1978 season.

The Mets got back Greg Field and a "player to be named later." On Feb. 7, 1979, that "player to be named later" was pitcher Jesse Orosco.

'Le Grand Orange' Gets His Number Called with Pinch Homer

Rusty Staub had a stellar 23-year career in the major leagues, but he was best known for his pinch-hitting prowess. That talent paid off in a Mets walk-off win.

Staub's pinch-hit home run with two outs in the ninth inning led the Mets to a 6–5 win over the San Francisco Giants at Shea Stadium before a crowd of 15,008.

Ron Hodges' two-run homer keyed a 3–0 lead for the Mets, but that quickly evaporated when San Francisco put up a four runs in the fifth.

Back-to-back home runs by Chili Davis and Johnnie LeMaster off Mets starter Pete Falcone accounted for the rally.

Dave Kingman's two-run homer in the sixth gave the Mets their second lead at 5–4, but a solo home run by the Giants' Tom O'Malley off Pat Zachry tied the score in the eighth.

Staub hit for Mets winning pitcher Craig Swan and drove a 1–0 sinker from losing pitcher Greg Minton into the bullpen in right field.

"He made a mistake," Staub said.

Minton was known as a pitcher who did not give up many home runs because of his sinker.

"If he makes a mistake," Staub said, "you've got a chance to drive the ball in the gap."

"Le Grand Orange" played nine years with the Mets in two separate stints. In 1983, Staub tied a record with eight consecutive pinch-hits.

At a Glance

WP: Swan (2–1)

HR: Hodges (1), Kingman (11), Staub (1)

Key stat: Staub walk-off HR wins it

Complete Game Shutout Is the Final One for Saberhagen

Bret Saberhagen made the most of a first-inning sacrifice fly as he tossed a complete game three-hitter in blanking the expansion Florida Marlins 1–0 at Shea Stadium.

The former two-time American League Cy Young Award winner walked one and struck out eight in pitching the final complete game shutout of his career.

A crowd of 20,234 watched the Mets get the only run of the game in the first inning against Marlins losing pitcher Ryan Bowen.

Vince Coleman singled to lead off the inning and stole second. He moved to third on a ground-out and scored on future Hall of Famer Eddie Murray's sacrifice fly to center field.

At a Glance

WP: Saberhagen (3–3)

Key stat: Saberhagen CG 3-hitter

The Marlins threatened to tie the game in the ninth. Chuck Carr singled and stole second. With two outs, former Met Dave Magadan hit a pop-up to short right field, but Mets second baseman Chico Walker made a nice running catch to preserve the game.

"I thought it was a base hit," Mets manager Jeff Torborg said.

After the game, Saberhagen said, "I'm just real happy he caught the ball and we're not still playing."

After being acquired from Kansas City in December 1991, Saberhagen spent parts of four years with the Mets. In July 1995, the Mets traded the former World Series Most Valuable Player to Colorado for right-handed pitcher Juan Acevedo.

Gooden Shows Prowess with Arm, Bat

Dwight Gooden was a one-man gang as he pitched and hit the Mets to a 9–4 win over the Los Angeles Dodgers at Shea Stadium.

At a Glance

WP: Gooden (2–3)

Key stat: Gooden 7 IP, 15 Ks; triple, 4 RBIs

Doc thrilled a crowd of 34,817 with his arm as he struck out 15 Dodgers in seven innings pitched. At the plate, Gooden lined a bases-clearing triple over the head of former Mets center fielder Juan Samuel and finished with four RBIs.

Gooden fanned the side in the first, second and fourth innings for nine of his 15 strikeouts.

Samuel, who struck out twice against the former National League Cy Young Award winner, said, "We didn't make him get the ball down. We chased his high stuff."

The Mets trailed 3–2 in the third but rallied for five runs (keyed by Gooden's triple) to grab a 7–3 lead.

The Tampa native was dominant, but he threw 127 pitches in seven innings, so manager Dave Johnson felt he had enough.

"He had a little trouble hitting spots," said the Mets skipper, "and he hung some breaking balls, but he got his rhythm and he got stronger as the game went on, and he didn't get arm weary."

For the 1990 season, Gooden would post a 19–7 record with a 3.83 ERA.

May 11, 1972

Mets Acquire Willie Mays

In one of the most famous trades in Mets history, Willie Mays was brought back to New York, where he began his illustrious career.

"It's a wonderful feeling," Mays said, "and I'm very thankful I can come back to New York."

Mays played the remainder of the 1972 season and 66 games of the 1973 season with the Mets.

A Pair of Walk-Off Homers Leads to First Doubleheader Sweep

The Mets thrilled a Polo Grounds crowd of 19,748 by winning not one, but two games by walk-off home runs.

Hobie Landrith and ol' favorite Gil Hodges hit walk-off "round trippers" to power the Mets to their first sweep of a doubleheader, 3–2 and 8–7 over the Milwaukee Braves.

In Game 1 the Mets trailed 2–1 heading to the ninth inning. Hodges stroked a leadoff single, but future Met and Hall of Famer Warren Spahn struck out pinch-hitter Cliff Cook and got pinch-hitter Gus Bell on a pop-up.

First baseman Gil Hodges holds his 1962 contract with the Mets. An artist's rendering of the club's new park, Shea Stadium, planned for construction in Flushing, N.Y., is behind him.

Spahn got ahead of Landrith with a called strike, but the Mets catcher drove the next pitch into the upper deck in right field for a dramatic 3–2 win.

Reliever Craig Anderson got the win, just as he would in Game 2.

Jim Hickman's leadoff homer against future Met Carl Willey gave the Mets a 1–0 lead. They made it 2–0 in the second on Elio Chacon's RBI single.

The Mets had a 4–1 advantage in the fifth, but the Braves rallied to score four runs to take a 5–4 lead. Tommie Aaron's sacrifice fly plated one run. Mack Jones tripled in a run to make it a one-run deficit and then future Hall of Famer Hank Aaron hit a two-run homer against Mets starter Bob Moorhead to give Milwaukee a the lead.

The Braves had a 7–6 lead in the eighth, but Chacon's RBI single tied the game 7–7 as the teams went to the ninth.

Left-hander Vinegar Bend Mizell was brought on to start the ninth for the Mets but he walked future Met Roy McMillan. Anderson replaced Mizell and got Aaron and Jones to ground out with the go-ahead run at third to keep the game tied.

In the bottom of the ninth, right-hander Hank Fischer retired Frank Thomas for the first out. Hodges also found the upper deck in right field at the Polo Grounds to his liking and ended this historic day for the Mets with a walk-off home run off Fischer for an 8–7 victory that completed the sweep.

Anderson, who was an expansion draft pick from the St. Louis Cardinals, played three of his four major league seasons with the Mets. In 1962, Anderson made 50 appearances—14 as a starter—and posted a 3-17 record. His overall record with the Mets was 3–20, so he got two of those in one day. His final game came on May 31, 1964, in the second game of a doubleheader, when the Mets lost an epic 23-inning marathon to the San Francisco Giants at Shea Stadium.

Besides Anderson, Willard Hunter and Jesse Orosco are the only other Mets pitchers to win both ends of a doubleheader.

Hunter did it on Aug. 23, 1964, when he beat the Cubs 2–1 and 5–4. On July 31, 1983, Orosco totaled five scoreless innings in relief to beat the Pirates twice in 12 innings, 7–6 and 1–0.

Gentry Flirts with No-No in Complete Game Shutout

Right-hander Gary Gentry flirted with a no-hitter for 7 $^2/_3$ innings before settling for a complete game one-hit shutout as the Mets blanked the Chicago Cubs at Wrigley Field, 4–0.

Gentry sat down the first 12 Cubs hitters before walking Ron Santo to start the fifth, but the threat was erased with a 6–6–3 double play.

A crowd of 9,823 watched Gentry retire nine more hitters before future Hall of Famer Ernie Banks batted with two outs in the eighth.

Banks worked the count to 2–2 and then hit a line drive toward left field. Mets left fielder Dave Marshall momentarily slipped on the wet grass. He then ran in and got his glove on the ball but could not hold it.

"The ball hit the tip of my glove," Marshall said. "The third base umpire, Chris Pelekoudas, said if I had scooped it more, I would've caught it."

The play was ruled a hit and after the game, Gentry defended his teammate.

"There was nothing Marshall could do about it," Gentry said. "It was a fastball up and in and Banks gave it a tomahawk chop. I've had better stuff, but never better control."

Banks didn't think he had a hit.

At a Glance
WP: Gentry (4–1)
HR: Shamsky (4)
Key stat: Gentry CG 1-hitter, 7 Ks

"I thought it would be caught by the outfielder," Banks said after the game.

Before Banks' hit, the closest the Cubs came to getting a hit was in the first inning. Billy Williams hit a ball wide of first base, but Mike Jorgensen made a terrific backhanded stop and flipped to Gentry, who covered first.

Gentry's "gem" was the fifth one-hitter in Mets history.

Say Hey! Mays Makes Marked Return to New York with Homer

You couldn't have written a better script for Willie Mays' return to New York.

Mays played in his first game since he was acquired from the Giants and he helped power the Mets to a 5–4 win over his old team before a crowd of 35,505 fans at Shea Stadium.

"It's a strange feeling to be batting against the club I played with for 20 years," Mays said as he reflected on the whole experience of joining only his second team in the big leagues. "You look up and you see 'GIANTS' written on their shirts, and you feel you should be out there."

The legendary center fielder hit in the leadoff spot and played first base in his first game back where he began his illustrious career.

Because the start of the game was delayed by rain for 30 minutes, Mays did not get to bat until 2:40 pm. But he received a thunderous ovation as he stepped to the plate, where he walked on five pitches against Giants starter Sam McDowell.

McDowell's control troubles were costly in the first inning as he walked Bud Harrelson and Tommie Agee to load the bases.

Rusty Staub smacked an 0–1 fastball off the scoreboard in right-center field for a grand slam and a 4–0 lead with Mays scoring his first Mets run.

The Giants rallied with four runs in the fifth inning against Mets lefty Ray Sadecki. Fran Healy walked and scored on a pinch-hit triple by the Giants' Bernie Williams. Chris Speier's double scored Williams and a two-run homer by Tito Fuentes tied the game, but Mays provided the fans with a little bit of "Say Hey" magic in the home half of the inning.

Giants	AB	R	H	RBI
Speier ss	5	1	1	1
Fuentes 2b	4	1	4	2
Bonds rf	5	0	0	0
Kingman 1b	4	0	0	0
Henderson cf	4	0	0	0
Hart 3b	4	0	2	0
Maddox lf	4	0	1	0
Healy c	1	1	0	0
Rader ph-c	1	0	0	0
McDowell p	1	0	0	0
Williams ph	1	1	1	1
Carrithers p	0	0	0	0
Howarth ph	1	0	0	0
Barr p	0	0	0	0
Gallagher ph	1	0	0	0
Totals	36	4	9	4

Mets	AB	R	H	RBI
Mays 1b	2	2	1	1
Harrelson ss	3	1	0	0
Agee cf	2	1	0	0
Staub rf	3	1	1	4
Jones lf	4	0	0	0
Fregosi 3b	3	0	1	0
Martinez 2b	3	0	1	0
Grote c	2	0	0	0
Sadecki p	2	0	0	0
McAndrew p	1	0	0	0
Totals	25	5	4	5

SF	0 0 0 0 4 0 0 0 0 -	4 9 0
NYM	4 0 0 0 1 0 0 0 X -	5 4 0

Giants	IP	H	R	ER	BB	SO
McDowell	4	2	4	4	4	7
Carrithers L (1-3)	1	1	1	1	2	1
Barr	3	1	0	0	1	5
Totals	8	4	5	5	7	13

Mets	IP	H	R	ER	BB	SO
Sadecki W (1-0)	5	6	4	4	2	2
McAndrew S (1)	4	3	0	0	1	2
Totals	9	9	4	4	3	4

DP—San Francisco 2. 2B—San Francisco Maddox, Speier; New York Fregosi. 3B—San Francisco Williams. HR—San Francisco Fuentes (2); New York Staub (3), Mays 1). LOB—San Francisco 8; New York 3. SB—New York Agee. Attendance: 35,505.

Don Carrithers replaced McDowell to start the fifth and Mays was the first batter that the right-hander would face. The 41-year-old living legend was exactly two weeks shy of the 22nd anniversary of his first major league home run when he connected on a 3–2 pitch from Carrithers and drove it over the wall in left field for his 647th career round-tripper.

In the clubhouse after the game, Mays noted the historical footnote to his first home run as a Met.

"That was my first hit as a Met," Mays said, "and my first hit as a Giant was a home run, too."

Mays' first big-league home run (and first big-league hit to snap an 0-for-12 skid to start his career) came on May 28, 1951, at the Polo Grounds against the Milwaukee Braves off future Hall of Famer and future Met, Warren Spahn.

Mets reliever Jim McAndrew made Mays' home run stand up as he relieved Sadecki to start the sixth inning and tossed four scoreless innings to earn the save.

Mays was dealt to the Mets on May 11, 1972, in exchange for Charlie Williams and $50,000 in cash. Mays played 135 games as a New York Met and hit 14 home runs and had 44 RBIs.

Following his retirement as a player in 1973, Mays was a member of the Mets coaching staff from 1974–1979.

Did You Know?

Ed Kranepool is the youngest player to ever appear in a game for the Mets. When he made his major league debut on Sept. 22, 1962, Kranepool was 17 years, 10 months and 14 days old.

Seaver's 1-Hitter Includes 15 Ks

Just two days after Gary Gentry tossed the Mets' fifth complete game one-hitter, Tom Seaver tossed his second career complete game one-hitter in blanking the Philadelphia Phillies 4–0 before a crowd of 6,373 at Connie Mack Stadium.

Phils rookie catcher Mike Compton singled with one out in the third inning for Philadelphia's only hit of the game. Compton was brought up from the minors two weeks earlier because Mike Ryan and Tim McCarver were injured.

Despite a severe chest cold, Seaver struck out 15 and walked three in his second career one-hitter.

The Mets took a 2–0 lead in the fourth inning as two runs scored on Phils pitcher Woodie Fryman's wild pitch. Donn Clendenon scored the first run and when Compton threw back toward home plate, no one covered, so the ball went down the first base line to enable Ron Swoboda to score from second.

The Mets padded their lead in the fifth to 4–0 on RBI singles from Joe Foy and Jerry Grote.

In the second inning, Foy was called out for passing Swoboda on the bases. Foy hit a fly ball to center field, but the Phils' Oscar Gamble, who was just recalled from the minors, dropped the ball. When Swoboda went back to first, thinking the ball would be caught, Foy passed him and was called out.

Seaver would throw five one-hitters for the Mets, including one on July 4, 1972, when he took a no-hitter into the ninth inning against San Diego. That day, the Padres' Leron Lee spoiled the bid with a one-out single.

At a Glance

WP: Seaver (7–1)

Key stat: Seaver CG 1-hitter, 15 Ks

Delgado's Hit Caps Ninth-Inning Rally Against Cubs

Down 5–1 in the ninth inning, the Mets stunned the Chicago Cubs by scoring five runs to pull out a thrilling 6–5 victory at Shea Stadium.

Carlos Delgado's walk-off, two-run single in the ninth was the key blow that delighted the crowd of 42,667.

Second baseman David Newhan singled to lead off the ninth against Cubs closer Ryan Dempster. After Ramon Castro lined out, Carlos Gomez singled, putting two runners on. Back-to-back walks to pinch-hitter Carlos Beltran and Endy Chavez made it 5–2.

After Ruben Gotay singled to make it a 5–3 game, the Cubs replaced Dempster with left-hander Scott Eyre.

At a Glance

WP: Burgos (1–0)

Key stat: Mets score five in ninth to stun Cubs; Delgado walk off, 2-run single

David Wright batted for Shawn Green and stroked a run-scoring single to center on the first pitch from Eyre to cut the deficit to 5–4.

With the bases loaded and one out, Delgado singled to right to score Chavez and Gotay with the tying and winning runs, making a loser of Dempster.

"I just lost the game," Dempster said, "not much more to say."

"I made the pitches I wanted to make," Eyre said, referring to ground ball hits by Wright and Delgado. "I'm not going to sit here and whine about it."

The game was tied at one in the sixth when the Cubs plated four runs against Mets starter Jason Vargas on a pair of two-run home runs from future Met Angel Pagan and third baseman Aramis Ramirez.

Ambiorix Burgos, a 23-year-old who would appear in 17 games with the Mets, pitched two scoreless innings to get the win.

Todd Overcomes Cancer, Then the Giants

Jackson Todd tossed 7 $^2/_3$ innings to pick up his first major league win as the Mets nipped the San Francisco Giants 4–3 at Shea Stadium.

This wasn't just your ordinary, initial big-league victory because 2 ½ years earlier, Todd was diagnosed with cancer and was given a 10 percent chance to live.

The 6-foot-2 right-hander underwent surgery in October 1974 to remove malignant lymph nodes from his chest. Todd underwent nine months of chemotherapy and turned to a diet of "healthy food and vitamins" to enable him to make his major league debut two weeks earlier.

At a Glance

WP: Todd (1–0)

HR: Milner (4), Randle (2)

Key stat: Todd 7 $^2/_3$ IP; 1st win in return from cancer

"After months of not being able to raise up, not being able to eat, wondering if I would live, much less, run or pitch again," the 25-year-old Todd said, "it's hard to get excited over winning a game. I guess it'll catch up to me later."

John Milner and Lenny Randle powered the offense with solo home runs as the Mets gave Todd a 4–0 lead.

After seven scoreless innings, Todd finally faltered as the Giants' Terry Whitfield clubbed a three-run homer to make it a one-run game.

Manager Joe Frazier lifted his starter for closer Skip Lockwood, who tossed 1 $^1/_3$ scoreless innings to pick up the save.

The newest Met put the whole experience in perspective.

"I don't put things off anymore," Todd said. "You learn how short life really is and to enjoy it while you're here."

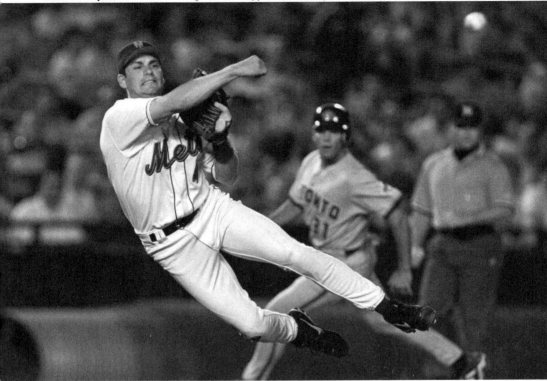

Ventura Gets Historic with Pair of Grand Slams in Doubleheader

Third baseman Robin Ventura became the first player in Major League Baseball history to hit a grand slam in both ends of a doubleheader as the Mets swept a pair from the Milwaukee Brewers at Shea Stadium, 11–10 and 10–1.

Ventura was well known for his success with the bases loaded (he had a total of 18 slams in his career), so it comes as no surprise that he would be the first to hit two in a twinbill. (On Sept. 4, 1995, Ventura hit two grand slams in one game against the Texas Rangers.)

In the opener, Ventura connected for his first slam against Brewers left-hander Jim Abbott to give the Mets a 4–0 lead in the first inning.

Benny Agbayani hit two home runs to make a winner of Al Leiter, who

Third baseman Robin Ventura, shown making a throw to first base, became the first player in Major League Baseball history to hit a grand slam in both games of a doubleheader on May 20, 1999.

didn't have his best game. Leiter gave up five earned runs in five innings pitched, but the Mets bailed him out after he gave up the lead in the fifth.

Agbayani's first home run off the Brewers' Steve Falteisek in the fifth inning gave the Mets an 8–6 lead. The native Hawaiian was 4-for-4 with four RBIs, but Ventura stole the show with his "slam-fest."

The Mets took a 10–6 lead in the sixth inning on a two-run, mammoth home run (an estimated 418 feet to dead-center field) by Mike Piazza.

The Mets had a two run lead entering the ninth. Closer John Franco gave up an unearned run thanks to a dropped pop-up with two out (sound familiar Met fans?) by 2B Edgardo Alfonzo but on the same play, Alex Ochoa was thrown out at the plate by RF Roger Cedeno as he tried to score the tying run.

Even though Leiter struggled to get the win, Manager Bobby Valentine supported his left-handed ace.

"Words only go so far," said the Mets skipper. "You need action and the win today was action. Regardless of how it looked or how tough it was going to get, he's (Leiter) going home with one more win than he had before."

At a Glance

Game 1

WP: Leiter (2–4)

HR: Agbayani 2 (2,3), Ventura (7), Piazza (7)

Game 2

WP: Yoshii (4–3)

HR: Allensworth (3), Ventura (8)

Key stat: Ventura hits grand slam in each game

In the nitecap, Masato Yoshi gave the Mets seven solid innings and Ventura's second slam of the day powered New York to a 10–1 thrashing of the Brewers and a sweep of the doubleheader.

A crowd of 19,542 saw Ventura make baseball history when he clubbed his second slam of the day to key a six-run rally in the fourth inning.

With two runs in, Ventura went deep against Milwaukee left-hander Horatio Estrada to blow the game open and give the Mets a 9–0 lead.

After the sweep was complete, Ventura put his feat in perspective while reminiscing about the time when he hit two grand slams in one game.

"It's different because it affects two games," Ventura said. "It's a little more satisfying. It's a good day to have a doubleheader."

Mays Steals the Show from Seaver, Carlton

Three future Hall of Famers proved to be the key players in the Mets' 4–3 win over the Philadelphia Phillies before a packed house of 57,267 on Bat Day at Veterans Stadium.

The Mets' Tom Seaver outpitched the Phils' Steve Carlton, but it was Willie Mays who had the deciding blow.

Mays blasted a two-run homer off Carlton in the eighth that gave the Mets the lead for good.

"To me, I don't think I did anything exceptional," Mays said afterward.

> ## At a Glance
>
> **WP:** Seaver (7–1)
>
> **HR:** Agee (5), Mays (2)
>
> **Key stat:** Mays game-winning 2-run HR off Carlton

The crowd, the second largest for a single game in NL history, saw Carlton, who would win 27 games and the 1972 National League Cy Young Award, no-hit the Mets through five innings, but Mays broke up the bid with a leadoff double in the sixth.

It wasn't the best day for Seaver, who gave up three runs in seven innings of work, but he was glad to have Mays on his side.

"He's fantastic, isn't he? He just makes things happen," Seaver said of Mays. "First he comes up and gets the first hit, then he comes up with the winning run at the plate and boom, he puts it out."

Mays had yet to lose as a Met—it was their team record-tying 11th straight victory—and had played well since joining the team.

"I don't think I'm trying to prove anything now after 20 years," Mays said, "and I'm not trying to show anybody up. I'm glad to be with the Mets. They have great spirit and they made me relax by welcoming me with open arms."

Most Impressive Pickoff? Stealing Piazza in Trade

Mets pitchers picked off two runners to secure a 3–2 victory over the Milwaukee Brewers at Shea Stadium, but the game took a back seat to what management did by picking off a superstar.

Before the game, the Mets acquired slugging catcher Mike Piazza from the Florida Marlins in exchange for outfielder Preston Wilson, pitcher Ed Yarnall and a pitching prospect named Geoff Goetz, who was the team's top draft pick in 1997.

The 22,307 fans at Shea were thrilled with the news. Some made signs acknowledging the acquisition, others cheered when Piazza's name was announced over the public address system.

The "picks" came in the top of the eighth inning. With runners at first and second and no one out for Milwaukee, Mets reliever Dennis Cook picked off Marquis Grissom, who was tagged out trying for third.

Without throwing another pitch, Cook picked off former Met Fernando Vina to effectively kill a rally without retiring a batter.

At a Glance

WP: Reed (5–2)

Key stat: Olerud 2 RBIs, Reed 9 Ks in 7 innings

Mets closer John Franco, who already switched his No. 31 in deference to Piazza and wore No. 45 for the first time, pitched 1 $\frac{1}{3}$ innings of scoreless relief to get the save for winning pitcher Rick Reed.

Mets general manager Steve Phillips was thrilled as he announced the trade.

"I'm ecstatic to be able to acquire an offensive force that instantly adds credibility to our lineup," Phillips said.

At a news conference in Miami, Piazza said he was happy to be going to the Mets.

"I know the media in New York is bigger than Los Angeles, so it's not going to be easy," said the hard-hitting backstop, who played for the Dodgers from 1992 to 1998. "I'm definitely not Superman, so I just want to try to get in there and help the team as much as possible and contribute and just kind of settle down a little bit."

Just about every Met was on board with the deal, but it left incumbent catcher Todd Hundley (who was rehabbing an elbow injury) in limbo.

Once the rumors of a Piazza deal intensified in recent days, the switch-hitting Hundley knew the writing was on the wall, but he still took it personally.

On a conference call from Florida, where he was rehabbing, Hundley said, "It just shows you have to look after yourself. I've been an organization guy. I played through broken bones and torn ligaments. The Mets have got to do what they've got to do."

There were rumors that Hundley could be moved to another position, possibly the outfield, but manager Bobby Valentine would not answer any hypothetical questions about how he would handle both players.

In a veiled shot at Hundley, who had never been one of his favorites, Valentine said, "What I do know is the four at-bats I have been getting out of my catching has been very upgraded."

The Mets were "under the gun" to sign the 29-year-old Piazza, who would be a free agent at the end of the season.

"I'm really not in a position to speculate on my future past this season," Piazza said.

Following the 1998 season, Piazza signed a record-breaking, seven-year, $91 million dollar deal to with remain with the Mets through the 2005 season. Piazza's career with the Mets included 220 home runs, which placed him second all-time on the club. He also established a single-season club record with 124 RBIs in 1999. In 2000, Piazza drove in at least one run in 15 consecutive games, a franchise record.

Piazza's Debut Brings Late Ticket Sales, and Seinfeld

It was a moment that Mets fans came to see.

Mike Piazza's debut was a complete success as he contributed an RBI double to the Mets' 3–0 shutout of the Milwaukee Brewers at Shea Stadium.

Al Leiter went the distance on a four-hitter, but it was Piazza who generated a buzz amongst the crowd of 32,908. (According to the game story in *The New York Times* editions of May 24, 1998, the Mets sold 13,000 of those tickets after the trade was completed.)

Piazza batted third in the lineup and got a standing ovation when he stepped to the plate in the first inning. Even after he grounded out, Piazza received another round of applause.

The Mets had a 1–0 lead in the fifth when Piazza brought the crowd to its feet.

With one out and a runner at first, Piazza lined a Jeff Juden pitch into the gap in right-center field to score Matt Franco with the second run. The slugging catcher took third on the throw home and the crowd (which included noted Mets fan and comedian Jerry Seinfeld) was in a frenzy.

At a Glance

WP: Leiter (4–3)

Key stat: Piazza 1-for-4, RBI in Mets debut; Leiter CG 4-hitter

"It feels good to get cheered again," said Piazza, who was being booed in Los Angeles earlier in the year.

Piazza acquitted himself well behind the plate as he handled Leiter to the tune of a complete-game shutout.

Leiter intimated that he and Piazza were able to get on the same page very quickly.

"I thought he did a fine job," Leiter said, "and I'm kinda tough to catch."

In the early stages of the game, Leiter shook off a couple of signs, but after a couple of meetings on the mound, the battery was in sync by the midway point of the game.

"We noticed Seinfeld in the stands," Leiter joked.

Nineteen-Inning Game a Hit Parade for Staub

Rusty Staub had five hits, including the tie-breaking, RBI double in the top of the 19th inning to lead the Mets to a 7–3 win over the Los Angeles Dodgers at Dodger Stadium.

Five hours and 42 minutes after it began, the third-longest game in Mets history was completed when Jim McAndrew induced Davey Lopes to ground into a game-ending force-out at second.

The Mets used five pitchers, including the winner, left-hander George Stone, who tossed six scoreless innings in relief.

Tom Seaver started and went six innings, giving up two earned runs (three in all) on nine hits. Tug McGraw walked five in five innings of relief but was able to keep the Dodgers off the board thanks to three of the Mets' five double plays, two that included outs at home plate.

"I can't remember that much trouble in a game I pitched," McGraw said.

The teams turned a total of nine double plays, one short of the National League record for a single game.

The Mets trailed 3–1 but scored a run in the seventh on a RBI double by Bud Harrelson and then tied the game in the eighth on a run-scoring single by George Theodore.

The Dodgers had the winning run on base in six of the last 10 innings, but McGraw, Stone and McAndrew were able to keep them off the board.

Cleon Jones led off the 19th with a single and scored on Staub's double. Pinch-hitter Ken Boswell drove in Staub with a RBI single off Dodgers lefty reliever Doug Rau, and then two more came home on a two-run double by Ed Kranepool.

Staub was 5-for-9 with the tie-breaking RBI and a run scored. Los Angeles center fielder Willie Davis tied a National League record with six hits, all singles. L.A. right fielder Willie Crawford had four hits while left fielder Manny Mota took an 0-for-9 collar in the game. The Dodgers also left 22 runners on base.

Jones and Theodore had three hits apiece for the Mets, who totaled 22 hits, 18 of which were singles.

At a Glance

WP: Stone (1–0)

Key stat: Staub 5-for-9, game-winning RBI in 19th

A crowd of 27,580 that included former Mets manager Casey Stengel was whittled down to a few thousand by the time the game ended at 1:45 AM. The 82-year-old Stengel, in his own inimitable manner, lamented, "I thought I'd beat the crowd so I left in the seventh inning."

A weary Staub was asked how it felt to finally break up a tie game in the 19th inning.

"I was already famous for playing all 24 innings in Houston against the Mets five years ago," said "Le Grande Orange." "I went 2-for-7 [actually 2-for-9] with a couple of walks [one walk]. I hadn't eaten anything since 1 o'clock yesterday afternoon, but somehow didn't get hungry during the game. Your spikes feel as though they're up in your ankles by the [19th] inning, though, especially on that hard infield here."

When Harrelson returned to the Biltmore Hotel, where the team was staying in Los Angeles, the shortstop immediately fell into an armchair seat.

"My feet are killing me," sighed Harrelson.

SS Bud Harrelson

Bud Harrelson was the anchor of the Mets' infield for 13 seasons.

Harrelson was an average hitter, but he also was an outstanding defensive shortstop who won a Gold Glove in 1971.

The 5-foot-11, 160-pound Harrelson is well known for an incident with 5-foot-11, 192-pound Pete Rose that occurred during Game 3 of the 1973 National League Championship Series.

In the fifth inning, Rose slid hard into Harrelson as Rose tried to break up the double play. The two were embroiled in a scuffle at second base as both benches and bullpens emptied onto the field. Order was eventually restored and play resumed, but Reds manager Sparky Anderson had to pull his team off the field because the fans in the left-field stands were throwing objects at—and harassing—Rose.

Mets manager Yogi Berra and a contingent of players that included Willie Mays, Tom Seaver, Cleon Jones, Rusty Staub, and Tug McGraw were actually summoned by NL President Chub Feeney to walk to out to left field to calm the fans.

In 1986, Bud Harrelson was inducted into the Mets Hall of Fame.

Aspromonte Provides the Heroics with His Bat

In a sweet taste of irony, Brooklyn's Bob Aspromonte's walk-off RBI single in the 12th inning gave the Mets a 5–4 win over Jim Bunning and the Philadelphia Phillies at Shea Stadium.

Both Bunning and Aspromonte were in the final years of their big-league careers, but the Phillies right-hander, who had started 512 games in his 17-year career, was demoted to the bullpen in time for this game. Aspromonte began his career with the Brooklyn Dodgers and ended his career with the New York Mets.

> **At a Glance**
>
> **WP:** Frisella (2–1)
>
> **Key stat:** Foli 3-for-6; Frisella 3 IP, 1 hit; Aspromonte walk-off single

The Phillies had a 4–3 lead in the fifth but the Mets tied the game as Jerry Koosman scored from third on a balk called against Phillies starter Ken Reynolds, who was Bunning's replacement in the rotation.

Phils manager Frank Lucchesi came out to argue the call with second-base umpire Shag Crawford to no avail and the game went to extra innings.

Mets second baseman Tim Foli was thrown out at home twice in extra innings, while the Phils had two on and one out in the 10th but were stymied by a diving stop from Mets shortstop Bud Harrelson that killed the rally.

In the 12th, Foli reached on a rare error by Phils shortstop Larry Bowa. Tommie Agee walked and Donn Clendenon hit what should've been a double-play grounder to Bowa at short, but Agee went in hard and took out Phils second baseman Terry Harmon with a "flying block" slide.

Foli took third base on the play, but the next batter, Cleon Jones, hit a grounder to shortstop. Foli tried to score but was thrown out by Bowa for the second out.

With two outs and two on, Aspromonte, a 13-year veteran, lined a 1–1 pitch from Bunning to right field to score Clendenon with the winning run.

Mets Turn Up the Heat at Wrigley with Record 23 Hits against Cubs

It was a record-setting day at Wrigley Field as the Mets clobbered the hometown Chicago Cubs 19-1 before 2,503 disbelieving fans.

The Mets amassed a club-record 23 hits that included 17 singles, three doubles, two triples and one home run. Every player in the starting lineup had at least one hit and one RBI.

Mets first baseman Dick Smith became the first player in franchise history to have five hits in a game, while third baseman Charley Smith drove in five runs.

The tone of the game was set in the top of the first, when the Mets scored four times off Cubs starter and loser Bob Buhl.

The first four Mets reached safely to produce one run. Smith plated two more with a single to make it 3–0 and Roy McMillan drove in the fourth run with a single that knocked out Buhl.

It was no better for Cubs relievers Wayne Schurr, Sterling Slaughter and Glen Hobbie, who combined to allow nine runs (six earned) on 13 hits in 5 $^2/_3$ innings pitched.

The Mets scored three times in the second on singles by Frank Thomas and Jim Hickman, a triple by Joe Christopher and a passed ball.

Singles by McMillan, winning pitcher Jack Fisher and Ron Hunt, a hit batsman, a balk and a double off the wall by Dick Smith made it a 13–1 runaway in the seventh.

The Mets continued their assault with five hits and six more runs in the ninth. The Smiths pounded Cubs reliever Don Elston. Dick had a triple and Charley popped a three-run homer to complete the

Mets	AB	R	H	RBI
D Smith 1b	6	3	5	2
Hunt 2b	5	2	4	1
Thomas lf	5	3	2	1
Stephenson lf	0	0	0	0
Hickman cf	5	3	3	3
Christopher rf	5	2	1	2
C Smith 3b	6	2	3	5
McMillan ss	5	1	2	1
Samuel ss	1	0	0	0
Cannizzaro c	5	2	2	1
Fisher p	6	1	1	1
Totals	49	19	23	17

Cubs	AB	R	H	RBI
Stewart 2b	4	0	0	0
Brock rf	4	0	0	0
Williams lf	4	0	1	0
Santo 3b	4	0	1	0
Banks 1b	3	1	1	0
Rodgers ss	3	0	0	0
Ranew c	3	0	0	0
Cowan cf	3	0	1	1
Buhl p	0	0	0	0
Schurr p	0	0	0	0
Burton p	0	0	0	0
Slaughter p	0	0	0	0
Amalfitano ph	1	0	0	0
Hobbie p	0	0	0	0
Spring p	0	0	0	0
Burke ph	1	0	0	0
Elston p	0	0	0	0
Totals	30	1	4	1

NYM	4	3	0	0	2	0	4	0	6	-	19	23	0
CHI	0	0	0	0	1	0	0	0	0	-	1	4	1

Mets	IP	H	R	ER	BB	SO
Fisher W (2-3)	9	4	1	1	1	3
Totals	9	4	1	1	1	3

Cubs	IP	H	R	ER	BB	SO
Buhl L (4-2)	0.1	5	4	4	1	1
Schurr	2.2	3	3	2	0	3
Slaughter	2	6	2	2	0	1
Hobbie	1	4	4	2	1	1
Spring	2	0	0	0	0	1
Elston	1	5	6	6	1	1
Totals	9	23	19	16	3	8

E—Chicago Rodgers. DP—New York; Chicago. 2B—New York D Smith, Cannizzaro 2; Chicago Banks, Williams. 3B—New York Christopher, D Smith. HR—New York C Smith (2). HBP—New York Christopher, Cannizzaro. LOB—New York 8; Chicago 3. SB—New York D Smith. Attendance: 2,503.

scoring barrage. Fisher took full advantage of the offensive support as he went the distance, giving up a run on four hits.

If there was a Cubs "star of the game," it had to be reliever Jack Spring, who pitched two hitless and scoreless innings.

In took just two hours and 49 minutes for the Mets to set six club records with their offensive outburst.

The game was probably summed up best in a book titled, *The New York Mets: 25 Years of Baseball Magic*, written by Jack Lang and Peter Simon.

In describing the game, the book tells the story of one anxious Mets fan who wanted the "lowdown" on the game.

"The Mets went into Chicago and erupted for an incredible nineteen runs in a twenty-three hit attack against Cubs pitchers that produced a 19-1 victory. Radio and TV broadcasts in New York carried the startling news that the Mets had scored nineteen runs. But one Connecticut fan, catching only the final words of the bulletin, was in a quandary. He called the *Waterbury Republican* to check: "I just heard that the Mets scored nineteen runs today. Is that right?" he asked the sports department.

"That's right, nineteen runs" he was assured.

"Did they win?" the fan inquired.

Did You Know?

Tom Seaver and Walt Terrell hold the team record for hitting the most home runs in one season as a pitcher. Seaver hit three home runs in 1972. Terrell hit three in 1983, including two in one game on Aug. 6, 1983, against the Chicago Cubs.

Darling Shows His Fight with 12 Ks

Ron Darling struck out a career-high 12 batters and George Foster smacked a grand slam to lead the Mets to a brawl-filled 8-1 win over the Los Angeles Dodgers at Shea Stadium.

The brawl, in front of a crowd of 35,643, came right after Foster's slam in the sixth inning gave the Mets a 7–1 lead. Dodgers reliever Tom Niedenfuer gave up the big blow and then plunked the next batter, Ray Knight, on the left forearm.

Knight charged the mound and both benches emptied, but, in the end, no one was ejected.

Darling gave up a first-inning home run to Dodgers center fielder Ken Landreaux, but just three singles and a double after that. Darling's curveball and split-finger fastball were so good that eight of the 12 strikeouts were of the "caught looking" variety.

At a Glance

WP: Darling (6–0)

HR: Foster (5), Hernandez (3)

Key stat: Darling CG 5-hitter, 12 Ks; Hernandez 3 hits; Foster grand slam, 4 RBIs

With the score tied at one, the Mets got to Dodgers starter Bob Welch. Len Dykstra singled and scored on a RBI double by Wally Backman to give the Mets a 2–1 lead.

Keith Hernandez singled to put runners on first and third. Gary Carter's single brought in Backman and then Danny Heep singled to reload the bases.

With Foster due up, Dodgers manager Tommy Lasorda elected to replace Welch with Niedenfuer, who had struck out the Mets' outfielder in two previous encounters.

Foster knew this and after taking strike one, he unloaded on a fastball and lined it over the 338-foot sign in left-center field for his 13th career grand slam.

After the home run, Niedenfuer backed off the mound, got back on the rubber and hit Knight with the very next pitch.

Lasorda argued that Knight should've been ejected, but neither player was. Niedenfuer denied that he was throwing at Knight.

"The pitch to Foster wasn't where I wanted it," said the 6-foot-5 reliever. "The pitch to Knight wasn't where I wanted it."

Koosman's 15 Strikeouts Set Table for Harrelson

Jerry Koosman pitched 10 scoreless innings and set a club record (later broken by Tom Seaver) with 15 strikeouts, but it was Bud Harrelson's walk-off single in the bottom of the 11th that gave the Mets a 1–0 win over the San Diego Padres at Shea Stadium.

Koosman was brilliant, but so was Padres rookie Clay Kirby, who tossed nine scoreless innings and worked out of jams in the second, fifth and seventh innings.

In the fifth, the Mets had the bases loaded with no one out, but Kirby got Tommie Agee to pop out to second and then induced Wayne Garrett to hit into an inning-ending 4–4–3 double play.

Left-hander Jerry Koosman ranks third in club history with 140 wins. Koosman went 17–9 with a 2.28 earned-run average and 180 strikeouts during an All-Star season in 1969.

Cleon Jones began the 11th by reaching first base on an error by Padres shortstop Tommy Dean. Ed Kranepool struck out while trying to bunt.

Ron Swoboda was due up, so Padres manager Preston Gomez went to right-hander Frank Reberger. The Mets' right fielder crossed up the strategy by lining a single to right-center to send Jones to third.

Jerry Grote was intentionally walked to load the bases and Harrelson connected for a game-winning single down the left-field line to score Jones.

Tug McGraw pitched a scoreless inning for the win, but even he would agree that Koosman deserved the victory. The Mets' 26-year-old southpaw had 14 strikeouts through eight innings to tie Nolan Ryan's record for a nine-inning game. He added his 15th strikeout in the top of the 10th, when he fanned Padres pinch-hitter Ivan Murrell.

LHP Jerry Koosman

Jerry Koosman is the winningest left-handed pitcher in Mets history.

In 1976, Koosman was 21–10 with a 2.69 ERA and finished second in the National League's Cy Young Award vote.

The Appleton, Minn., native won two games in the 1969 World Series, including the decisive Game 5, when he went the distance to clinch the Mets' first World Championship.

Koosman is among the club's all-time leaders in wins (140), starts (346), complete games (108) and shutouts (26).

"Kooz" joined the Mets Hall of Fame in 1989.

At a Glance

WP: McGraw (4–1)

Key stat: Koosman 10 IP, 4 hits, 15 Ks

Delgado Stuns Ex-Met in Comeback

Carlos Delgado hit a walk-off home run off former Mets closer Armando Benitez in the bottom of the 12th inning to give the Mets an exciting 5–4 win over the San Francisco Giants at Shea Stadium.

Benitez came on to protect a 4–3 lead, but he walked Jose Reyes leading off the 12th. Reyes executed his job to perfection as he distracted Benitez into committing a balk that sent him to second.

Endy Chavez laid down a successful sacrifice bunt to move Reyes to third.

"I just tried to put some pressure on him (Benitez) and it worked," the shortstop said.

It worked all right. Benitez comitted another balk, sending Reyes home with the tying run.

> ### At a Glance
> **WP:** Smith (2–0)
> **HR:** Delgado 2 (6, 7)
> **Key stat:** Delgado 2-for-4, 3 RBIs

Benitez was distracted enough to feed Delgado a pitch that he clobbered for his second home run of the night, sending the 47,940 fans home happy.

The Giants had taken a 4–3 lead in the top of the 12th. Omar Vizquel reached first on a leadoff walk from Mets reliever Joe Smith and eventually scored the go-ahead run on Randy Winn's ground-out.

Delgado's first home run, a two-run shot, came off Giants phenom Tim Lincecum, who was making only his fifth major league start. The blast tied the game at two in the fourth.

Smith got the win in relief while Benitez took the loss.

Rookie Wilson Shuts Down Bonds, Giants

The Mets had the first overall pick in the 1994 draft. They chose a 6-foot-5 right-handed pitcher named Paul Wilson out of Florida State University.

Wilson made 26 starts in 1996 as a rookie for the Mets, but he never pitched a better game than when he tossed eight shutout innings and beat the San Francisco Giants and Barry Bonds 1–0 at Shea Stadium before a crowd of 15,781.

"This is the kind of game I've been waiting for," Wilson said. "I feel I'm capable of doing that every time out."

A run-scoring single in the eighth by Jose Vizcaino brought home Rey Ordonez with the only run of the game.

Mets closer John Franco overcame a leadoff bunt single by Stan Javier to finish it off for Wilson's second big-league win and his 10th save.

Mets manager Dallas Green was pleased with the performance.

"Today he (Wilson) was dominating," Green said. "He got the ball over the plate and had command of his pitches. He pitched like a pitcher."

Giants lefty Allen Watson, who grew up in nearby Middle Village, Queens, was just as stingy as Wilson as he held the Mets scoreless through seven.

Ordonez led off the eighth with a single and moved to second on a sacrifice bunt by pinch-hitter Edgardo Alfonzo. After taking third on a groundout, Ordonez scored when Vizcaino slapped a 1–1 pitch past a diving Shawon Dunston (a future Met) for the RBI single.

"He (Watson) had pitched me inside the whole game," Vizcaino said. "I wanted to put the ball in play and see what happened. Luckily, it found a hole."

On this day, Wilson lived up to his billing as a No. 1 overall draft choice.

Giants	AB	R	H	RBI
Benard rf	4	0	1	0
Javier cf	4	0	2	0
Bonds lf	4	0	1	0
Williams 3b	4	0	0	0
Carreon 1b	3	0	0	0
Dunston ss	3	0	0	0
Scarsone 2b	3	0	0	0
Manwaring c	2	0	0	0
Watson p	3	0	0	0
Totals	30	0	4	0

Mets	AB	R	H	RBI
Johnson cf	4	0	0	0
Vizcaino 2b	4	0	1	1
Gilkey lf	4	0	1	0
Kent 3b	3	0	1	0
Hundley c	3	0	1	0
Huskey rf	2	0	0	0
Jones pr-rf	0	0	0	0
Bogar 1b	3	0	1	0
Ordonez ss	3	1	1	0
Wilson p	2	0	0	0
Alfonzo ph	0	0	0	0
Franco p	0	0	0	0
Totals	28	1	6	1

SF	0	0	0	0	0	0	0	0 - 0	4	1
NYM	0	0	0	0	0	0	1	X - 1	6	0

Giants	IP	H	R	ER	BB	SO
Watson L (5-5)	8	6	1	1	1	4
Totals	8	6	1	1	1	4

Mets	IP	H	R	ER	BB	SO
Wilson W (2-5)	8	3	0	0	0	8
Franco S (10)	1	1	0	0	0	1
Totals	9	4	0	0	0	9

E—San Francisco Dunston. DP—San Francisco; New York. 2B—San Francisco Bonds, Benard. SH—New York Alfonzo. HBP—San Francisco Carreon, Manwaring. LOB—San Francisco 5; New York 5. Attendance: 15,781.

May 31, 1964

A Long Doubleheader

A doubleheader that included a second game lasting seven hours and 23 minutes finally ended at 11:25 PM Eastern, when Mets second baseman Amado Samuel flied out to San Francisco Giants right-fielder Jesus Alou.

The Giants beat the Mets 8–6 in a record-setting, 23-inning marathon.

By the time the second game ended, many of the crowd of 57,037 had gone home.

The Mets' Joe Christopher hit a game-tying, three-run homer off Bobby Bolin in the seventh inning. The teams went scoreless for the next 15 innings until pinch-hitter Del Crandall broke the tie with an RBI double that gave San Francisco a 7–6 lead.

Alou drove in the second run of the inning with an RBI single. Future Hall of Famer Gaylord Perry pitched 10 innings in relief to get the win. Galen Cisco relieved Larry Bearnarth and tossed nine innings, but suffered the loss.

A total of 12 pitchers were used to compile a record 36 strikeouts for one game and a record 47 "Ks" for the day.

The Mets even turned a triple play in the 14th inning. Numerous records were set on "The Longest Day" at Shea. The game was the longest in major league history in time elapsed (seven hours and 23 minutes). It was also the longest doubleheader in history (nine hours and 52 minutes). Finally, it was the most innings ever played by two teams in one day and the fourth-longest game in baseball history (Brooklyn and Boston played a 26-inning tie on May 1, 1920).

The Giants swept the twinbill with a 5–3 win in the opening game.

JUNE

Ron Darling, who pitched for the Mets from 1983–1991, went 15–6 with a 2.81 earned run average in the team's 1986 World Championship season.

A Pair of Walk-Offs, A Pair of Victories

It was a very pleasant Sunday afternoon for 18,844 fans at the Polo Grounds as the Mets swept a twinbill from the Pittsburgh Pirates, 2–1 and 4–3.

A pair of walk-off hits gave the Mets an impressive two-win day.

With the score tied in the 10th in the opening game, Mets pitcher Larry Bearnarth led off with a single. Pinch runner Rod Kanehl was sacrificed to second.

Tim Harkness was intentionally walked, bringing up Ron Hunt.

The Mets' second baseman hit a fly ball to left. Pirates left fielder Jerry Lynch originally broke back on the ball, but had to reverse field to come racing back. Bucs center fielder Bill Virdon saw the problem Lynch was having, so he went over toward left to catch the ball, but as it settled into the leather, Lynch collided with Virdon. Both fielders crashed to the ground, the ball came loose and Kanehl raced home from second on the error (charged to Lynch) with the winning run.

In the nightcap, Jim Hickman slammed a long home run off the Pirates' Elroy Face with one out in the 10th to lift the Mets to a 4–3 win.

The Mets had a 3–0 lead going to the seventh, but the Pirates came back with single runs in the seventh, eighth and ninth innings. Pittsburgh tied the game on an error by Mets catcher Choo Choo Coleman, who failed to hold on to the ball after a collision at home with future Met Donn Clendenon.

Hickman's game-winner, estimated at 420 feet, landed in the upper deck in left-center field at the Polo Grounds.

At a Glance

Game 1

WP: Bearnarth (2–1)

HR: Snider (9)

Key stat: Fernandez 3-for-3

Game 2

WP: Hook (3–5)

HR: Hickman (6)

Key stat: Stallard 1 run in 6 IP

Pair of Kranepool Homers Beat Dodgers

Ed Kranepool slammed two home runs to lead the Mets over the Los Angeles Dodgers 5-2 before a crowd of 24,212 at Shea Stadium.

At a Glance

WP: Seaver (8–3)

HR: Kranepool 2 (4,5)

Key stat: Kranepool 2-for-3, 3 RBIs

Kranepool's first home run in the fifth was the first hit off Dodgers starter and losing pitcher Alan Foster.

With two outs in the sixth, Wayne Garrett singled and Cleon Jones hit a fly ball to right-center field. Dodgers center fielder Willie Davis ran in front of right fielder Andy Kosco and caught the ball, but he dropped it when he bumped Kosco. It was ruled a triple for Jones, who came home to score on Kranepool's second home run of the game and it was 4–0.

Tom Seaver tossed one-hit shutout ball for six innings, but he gave up a two-run homer to Kosco in the seventh to make it a 4–2 game.

The Mets scored their last run in the eighth. With the bases loaded and two outs, Dodgers pitcher Jim Brewer tried to pick off Jones at second. Wayne Garrett, meanwhile, stole home on the attempted pickoff to score an important fifth run.

June 3, 1980

Mets Pick Strawberry No. 1 in Draft

For the third time in their history, the Mets had the number one overall pick in the amateur draft. They chose 18-year-old outfielder Darryl Strawberry out of Crenshaw High School in Los Angeles.

The young left-handed hitter drew comparisons to Hall of Famer Ted Williams. Respected Philadelphia Phillies scout Hugh Alexander was quoted as calling Strawberry, "the best prospect I've seen in the last thirty years."

Kingman Sets Records with 3 Homers, 8 RBIs

Dave Kingman became the second Met (see: Sept. 3, 1965) to hit three home runs in one game as he powered the Mets to an 11–0 whuppin' of the Los Angeles Dodgers at Dodger Stadium.

Kingman drove in a club-record eight runs (since surpassed by Carlos Delgado, see: June 27, 2008) to support the three-hit shutout spun by Mets ace Tom Seaver in front of a crowd of 52,516 at Dodger Stadium.

"Kong" touched Dodgers starter and loser Burt Hooton for two of his home runs.

In the fourth, Kingman hit a two-run shot that went over the 370-foot mark in left field for a 2–0 lead.

> ## At a Glance
>
> **WP:** Seaver (5–4)
>
> **HR:** Kingman 3 (18,19,20), Kranepool (4)
>
> **Key stat:** Kingman 3-for-5, 8 RBIs

With two outs in the fifth, Kingman unloaded on Hooton to just about the same spot in left field for a three-run homer and a 6–0 lead. The next hitter, Ed Kranepool, also homered, knocking Hooton out of the box.

With Dodgers left-hander Al Downing working the seventh in relief, Kingman took him deep for another three-run bomb as the Mets blew the game open with a 10–0 advantage.

As usual, Seaver was superb. In eight innings, "Tom Terrific" had allowed one hard-hit ball. The three-time Cy Young Award winner walked one and struck out eight in tossing a gem that was watched by Rod Dedeaux, who coached both Seaver and Kingman at the University of Southern California.

Dave Kingman hit three home runs and set a Mets record with eight RBIs in an 11–0 win over the Dodgers on June 4, 1976.

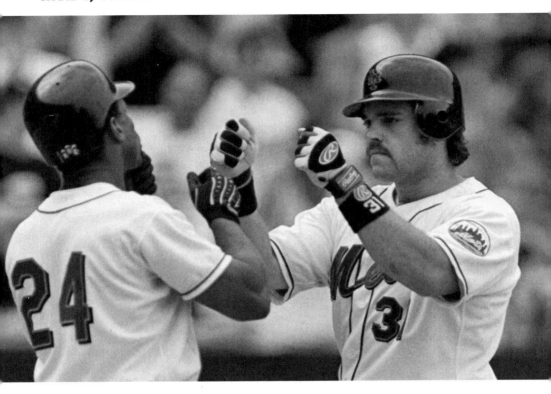

Piazza Helps to End Clemens' Win Streak at 20 Games

Mike Piazza continued his domination of Yankees pitcher Roger Clemens as he led the Mets to a 7–2 win over their crosstown rivals at Yankee Stadium.

A crowd of 56,294 packed the ol' ballpark to see the Mets put an end to Clemens' 20-game winning streak. The five-time Cy Young Award winner had not lost since May 29, 1998.

Piazza got things started in the second inning with a booming double that landed over the head of center fielder Bernie Williams.

Bobby Bonilla's two-run double and a two-run single by Benny Agbayani provided the four-run outburst.

Mike Piazza (right) delivered many memorable moments in his career with the Mets.

Al Leiter was on top of his game as he limited the Yankees to only two infield hits over the first four innings.

At a Glance

WP: Leiter (3–5)

HR: Piazza (10)

Key stat: Piazza 2-for-5, 2 runs, 2 RBIs; Agbayani 3 RBIs

"Easily my most satisfying moment of the season, thus far," Leiter said after the game.

John Olerud singled to begin the third and Piazza took Clemens deep for a two-run homer and a 6–0 lead.

The Mets knocked Clemens out of the box in the third as the right-hander gave up a total of seven runs on eight hits in 2 2/3 innings pitched.

The win came just one day after management shook up the club by firing three of manager Bobby Valentine's coaches.

Pitching coach Bob Apodaca, hitting coach Tom Robson and bullpen coach Randy Niemann were all let go and replaced by Dave Wallace, Mickey Brantley and Al Jackson, respectively.

Olerud was taken aback by the change in hitting coaches.

"He was the best hitting instructor that I've worked with," Olerud said of Robson.

C Mike Piazza

In the late 1990s, the Mets were lacking an "identity," but that changed when they acquired hard-hitting catcher Mike Piazza from the Florida Marlins in May 1998.

Piazza was a force behind the plate as he keyed many memorable victories while leading the Mets to consecutive postseason appearances in 1999 and 2000, the only time that has been accomplished in club history.

The 12-time All-Star is considered by many to be the "best hitting catcher of all time."

Piazza played 7 ½ seasons and a total of 972 games in New York. He had 1,028 hits with the Mets and is the club's all-time leader in slugging percentage (.542).

In addition, Piazza is second on the club's all-time list behind Darryl Strawberry in home runs (220) and third in RBIs (655).

Snider's 399th Homer Provides the Edge

Duke Snider's 399th career home run proved to be a game-winner as the Mets beat the Cardinals 3–2 before 15,268 fans at the Polo Grounds.

With one out in the ninth, the "Duke of Flatbush" smashed a three-run homer off Cardinals left-hander Diomedes Olivo to give the Mets an improbable win.

The Cardinals had right-hander Ron Taylor (who would go on to become a key member of the Mets' bullpen during their 1969 championship season and later a team physician for the Toronto Blue Jays) on the mound and the 25-year-old held the Mets down for eight shutout innings.

Taylor began the ninth by giving up a one-out single to pinch-hitter Frank Thomas and then he walked Ron Hunt to put the tying runs on base.

> ### At a Glance
> **WP:** Jackson (5–5)
> **Key stat:** Snider 2-for-4, 3 RBIs

Olivo, a 43-year-old left-hander from the Caribbean who did not speak much English, got behind Snider. On the 2–1 pitch, Snider took a called third strike but Cards catcher Gene Oliver was charged with a passed ball, putting the tying runs in scoring position.

The Cards then held a conference on the mound to no avail, as two pitches later Snider drove a curveball from Olivo into the left-field stands for a three-run blast and the walk-off win.

Snider said, "I'm sure he (Olivo) tried to get it on the outside corner, but he didn't, thank goodness."

Mets manager Casey Stengel added this little bit of "Stengelese" to the festivities.

"I think with the manager and eight infielders and outfielders all going out there to tell him what to do, I wonder what they all say now which one told him the right thing to do, or whether he got it."

Seaver's 14 Ks Give Mets Edge over Padres

Tom Seaver had a club record-tying 14 strikeouts (in a nine-inning game) and Wayne Garrett's RBI single capped off a two-run rally in the eighth inning that gave the Mets a 3–2 win over the San Diego Padres before 8,568 at San Diego Stadium.

The Mets trailed 2–1 in the eighth. Padres starter Al Santorini had allowed one run on three hits to that point, but pinch-hitter Ed Charles began the eighth with a single. Rod Gaspar hit for Seaver and bounced back to Santorini, but Charles was on the move and he took second.

After Bud Harrelson walked, Tommie Agee smacked a double off the wall in right field to score Charles, tie the game 2–2 and knock Santorini out of the game.

Left-hander Bill McCool was brought on to pitch to the left-handed hitting Garrett, but the redheaded third baseman spoiled the strategy as he lined a single off Padres rookie second baseman Johnny Sipin, who was playing in. Harrelson scored with the lead run.

Seaver was brilliant but still trailed 2–1 going into the eighth.

At a Glance
WP: Seaver (9–3)
Key stat: Seaver 7 IP, 14 Ks

In the third, the Padres scored an unearned run on Seaver's throwing error. Padres third baseman Ed Spiezio led off the fourth with a home run, but that was all they would get off the future Hall of Famer.

Seaver struck out the side in the first, fourth and sixth. Ron Taylor pitched the last two innings and struck out two (to make it 16 total Ks for Mets pitching) to pick up the save.

No Old Timer Yet, Mays Shows Off His Glove Again

It was Old Timers' Day at Shea, but it was a "living legend" who stole the show.

Future Hall of Famer and 42-year-old Willie Mays made a tremendous catch and hit a home run to power the Mets to a 4–2 win over the Los Angeles Dodgers.

With "dem bums" in town, former Mets manager and former Brooklyn first baseman Gil Hodges had his No. 14 posthumously retired in pregame ceremonies. Hodges died on April 2, 1972.

The Dodgers took a 1–0 lead against Mets winning pitcher Jon Matlack in the top of the first, but Rusty Staub's two-run double in the home half made it 2–1.

Los Angeles tied it in the third, but Mays broke the tie when he connected for career home run No. 655 and a 3–2 lead.

The "Say Hey" kid wowed the crowd of 47,800 fans with a vintage Mays catch in the top half of the third. Willie Davis hit a drive toward straight-away center. Mays initially misjudged the ball, then backtracked to make a remarkable over-the-head catch. After making the grab, Mays tumbled backward and rolled twice onto the dirt track in center field.

> ## At a Glance
>
> **WP:** Matlack (3–8)
>
> **HR:** Mays (1)
>
> **Key stat:** Mays 1-for-3, RBI; Staub 2-for-4, 3 RBIs

The catch snuffed out a rally because Matlack walked Joe Ferguson and Ron Cey with two outs, but ended the inning when he got Manny Mota to fly out to Mays in center.

The Mets' defense saved the game in the seventh, when two Dodgers were gunned down on a potential double steal. Davey Lopes was caught stealing second and when Tom Paciorek tried for home, the Mets gunned him down on a play where six men handled the ball. If you're scoring at home, the "caught stealing" on the back end of the double play sounded like a telephone number (1–3–6–3–4–3–4–9–2).

No Defense for Teufel's Clutch Hit

Tim Teufel's walk-off, pinch-hit grand slam home run in the bottom of the 11th inning gave the Mets an 8–4 victory over the Philadelphia Phillies and capped an exciting win in front of 27,472 delirious fans at Shea Stadium.

When Teufel came to bat against Phillies reliever Tom Hume, he saw an unusual defensive formation. The Phils brought in right fielder Glenn Wilson as a fifth infielder to play second base, while the other two outfielders were shallow.

"It looked there were people on top of me," Teufel said.

Hume got behind 2–0 and then Teufel connected for his first career grand slam.

Teufel had been struggling in the clutch, so the game-ending blow took a "monkey off his back."

"I didn't want to hit through the middle where Wilson was standing, I might've hit into a double play," Teufel said. "I took a very compact swing, not a vicious swing. Hume's a sinkerball pitcher, but he got it up and I hit it on the nose."

Mets starter Bob Ojeda did not have his best stuff, but he managed to keep the team in the game by tossing 7 2/3 innings. The Phils took a 4–3 lead in the eighth on Ron Roenicke's RBI single.

Doug Sisk replaced Ojeda and after a wild pitch put a runner on third, the Mets' reliever got Juan Samuel to line out to left to end the threat.

At a Glance

WP: McDowell (6–0)

HR: Carter 2 (9,10), Teufel (2)

Key stat: Carter 3-for-5, 4 RBI; Teufel grand slam

The Mets came right back and tied the game on Gary Carter's second home run of the game. Carter had given the Mets a 3–2 lead in the sixth with a two-run "bomb" off Charles Hudson that landed in the bleachers in left-center field.

After the game, Carter said, "It's been frustrating, then I broke out."

Carter's second home run came off right-hander Steve Bedrosian, who was brought in to replace left-hander Don Carman, who was always tough on the Mets.

On the 2–2 pitch, Carter lined a bullet that slammed into the barrier in left-center field.

Mets 8, Phillies 4 (11 innings)

"That's strength against strength," Mets manager Dave Johnson said, "fastball pitcher against fastball hitter, and the hitter won."

With the game tied 4–4 in the ninth, the managerial wheels were spinning as both skippers tried to maneuver their teams to a win.

The Phils had two on with two outs. Milt Thompson reached on an error by Mets shortstop Rafael Santana and Rick Schu was hit by a Sisk pitch. Phils manager John Felske sent up left-handed hitter Greg Gross to bat for shortstop Steve Jeltz, so Johnson countered with left-hander Jesse Orosco.

Felske went to Mike Schmidt to bat for Gross, but Orosco got the future Hall of Famer on a fly out to center field.

Roger McDowell entered the game in the 10th and gave the Mets two scoreless innings to pick up the win in relief.

In the home half of the 11th, Ray Knight started the inning with a "bad hop" single.

On a hit-and-run play, Santana grounded out, sending Knight to second.

Pinch-hitter Barry Lyons was intentionally walked and then Phils lefty Randy Lerch walked Len Dykstra, loading the bases.

Hume entered the game to face Teufel, and for the only the third time in franchise history, a Mets player hit a pinch-hit grand slam.

Teufel saw "a lot of people on top of me" when he stepped on home plate to officially end the game.

Did You Know?

John Olerud holds the club record for the highest batting average in a single season when he hit .354 in 1998.

Mets 5, Angels 3 (10 innings)

Inside-the-Park or Over the Wall, Homers Prevail

Cliff Floyd blasted a walk-off, three-run homer in the bottom of the 10th inning to give the Mets a stunning 5–3 interleague win over the Anaheim Angels at Shea Stadium.

It was wildly entertaining for the 33,889 on hand for a game that featured a game-tying, pinch-hit, inside-the-park home run in the bottom of the ninth.

The Mets were trailing 2–1 and facing closer Francisco Rodriguez, a future Met. With one out, pinch-hitter Marlon Anderson drove a 3–1 pitch from Rodriguez into the gap in right-center field. Angels center fielder Steve Finley decided to attempt a spectacular backhanded catch instead of keep the ball in front of him, but was burned when he missed and kicked the ball into right field.

"It just tipped the end of my glove, hit my knee," Finley said. "Tough luck play. Freak play. Can't really defend that."

Finley chased the ball down and hit Angels second baseman Adam Kennedy with the relay, but the throw to the plate was late. Anderson had a collision with Angels catcher Jose Molina and came out of it with a bloody lip, but the game was tied 2–2.

It was the first inside-the-park home run at Shea since Darryl Strawberry had one on May 3, 1989.

The Angels regained the lead in the top of the 10th on a two-out RBI single by Darin Erstad that was set up by an error by Mets first baseman Doug Mientkiewicz.

Brendan Donnelly was brought on for the save, but a bloop single by Jose Reyes and a walk to Mike Cameron put two runners on with no one out.

Donnelly struck out Carlos Beltran and Mike

Angels	AB	R	H	RBI
Erstad 1b	5	0	1	1
Finley cf	5	0	0	0
Donnelly p	0	0	0	0
Guerrero rf	4	0	1	0
Anderson lf	4	1	3	0
Paul c	0	0	0	0
McPherson 3b	4	1	2	0
Molina c	3	0	0	0
Shields p	0	0	0	0
Rodriguez p	0	0	0	0
Figgins ph-cf	1	0	0	0
Kennedy 2b	3	1	1	1
Cabrera ss	4	0	0	0
Washburn p	2	0	0	0
Molina c	1	0	0	0
DaVanon ph-lf	1	0	0	0
Totals	37	3	8	2

Mets	AB	R	H	RBI
Reyes ss	5	1	1	0
Cameron rf	4	1	1	0
Beltran cf	5	0	0	0
Piazza c	5	1	2	0
Floyd lf	5	1	2	3
Wright 3b	4	0	0	0
Woodward 1b	3	0	1	0
Anderson ph	1	1	1	1
Looper p	0	0	0	0
Matsui 2b	3	0	0	0
Benson p	1	0	0	1
Cairo ph	1	0	1	0
Heilman p	0	0	0	0
Mientkiewicz ph-1b	1	0	0	0
Totals	38	5	9	5

```
LAA  0 1 0 0 1 0 0 0 1 - 3 8 0
NYM  0 1 0 0 0 0 0 1 3 - 5 9 1
```

Angels	IP	H	R	ER	BB	SO
Washburn	6.1	6	1	1	2	3
Shields	1.2	0	0	0	0	1
Rodriguez	1	1	1	1	0	3
Donnelly L (4-2)	0.2	2	3	3	1	2
Totals	9.2	9	5	5	3	9

Mets	IP	H	R	ER	BB	SO
Benson	7	4	2	2	0	2
Heilman	2	2	0	0	0	2
Looper W (2-1)	1	2	1	0	0	0
Totals	10	8	3	2	0	4

E—New York Mientkiewicz. DP—New York. 2B—Los Angeles McPherson, Anderson; New York Cameron, Piazza. HR—New York Floyd (15), Anderson (1). SF—Los Angeles Kennedy. LOB—Los Angeles 5; New York 7. SB—Los Angeles Kennedy; New York Reyes. Attendance: 33,889.

Piazza and then faced the left-handed hitting Floyd. The count went to 3–2 when Floyd lined a drive that went foul and landed in the third deck, just to the right of the pole.

Before the next pitch, Reyes stole third and that put pressure on Donnelly to think twice about throwing a splitter in the dirt.

Floyd hit a drive that went over the wall in right-center field and the Mets had an incredible come-from-behind victory.

The clubs traded runs in the second, but the Angels took a 2–1 lead in the fifth on a sacrifice fly by Kennedy before Anderson's unique pinch-hit home run.

Cliff Floyd was signed as a free agent in January 2003 and only injuries prevented him from having a more productive Mets career.

The Chicago native played four years in Queens, averaging 117 games played each year. In 2005, Floyd played in 150 games and had his best season with the Mets. The left-handed power hitter had a team-leading 34 home runs with 98 RBIs.

Did You Know?

Edgardo Alfonzo is the club's all-time leader with 26 postseason hits and 17 RBIs. Mike Piazza holds the club's record for the most home runs in postseason play with five.

Seaver Shines as Trade Rumors Swirl

A crowd of 10,439 fans came out to the Houston Astrodome to see what would be Tom Seaver's final act in his first stint as a New York Met.

Seaver tossed a complete game five-hitter to lead the Mets to a 3–1 win over the Astros in a game that was played amidst an atmosphere of intense trade rumors involving the most prominent player in franchise history.

The relationship between Seaver and the Mets' front office had broken down, and with the June 15 trade deadline fast approaching, the popular right-hander wanted to be dealt away from the team where he made his mark and was appropriately nicknamed "The Franchise."

Seaver gave up his only run in the first. Cesar Cedeno led off with a triple and scored on Jose Cruz's sacrifice fly. From that point, Seaver allowed only four total base runners until the ninth, when he ran into some trouble.

The future Hall of Famer got the first two outs, but Astros catcher Joe Ferguson singled to left and Cliff Johnson walked.

Mets manager Joe Torre went out to the mound to talk to his ace, but there was no way he was going to take Seaver out of the game.

"I hadn't the faintest notion of taking him out," Torre said after the game. "He'd thrown only 108 pitches. I just went out to break up the mood."

In order to close out the game, Seaver would have to go through Astros third baseman (and future Mets manager) Art Howe, who fouled off the first five pitches. With the count at 1–2, Howe lifted a deep fly ball to left field, where Dave Kingman backed up against the wall and hauled in the long drive.

"I was scared, let me tell you," Torre said.

Seaver did not want to deal with the postgame questions about his status with the Mets.

"Leave me alone, please," Seaver said.

According to a June 13, 1977, game story in *The New York Times*, Mets general manager Joe McDonald was quoted about a potential deal.

At a Glance

WP: Seaver (7–3)

Key stat: Seaver 5-hitter

"We're talking to clubs as we have been," McDonald said. "I have nothing else to report. There's no trade until it's consummated."

Longtime *New York Daily News* columnist Dick Young had been writing a series of negative articles about Seaver after he requested a contract that would put the right-hander's salary in line with other top pitchers. The rift between Seaver and Mets management came to a head when Young wrote that Nancy Seaver (Tom's wife) was trying to persuade him to ask for more money because she was jealous of Nolan Ryan's wife and what the former Met was making.

This proved to be the last straw. Seaver demanded a trade and the Mets brass went to work to accommodate him.

While Young took management's side, other noted columnists did not see it that way.

From Pulitzer Prize-winning *New York Times* columnist Dave Anderson's article of June 8, 1977, titled, "The Tom Seaver Trade Talks." "During the week, M. Donald Grant was quoted as having said that Tom Seaver 'has destroyed his market.'" "If no market exists for Seaver," wrote Anderson, "then M. Donald Grant should blame himself, not Tom Seaver. As the Mets Chairman of the Board, M. Donald Grant created the hassle with Tom Seaver by humiliating him during contract negotiations early last year."

Three days later, "The Midnight Massacre" was born.

June 12, 1979

Mets Score 10 in One Inning

For the first time in franchise history, the Mets scored 10 runs in one inning as they coasted to a 12–6 win over the Cincinnati Reds at Shea Stadium.

A crowd of 9,805 saw the Mets put up a 10-spot in the bottom of the sixth inning, after Cincinnati had scored five runs in the top half to take a 5–2 lead.

With the bases loaded and no one out, Ron Hodges walked to drive in the first run. With one out, Frank Taveras doubled in two more runs to tie the game 5–5.

Richie Hebner's two-run single and another run on an error preceded Steve Henderson's RBI single. Doug Flynn capped the rally with a three-run, inside-the-park home run.

Singleton's Sac Fly Makes the Mets a Winner over Giants

Ken Singleton's sacrifice fly scored Bud Harrelson with the winning run in the 10th inning as the Mets "walked-off" with a 5–4 win over the San Francisco Giants at Shea Stadium.

The game lasted three hours and five minutes, but it didn't end until 5 ½ hours after the first pitch because of rain, which stopped the game three separate times (a total of two hours and 26 minutes worth of rain delays).

At a Glance

WP: McGraw (4–3)

HR: Singleton (2)

Key stat: Singleton 2-for-3, 3 RBIs

Mets starter Gary Gentry did not have it, but relievers Jim McAndrew, Danny Frisella and Tug McGraw combined for 5 ²/₃ scoreless innings.

The Mets trailed 1–0 in the home half of the second when Singleton blasted a two-run homer off future Hall of Fame pitcher Juan Marichal.

Ken Henderson's solo home run and an RBI single by Bernie Williams in the fourth tied the game 3–3.

The Mets took a 4–3 lead in their half of the fourth on a sacrifice fly by catcher Duffy Dyer, but the Giants came right back to tie it again in the fifth on a solo home run by Bobby Bonds.

Harrelson opened the 10th with a double down the left-field line. After Al Weis was intentionally walked, Ed Kranepool moved the runners to second and third with a sacrifice bunt.

Donn Clendenon was walked intentionally to load the bases. Singleton stepped up and hit a fly ball to center, where Bobby Bonds made an accurate throw home. Harrelson eluded the tag of Giants catcher Russ Gibson and the Mets treated a crowd of 52,010 to a thrilling win.

Lewis Homer Makes Mets an Unlikely Winner vs. Maloney

In one of the most improbable wins in franchise history, a solo home run by Johnny Lewis in the top of the 11th inning gave the Mets a 1–0 win over Jim Maloney and the Cincinnati Reds at Crosley Field.

Maloney did not allow a hit until Lewis led off the 11th inning with a homer, but he ended up being the losing pitcher despite a pitching line that read: 11 IP, 2H, 1R, 1BB and 18K.

The Reds' right-hander struck out at least one Mets batter in every inning except the sixth.

The Mets did not even come close to a hit until the seventh. Mets second baseman Chuck Hiller led off and hit a bouncer toward first. Reds first baseman Gordy Coleman made a tumbling stop near the line and beat Hiller to the bag for the out.

The Reds had a few chances to score, beginning in the fourth inning. With Vada Pinson at second, Coleman struck out but the ball got past Mets catcher Chris Cannizzaro. Pinson tried to score but Cannizzaro got the ball to pitcher Frank Lary, who covered the plate and applied the tag.

Pete Rose came up in the eighth with a runner on third. Lary escaped when the Reds' second baseman bounced back to the mound.

In the bottom of the 10th, Reds catcher Johnny Edwards singled and pinch runner Chico Ruiz was sacrificed to second.

Mets reliever and winning pitcher Larry Bearnarth got Maloney to ground to short and then ended the threat by retiring Tommy Harper on a grounder to third that was anything but routine.

Third baseman Charley Smith's throw to first base was low, but first baseman Ed Kranepool scooped it cleanly and held it for the final out.

At a Glance

WP: Bearnarth (2-1)

HR: Lewis (8)

Key stat: Lewis solo HR in top of 11th; Lary, Bearnarth combine for 7-hit shutout as Mets win 10th in a row

The Mets got their first base runner in the second inning, when Kranepool led off with a walk. In the fourth, Smith struck out but reached on a wild pitch and was quickly erased on a double play.

From there, Maloney retired the next 18 hitters (including striking out the side in the eighth) until Lewis blasted his homer in the 11th.

Before Maloney's gem, only four other pitchers had carried a no-hitter beyond nine innings. (The most famous one is Pirates pitcher Harvey Haddix, who, in 1959, had a perfect game for 12 innings but lost the bid and the game to the Milwaukee Braves in the 13th.)

A crowd of 5,989 was on hand watching this amazing pitching feat when Lewis stepped to the plate to lead off the 11th.

Lewis, who had struck out in his three previous at-bats, worked the count to 2–1 and then sent Maloney's fastball deep to center field. The ball went over the fence and slammed into the outer wall that had been erected at Crosley Field to ward off the glare of a highway that ran past the ballpark.

Understandably, Maloney was frustrated and dissapointed after the game.

"No-hitters are fine, I knew I was working on one and I go for one every time I pitch," he said, "but I'd settle for a victory any time instead."

As far as the home run, the 25-year-old pitcher admitted that Lewis did hit a fastball.

"I was trying to pitch him inside, but I got the ball a little too far out over the plate," Lewis said.

Lary gave the Mets eight scoreless innings while Bearnarth tossed the final three. In the bottom of the 11th, Bearnarth retired Rose and Pinson rather easily, but future Hall of Famer Frank Robinson singled with two outs.

Bearnarth ended the game when he induced Coleman to ground out to Mets shortstop Roy McMillan.

The Mets acquired Lewis and left-handed pitcher Gordie Richardson from the Cardinals for pitcher Tracy Stallard and infielder Elio Chacon in December 1964.

Lewis played three years in Queens, having his best season in 1965, when he hit 15 home runs and had 45 RBIs.

Bearnarth was an alumnus of St. John's University in New York. He was signed as a free agent in 1962 and pitched four seasons with the Mets.

Maloney (who would go on to throw two no-hitters, including a 10-inning masterpiece) always had success against the Mets in his career. The two-time 20-game winner started 30 games against the Mets and posted a 19-8 record with a 2.78 ERA.

'Midnight Massacre' Leaves the Mets with No 'Franchise'

The Mets beat the Atlanta Braves 6–5 at Atlanta-Fulton County Stadium, but that couldn't hide the fact that Tom Seaver was no longer a New York Met.

During the game, the Mets and Reds had agreed on a deal that would send "The Franchise" to Cincinnati in exchange for second baseman Doug Flynn, outfielders Steve Henderson and Dan Norman and right-handed pitcher Pat Zachry.

The trade could not be announced in Atlanta until the Reds' game with the Phillies in Cincinnati was completed, so everyone anxiously waited a long time after the Mets had won their game.

Thanks to future Met George Foster's solo home run in the ninth, the Reds tied the game and then won it in the 10th. When the game was over in Cincinnati, the Mets' board of directors issued a statement announcing the deal.

Seaver had veto power over any trade and reportedly he used that option in a phone call to the president of the Mets, Lorinda de Roulet.

The day after the phone call, Seaver saw a column written by *New York Daily News* columnist Dick Young that brought his wife, Nancy, into the fray, and that was the last straw.

"Dick Young dragged my wife and family into it and I couldn't take that," an emotional Seaver said at his farewell press conference at Shea Stadium. "I called the Mets and said, 'That's it, it's all over.'"

The rift between the two sides began when Seaver had blasted board chairman M. Donald Grant in spring training of 1977 for his blasé attitude in trying to improve the team.

During the spring, Seaver held an impromptu press conference at the Mets' training camp in St. Petersburg, Fla., where he spoke about his own contract, which had been finally settled after a lot of public acrimony with Grant. Seaver said: "I was made an example of. I was pictured as the ingrate after nine years with the club. I was to be punished. And even now, a year later, I still resent the way they did it."

At a Glance

WP: Apodaca (2-2)

HR: Boisclair (2)

Key stat: Milner 2-for-4, 3 RBIs, 3B; Boisclair 1-for-2, HR, 2 RBIs

Thirty years after the trade, Seaver told Bill Madden of the *Daily News*, "There are two things Grant said to me that I'll never forget, but illustrate the kind of person he was and the total 'plantation' mentality he had," Seaver said. "During the labor negotiations, he came up to me in the clubhouse once and said: 'What are you, some sort of Communist?' Another time, and I've never told anyone this, he said to me: 'Who do you think you are, joining the Greenwich Country Club?' It was incomprehensible to him if you didn't understand his feelings about your station in life."

Teammates and club personnel alike were still trying to deal with something that seemed so "surreal" to those who were close to Seaver.

Mets equipment manager Herb Norman was teary eyed when he said, "No one will ever wear Tom's number," he said, "no matter who asks me, even if M. Donald Grant orders me to give out number 41 to another player, I won't do it. I don't care if I'm fired."

Ed Kranepool tried to put the deal in perspective. "I hope our scouts did their homework in who we got for Seaver," he said.

Shortstop Bud Harrelson, Seaver's longtime roommate, was distraught.

"I'm selfish," Harrelson said. "Who we got for Tom is trivia as far as I'm concerned. I lost my friend."

Fellow pitcher Jon Matlack wouldn't "toe the company line." "I don't want to get in trouble, so I want to be careful of what I say, but I don't think this deal was made, per se, to help our ball club. It was a deal that had to be made."

Mets manager Joe Torre hated to lose Seaver but was diplomatic when he addressed the principals that the Mets got from the Reds in return.

"We've added speed and we've added youth," Torre said, "we've got a deeper ballclub and we won't strike out as much."

Nor would they strike out as many once "The Franchise" was gone.

Subway Series Kicks Off with a Gem by Mlicki

Dave Mlicki scattered nine hits in going the distance and the Mets outperformed the defending World Champions as they whipped the Yankees 6–0 at Yankee Stadium in the first regular-season "Subway Series" game between the two rivals.

With the advent of "interleague play," the "intra-city cousins" would be paired against each other in a three-game series at Yankee Stadium. (In 1998, the teams played a three-game series at Shea. In 1999, the teams began playing an annual three-game series at each ballpark.)

This time it wasn't a "Mayor's Trophy" that was on the line. (The Mets played the Yankees in a series of exhibitions from 1963-1983 called the Mayor's Trophy Game.) This was a regular-season game, which counted in each of the team's standings. So, for the first time, there was a lot at stake.

The Mets didn't waste any time as they scored three runs in the top of the first inning. Bernard Gilkey hit a check-swing double to right field and scored the first run on John Olerud's double.

After Mets catcher Todd Hundley walked, Butch Huskey's RBI single scored Olerud and put runners on first and third.

Next came the play that epitomized the first regular-season game played between two New York teams in 40 years.

> ### At a Glance
>
> **WP:** Mlicki (3-5)
>
> **Key stat:** Mlicki complete game 8-hitter, 8 Ks, 2 walks; Olerud 2-for-5, 3 RBIs, 2B

Yankees losing pitcher Andy Pettitte had Huskey picked off at first base. Yankees first baseman Tino Martinez threw to Derek Jeter, but on the throw back to Pettitte, (who was covering the rundown) Hundley took off for home and slid around the tag of catcher Joe Girardi.

It was an exhilarating feeling for the Mets and an embarrassment to the Yankees in their own ballpark.

Mlicki was in total command by using an array of change-ups and curveballs. The 29-year-old right-hander struck out eight, four looking.

"His hammer was unbelievable. That thing was going 12 to 6," said Hundley.

Mlicki was particularly stingy when the Yankees had runners in scoring position, holding them to 0-for-11 on the evening.

In the third, Mlicki threw a pair of nasty curves to strike out Jeter and Pat Kelly.

"I felt focused," Mlicki said. "I felt I could throw any pitch for a strike at any time."

A crowd of 56,188 jammed into Yankee Stadium for this historic game. Chants of "Let's Go Mets!" rang around the packed house, followed by boos from the Yankee fans.

The Mets didn't give their "cousins" much to cheer about.

In the seventh, Olerud's two-run single essentially put the game away as the Mets took a 5–0 lead.

The clutch hit also lifted Mlicki, who felt like he got a "second wind" for the chance to toss his first complete game.

"That's when I really started to want it bad," he said.

In the bottom of the ninth, the Yankees staged a mini-rally and had two on with two outs and Jeter at the plate.

At this point, Hundley walked to the mound for one final "support session" for his pitcher.

"You've got to throw strikes," Hundley said. "Bear down."

Mlicki caught Jeter looking at a called third strike and he raised his arms in triumph.

The Mets had "drawn first blood" and it never tasted any sweeter for Mlicki, who walked off the field with the best game he ever pitched and a very satisfying win.

One of the last to greet him was manager Bobby Valentine.

"I hope you enjoyed it," Valentine said.

"Oh yeah," Mlicki said as he tipped his cap to the Mets fans who gathered to honor him for his effort.

The Mets acquired Mlicki from the Cleveland Indians as part of a six-player trade in December 1994. The Cleveland native pitched parts of four seasons in New York and finished his Mets career with a 24–30 record.

In June 1998, Mlicki was traded along with pitcher Greg McMichael to the Los Angeles Dodgers for pitchers Brad Clontz and Hideo Nomo.

Swan's Day Uplifted by Kingman Blast

Dave Kingman ended a terrific pitchers' duel with a walk-off home run in the 14th inning to give the Mets a 1–0 win over the Los Angeles Dodgers at Shea Stadium.

Kingman connected off Dodgers knuckleballer Charlie Hough to end a scoreless thriller.

A crowd of 20,268 watched Dodgers starting pitcher Don Sutton toss nine scoreless innings, but Mets starter Craig Swan did one better with 10 shutout innings.

"My fastball was really moving, my control was almost perfect and my curve was on the money," the 25-year-old from Van Nuys, Calif., said. "It's the best I've felt all year."

Kingman's home run was a high, deep drive that landed in the left-field bullpen for the game-winner.

After the game, "Kong" said Hough's first pitch "probably didn't knuckle and I was thinking home run all the time."

Hough said, "You've got to throw good knucklers to that guy because he can hit the ball out of the park."

Reliever Mike Marshall combined with Hough for 4 1/3 scoreless innings before the home run. Skip Lockwood pitched four scoreless innings in relief for the Mets and picked up the win.

> ## At a Glance
> **WP:** Lockwood (3–2)
>
> **HR:** Kingman (23)
>
> **Key stat:** Swan 10 IP, 3H, 8 Ks

Swan spent parts of 12 years with the Mets, posting a 59–71 record. In 1978, Swan led the National League with a 2.43 ERA.

Kingman spent parts of six seasons with the Mets in two separate tenures. "Kong" is one of seven Mets to have hit three home runs in a game and he still shares the franchise record for most home runs in a month when he slammed 13 in July 1975. Mets catcher Gary Carter equaled that feat with 13 in September 1985.

Legend of 'Marvelous' Marv Throneberry Comes to Fruition

Marv Throneberry was a journeyman major leaguer who became the symbol of the Mets' futility in their very first season.

A crowd of 13,128 fans watched one of Throneberry's most famous gaffes. It occurred in the first game of a doubleheader against the Chicago Cubs.

In the top of the first inning, Cubs outfielder Lou Brock became the second major leaguer to hit a home run into the center-field bleachers at the Polo Grounds to cap off a four-run inning that gave Chicago a 4–0 lead.

In the bottom of the first inning, the Mets rallied to tie it at 4–4, but not before Throneberry would extinguish any chance of taking the lead.

Future Hall of Famer Richie Ashburn singled. After a sacrifice, Gene Woodling, who was making his debut for the Mets, walked to put runners on first and second. Ashburn scored on a Frank Thomas RBI single to make it 4–1.

Throneberry hit a deep drive to right field to score Woodling and Thomas, and the first baseman ended up at third with a triple. Or did he?

Throneberry had missed first base, so he was called out for the second out and the tying run was taken off third base.

When Mets manager Casey Stengel bolted from the dugout to argue the call, first base coach Cookie Lavagetto intercepted him and said "Don't argue, Case, he missed second base, too."

Throneberry later admitted that he missed second as well, as his "hit" was wiped off the scoresheet.

Cone Comes Up Short
of Mets' First No-Hitter

David Cone flirted with a no-hitter for 7 $^2/_3$ innings but settled for a complete game, two-hit shutout to lead the Mets to a dominant 6–0 win over the Philadelphia Phillies at Shea Stadium before a crowd of 46,773.

Cone had two outs in the eighth when Steve Jeltz hit a lazy line drive to the left of second base that Mets shortstop Kevin Elster could just not reach, and the bid for the first no-hitter in team history was over.

"When it was hit, I thought I had a chance," said Elster, a rookie shortstop who was inserted into the game as a pinch runner for Gary Carter in the seventh. "The wind was also blowing that way and it helped it."

"Definitely it is a letdown," Cone said, "and so I was just trying to control my emotions."

The 25-year-old right-hander clamped down to polish off his gem, but the disappointment was apparent when he addressed the media after the game.

"You dream all your life about being in that situation," he said. "You want to make the most of it. But you need luck to get there. And then you need another bit of luck to finish it. I didn't have that second bit of luck."

"David's got the stuff so that it makes no sense to fool around," said catcher Barry Lyons, who worked behind the plate because Carter started at first base.

Cone walked two and struck out seven as he and Lyons were on the same page all game long.

At a Glance

WP: Cone (8–1)

HR: McReynolds (7), Strawberry (16)

Key stat: Cone 7 $^2/_3$ no-hit IP; McReynolds, Teufel 2 hits apiece

Second baseman Tim Teufel said, "There was absolutely no action out there."

Home runs from Kevin McReynolds and Darryl Strawberry helped the Mets build a 5–0 lead after four innings.

David Cone nearly became the first Met to throw a no-hitter.
On June 19, 1988, Cone did not allow a hit through 7 $^2/_3$ innings.
He ended up with a two-hit shutout.

Ryan Hands Off to McGraw for Big Win over Gibson

In a battle of future Hall of Famers, Nolan Ryan—with a little help from Tug McGraw—outpitched the Cardinals' Bob Gibson and the Mets got by St. Louis 4–3 before a crowd of 54,083 at Shea Stadium.

The Mets roughed up Gibson and the two-time defending National League champions for four runs in the first two innings.

A two-run single by Cleon Jones keyed a three-run first-inning rally. It was 4–0 after two innings thanks to an RBI triple by Mets second baseman Ken Boswell.

Ryan went six innings and allowed one earned run on six hits.

McGraw began the seventh by giving up a home run to Gibson that cut the Mets' lead to 4–3, but that was all the Cardinals would get. McGraw settled down and retired the last nine Cardinal hitters. He struck out the side in the ninth with Gibson going down as the final out.

Allowing Gibson to bat in that spot was a tribute to his hitting abilities, according to St. Louis manager Red Schoendienst.

The Mets' defense came up with some big plays early on to support Ryan.

In the first, Vada Pinson singled with two outs. Joe Torre doubled, but Pinson was cut down at home on a nice relay throw from Mets shortstop Bud Harrelson.

> **At a Glance**
>
> **WP:** Ryan (3–0)
>
> **Key stat:** Agee 2-for-4, 2 runs

In his eight innings of work, Gibson gave up four runs (three earned) on eight hits with four walks and seven strikeouts.

In his career against the Mets, Gibson started 47 games, completed 27 and was 28–14 with a 2.57 ERA.

Henderson Rolls Out the Welcome Mat with Walk-off Homer

Six days after joining the Mets in the most controversial trade in franchise history, Steve Henderson slammed a walk-off three-run homer in the bottom of the 11th inning to power a 5–2 win over the Atlanta Braves at Shea Stadium.

The game-winning blow was Henderson's first big-league home run and it came off Braves left-handed reliever Don Collins. Among the crowd of 10,613 on hand was the Mets chairman of the board, M. Donald Grant, who had been taking a large amount of criticism for trading Tom Seaver to the Cincinnati Reds. Henderson was among the players shipped to the Mets in exchange for Seaver.

"Way to go," the beleaguered Grant told Henderson in the clubhouse after the game.

"Thank you," the 24 year-old rookie responded. "I'm happy to be here."

Grant was making his first appearance at Shea since the "Midnight Massacre."

The Mets trailed 2–1 entering the bottom of the ninth, but Ed Kranepool tied the game with a solo home run on a 3–2 pitch from Braves starter Andy Messersmith, who was going for the complete game victory.

Atlanta scored both of its runs in the top of the first against Mets starter Jon Matlack on a two-run homer by future Met Willie Montanez.

In the 11th, John Stearns lined a one-out double to left. The Braves elected to intentionally walk Felix Millan to bring up Henderson.

"It makes you kinda mad," Henderson said, "because they don't have respect for me. In the major leagues, they don't have no respect for a rookie."

The first-year player made them pay when he drove Collins' 0–1 delivery into the stands in left field for his first round-tripper.

Henderson knows he'll always be linked with Seaver and the infamous trade.

"I can't compare myself to a great pitcher like that," he said, "all I can do is my best."

At a Glance

WP: Baldwin (1–0)

HR: Kranepool (7), Henderson (1)

Key stat: Henderson 1-for-1, HR, 3 RBIs

Ashburn Shows Hall of Fame Stuff with Homers

Future Hall of Famer Richie Ashburn hit two home runs to power the Mets to a 13–2 "mauling" of the Houston Colt .45s at the Polo Grounds before 6,425 fans.

Ashburn never hit more than four home runs in a season before joining the Mets. The 5-foot-10 left-handed hitter connected for his first home run of the game in the third inning off Houston's starting pitcher, right-hander Ken Johnson.

The very next inning, Ashburn thrilled the crowd of 6,425 with an inside-the-park home run.

Jay Hook was the beneficiary of a 16-hit attack as he went the distance, giving up two runs on eight hits.

The game didn't start well for the 25-year-old Hook, as he gave up a leadoff home run to Al Spangler to start the game.

Hall of Famer Richie Ashburn played only one season with the Mets, but he set a career high with seven home runs in his final season in 1962.

The Mets came right back with two runs in the first inning and then blew the game open in the third with a six-run rally. Hook singled to start the inning and scored on Ashburn's first home run, a ball that hit the façade in right field at the Polo Grounds.

Marv Throneberry's two-run triple was the other key hit as the Mets took an 8–1 lead after three.

Ashburn led off the fourth against left-hander Dean Stone and drove a ball to right-center field. Houston right fielder Roman Mejias had the ball tip off his glove and Ashburn raced around the bases for one of the most thrilling plays in baseball.

It was 11–1 after five innings and the Mets completed the scoring with two runs in the eighth. Ashburn had three hits, three RBIs and tied a personal best with four runs scored.

The five-time All-Star played one season with the Mets. He batted .306 with a career-high seven home runs and 28 RBIs in 1962, the final season of his career.

At a Glance

WP: Hook (5–8)

HR: Ashburn 2 (4,5), Christopher (3)

Key stat: Ashburn 3-for-4, 4 runs, 3 RBIs

June 23, 1963

Piersall Runs Bases Backward After 100th HR

Zany Mets outfielder Jimmy Piersall promised to run the bases backward once he hit his 100th career home run.

Piersall kept his word when he homered off the Phillies' Dallas Green in the opening game of a doubleheader and ran the bases backward to the amusement of 19,901 fans at the Polo Grounds.

The memorable blow came in the fifth inning. Piersall ran around the bases backward, but in the right order, of course, and the Mets came away with a 5–0 win in that opening game.

Rookie Mitchell Gets Quick Lesson in Appeal Play from Hernandez

Bill Almon's walk-off, RBI single in the bottom of the ninth inning gave the Mets a 2–1 win over the Chicago Cubs, but it was an alert Keith Hernandez who probably saved the game.

A crowd of 42,196 was on hand at Shea Stadium as Chicago held a 1–0 lead in the eighth when Leon Durham led off with a double. Keith Moreland hit a fly ball to right and Durham went to third on the out.

Hernandez thought Durham left early.

"I had nothing to do on that play so I watched the ball," he said.

The first baseman alertly notified Mets starter John Mitchell to make the appeal play at second base.

"How do I do that?" the rookie Mitchell asked.

> ## At a Glance
> **WP:** McDowell (4–2)
>
> **Key stat:** Mitchell 7 $2/3$ IP, 1 run, 11 hits

"Get on the mound and take your stretch," Hernandez said, "then step off the mound and throw it to second."

Mitchell threw the ball to Keith Miller at second and umpire Jim Quick threw up his right hand and called Durham out for leaving early.

Mitchell went 7 $2/3$ innings, giving up one run on 11 hits. The Mets tied the game in the eighth on Mookie Wilson's pinch-hit RBI single.

Kevin McReynolds and Howard Johnson stroked one-out singles to set up the winning rally.

Dave Magadan battled Cubs closer Lee Smith and drew a walk to load the bases.

The Cubs brought the infield and outfield in against Almon.

"I thought it was at least a 50-50 that I'd get the squeeze sign," the veteran infielder said.

Smith threw a 2–1 pitch that Almon bounced through the middle for the game-winner.

Mitchell appeared in 27 games and was 3–8 during his four-year career with the Mets.

No Assists Needed Behind Fernandez as Mets Take Out Phillies

The Mets tied a major league record by playing nine innings without recording a single assist as they beat the Philadelphia Phillies 5–1 at Shea Stadium.

A crowd of 47,692 saw the Mets set a National League record with the defensive oddity.

The Phillies made six outs by popping up in the infield or to the catcher, six by fly balls to the outfield, two on unassisted ground-outs and 13 on strikeouts.

Sid Fernandez put together one of his best seasons in 1989.
His 14–5 record produced a winning percentage of .767
that ranked best in the National League that year.

Mets 5, Phillies 1

Mets starter Sid Fernandez held the Phillies down with seven strong innings, giving up a run on five hits while walking three and striking out nine.

"I felt stronger as the game went on and I could have pitched longer," Fernandez said, "but I already had 130 pitches and I can't go much longer than that."

On the final play of the game, former Met Len Dykstra grounded a ball to first base that was fielded by Dave Magadan, who waved off Mets pitcher Rick Aguilera and took the out himself.

"In the eighth inning, I realized I hadn't thrown anybody out," Magadan said after the game, "but with Sid you're going to get a lot of fly ball outs and strikeouts."

With the game tied 1–1 in the third inning, Kevin McReynolds' two-run double keyed a four-run inning that gave the Mets a 5–1 lead.

At a Glance

WP: Fernandez (5–2)

Key stat: Fernandez 7 IP, 1 run, 5H, 9 Ks; Mets defense goes 9 innings without recording an assist

Fernandez took over from there by tossing shutout ball through the seventh. Rick Aguilera pitched scoreless ball over the final two innings.

The last team to record 27 outs without an assist was the 1945 Cleveland Indians, who turned the trick against the New York Yankees.

Did You Know?

Tim Harkness recorded the first hit for the Mets; Ron Hunt hit the team's first home run and Jesse Gonder had the first Met RBI at Shea Stadium in 1964.

Harkness Walk-Off Slam No Work of Fiction

This was a real life *Casey at the Bat* story, except Casey was in the dugout and the hero's name was Tim Harkness.

The 25-year-old first-baseman capped a memorable day at the Polo Grounds with a walk-off grand slam in the bottom of the 14th that powered the Mets to an 8–6 win over the Chicago Cubs before an excited crowd of 18,702.

"It was one of those good ones," Mets skipper Casey Stengel said. "We just about had to end it there because I'd run out of men."

Stengel wasn't using his patented "Stengelese," because he had used 20 players and only five pitchers were available.

The Cubs snapped a 4–4 tie in the top of the 14th thanks to a two-run, inside-the-park home run by Billy Williams. With a runner on first, Williams lined a low line drive to left. Mets left fielder Frank Thomas got a poor jump on the ball and tried to cut it off, but it rolled behind him and hit the wall.

Jim Hickman opened the home half of the 14th with a single, but he overran second on Ron Hunt's single and was thrown out. Jimmy Piersall walked and the Dodgers brought in right-handed reliever Paul Toth, who got Thomas on a pop out.

At a Glance

WP: Cisco (4-6)

HR: Harkness (7), Thomas (5)

Key stat: Harkness 4-for-7, 4 RBIs, game-winning grand slam in bottom of 14th; Thomas 4-for-7, 3 RBIs

Following the out, the Cubs again went to the bullpen. Left-hander Jim Brewer was brought on to face Mets left-handed hitting catcher Sammy Taylor, but he walked Taylor to load the bases.

The left-handed hitting Harkness was next and he worked the count to 3–2 before belting the game-winning blast into the seats in right field.

The Cubs built a 4–0 lead, but the Mets scored three times in the sixth inning (a two-run homer by Thomas was the big blow) to narrow the gap to one run.

The Mets tied the game in the eighth as Thomas drove in his third run of the game with a single that scored Choo Choo Coleman, who had walked.

The bullpen was the story of this game as Larry Bearnarth, Tracy Stallard, Carl Willey and Galen Cisco combined to allow two runs on one hit over eight innings of work.

June 26, 1963
Mets 8, Cubs 6 (14 innings)

The Mets had a chance to win in the 13th when they had the bases loaded and one out, but Chico Fernandez forced Thomas at home. With Stengel lacking players, Cisco had to bat and he grounded out to second to end the threat.

Harkness tied personal bests for a single game with four hits and four RBIs. Thomas also had four hits.

The Canadian-born Harkness played two seasons for the Mets. In July 1964, the Mets traded Harkness to the Cincinnati Reds in exchange for infielder Bobby Klaus.

June 27, 2008

Delgado Sets Club Record with 9 RBIs

Carlos Delgado set a club record with nine RBIs as the Mets battered the Yankees 15–6 at Yankee Stadium in the first game of a day-night doubleheader before 54,978 fans in the Bronx.

Delgado had a two-run double, a three-run home run and a grand slam to set the club's record for RBIs in a game. Delgado broke Dave Kingman's mark of eight, which was set in 1976.

With the game tied 4–4 in the top of the fifth inning, Delgado doubled to drive in runs for a 6–4 lead.

In the sixth, Delgado's slam off Ross Ohlendorf blew the game open and gave the Mets an 11–4 lead.

Delgado capped his day with a three-run homer in the eighth inning to give him the franchise's single-game record for RBIs.

Delgago wasn't the only one with impressive offensive numbers. Luis Castillo set a career high with five runs scored, while Carlos Beltran homered, drove in three runs and scored three runs.

Ventura's 3-Run Homers vs. Marlins Part of Career Year

Robin Ventura slammed a pair of three-run homers and tied a career high with six RBIs to power the Mets past the Florida Marlins 10–4 at Pro Player Stadium before a crowd of 12,444.

With one out in the fourth inning, Ventura connected for his first three-run shot off Marlins losing pitcher Brian Meadows to give the Mets a 3–2 lead.

Ventura's second round-tripper came off left-hander Vic Darensbourg. The blast capped a six-run fifth inning that gave the Mets a 9–2 lead.

Except for a 42-pitch third inning, Al Leiter benefited from Ventura's game to go 6 $\frac{1}{3}$ innings and get the win.

Mets second baseman Edgardo Alfonzo had a double and triple as part of the Mets' 14-hit attack.

At a Glance

WP: Leiter (7–5)

HR: Ventura 2 (14,15)

Key stat: Ventura 2-for-4, 2 HR, 6 RBIs

After the game, Mets manager Bobby Valentine had nothing but praise for his third baseman.

"It's hard to put into words what Robin has meant to this team," Valentine said. "He brings a real light-hearted, at times, and yet hard-nosed perspective to the bench and in the clubhouse, and his bat has been the missing link."

In 1999, Ventura had the best of his three seasons in Flushing as he batted .301 with 32 home runs and 120 RBIs.

The six-time Gold Glove third baseman was traded to the Yankees in December 2001 for outfielder David Justice, who never played a game for the Mets. One week later, Justice was dealt to the Oakland A's in exchange for pitchers Mark Guthrie and Tyler Yates.

Complete Game 1-Hitter Old Hat for Matlack

Jon Matlack tossed his second complete game one-hitter in less than two years as the Mets blanked the St. Louis Cardinals 4–0 before a crowd of 37,317 at Shea Stadium.

Matlack gave up his only hit when the opposing pitcher, John Curtis, singled to left with one out in the third inning.

"Curtis hit a fastball," Matlack said after the game. "It was a good pitch, too, outside and low. I was very happy with it. I never dreamed at that point it would be the only hit of the game."

Only one other Cardinal reached base the remainder of the game. Pinch-hitter Tom Heintzelman batted for Curtis and walked to lead off the sixth.

Heintzelman was left at third when Reggie Smith grounded out to end what was a rare threat for the "Redbirds."

Matlack, a 24-year-old left-hander from West Chester, Pa., walked three and struck out seven.

Cleon Jones drove a 2–2 pitch from Curtis over the fence in left field for a two-run shot in the first and a 2–0 lead.

> ## At a Glance
>
> **WP:** Matlack (6–5)
>
> **HR:** Jones (6), Garrett (7)
>
> **Key stat:** Matlack CG 1-hitter, 7 Ks

The Mets made it 3–0 in the fifth inning on Wayne Garrett's solo home run and added the final run in the seventh on an RBI double to right by Jones.

In parts of seven seasons with the Mets, Matlack posted an 82–81 record with a 3.03 ERA.

In December 1977, Matlack was traded to the Texas Rangers as part of a four-team, 10-player deal. The Mets ended up with first baseman Willie Montanez and outfielders Tom Grieve and Ken Henderson. Montanez, who was known for his animated antics on the field (some called it "hot-dogging"), played two seasons in Queens. Grieve played in 54 games for the Mets while Henderson lasted only seven games.

'Greatest Inning Ever' Ends with 10 Runs and a Piazza Blast

It was arguably the greatest single inning in the history of the New York Mets.

Trailing 8–1 entering the bottom of the eighth, the Mets scored 10 runs to capture a thrilling 11–8 victory over their National League East rivals, the Atlanta Braves, at Shea Stadium.

Mike Piazza's screaming line drive landed just inside the left-field foul pole for a three-run home run that capped this memorable comeback.

"It's a big game for us," Piazza said afterward. "It's a great win for us. Fortunately, we snuck up on them."

Atlanta was cruising with a four-run lead and when noted Met killer Brian Jordan smashed a three-run home run in the top of the eighth, the Braves led 8–1. (Jordan hit 19 of his 184 career home runs against the Mets.)

Braves starter Kevin Millwood held the Mets in check with seven innings of one-run ball, but Atlanta went to reliever Don Wengert to start the fateful eighth.

At a Glance

WP: Benitez (2-3)

HR: Piazza (22)

Key stat: Piazza 2-for-5, 3 RBIs, HR; Alfonzo 2-for-5, 2 RBIs

---

"Millwood said he was out of gas," Braves pitching coach Leo Mazzone said.

Braves closer John Rocker (who was labeled a "villain" in New York and who had recently caused a stir with his callous comments about riding the New York City subways) was unavailable because of a callus on his left thumb that split and began to bleed during the third inning.

"I really, literally let my team down," Rocker said after the game.

Derek Bell led off with a single and with one out, Piazza singled his first time up in the inning. Bell scored when Robin Ventura grounded out for an 8–2 lead with two outs.

At this point, things got very interesting.

Todd Zeile singled in Piazza to make it 8–3. After Jay Payton singled, the Braves replaced Wengert with right-hander Kerry Ligtenberg, who had problems with his control.

Benny Agbayani walked to load the bases. Pinch-hitter Mark Johnson drew a walk to score Zeile and Melvin Mora got a third straight walk to draw the Mets to within 8–5.

By this point, the Atlanta bullpen had thrown 60 pitches.

"It seemed like 170," said Mazzone, "you keep thinking when you're sitting there that you're going to make the pitch to get out of it."

Left-hander Terry Mulholland replaced Ligtenberg and promptly walked Bell to force in another run and it was a two-run deficit.

"I felt like I made good pitches to Bell," Mulholland said.

Edgardo Alfonzo frustrated Mulholland as he kept the rally going with a clutch two-run single to tie the game 8–8.

"He did what any good hitter would do with a bad pitch," Mulholland said.

Piazza didn't waste any time in delivering the knockout blow as he lined the first pitch from Mulholland just over the padding in left field as the 52,831 fans at Shea went crazy. The blast measured an estimated 342 feet.

"Mike gets in certain situations where you can feel that the pitcher is in trouble," Zeile said.

The total numbers for the historic inning were mind-boggling. Thirteen hitters came to bat. There were 56 pitches thrown; 10 runs scored, and nine scored with two outs. There were six hits, four walks (three with the bases loaded) and one huge home run.

Five Mets had two hits apiece in the game to key a 12-hit attack, including Piazza, who had three RBIs.

The Mets and Braves were battling for supremacy in the National League East, putting added importance on these head-to-head games.

"These are intense games," Zeile said. "You can feel beat up on after you've made a couple of mistakes, and you can get flat. But one positive is we didn't do that."

The loss left the Braves' locker room in a "state of shock." Catcher Javy Lopez said, "It's unbelievable, I've never seen a game like this."

Armando Benitez got the win and not the save because Eric Cammack, who was the pitcher of record at the time of the barrage, was ineffective, thus the official scorer was able to award the win to the Mets' closer.

As the face of the franchise in the 1980s, Darryl Strawberry was an All-Star seven years in a row

Koosman Makes Quick Work of Expos

In a nine-inning game that lasted less than two hours, Mets left-hander Jerry Koosman tossed a complete game four-hit shutout to beat the Expos 2–0 at Parc Jarry in Montreal before a crowd of 25,156.

Montreal's Mike Torrez, a future Met, was the tough-luck loser as he gave up two runs (one earned) on eight hits in going the distance.

The Expos featured an entirely right-handed hitting lineup, but the Mets southpaw struck out six and kept Montreal's hitters off balance, as evidenced by the seven putouts that were recorded in center and right field.

The Mets took a 1–0 lead in the third inning with an unearned run off Torrez. With two outs, Bud Harrelson reached on an infield hit and took second on a throwing error by Expos first baseman John Boccabella.

Right fielder Dave Marshall lined a single to left to score Harrelson for the first run. The Mets' outfielder was a one-man gang on offense as he hit a solo home run off Torrez in the fifth to cap the scoring.

Koosman was in total command as the Expos could get no more than one runner on base in any single inning. No stat could better exemplify that fact than the time of the game, which was an astounding, one hour and 49 minutes.

> **At a Glance**
>
> **WP:** Koosman (6–3)
>
> **HR:** Marshall (2)
>
> **Key stat:** Koosman CG 4-hitter; Marshall 2-for-4, HR, 2 RBIs

The Mets acquired Marshall and left-handed pitcher Ray Sadecki in December 1969 for infielder Bob Heise and outfielder Jim Gosger. Marshall played three seasons with the Mets before being dealt to the San Diego Padres after the 1972 season.

McGraw Holds Off Cardinals Late to Win in 14 Innings

The Mets took a punch to the stomach but still had enough grit to get a victory on the road.

Vic Davalillo clubbed a game-tying pinch-hit grand slam off reliever Ron Taylor in the eighth inning, but the Mets scored two in the 14th inning to walk away with a 6–4 victory over the Cardinals before 14,928 at Busch Stadium.

Tug McGraw gives the "thumbs-up" sign after a game later in his career. McGraw pitched six scoreless innings in relief during a win over the Cardinals in 14 innings on July 2, 1969.

July 2, 1969

Mets 6, Cardinals 4 (14 innings)

An RBI single by Ken Boswell and a bases-loaded walk to Wayne Garrett plated the go-ahead runs while Mets closer Tug McGraw closed out the win by holding the Cards down in the home half of the 14th, his sixth scoreless inning of the game.

The winning rally came with two outs. Tommie Agee singled, stole second and scored on Boswell's single. Cards pitcher Ron Willis hit Cleon Jones, walked Rod Gaspar to load the bases and then walked Garrett to make it a two-run game.

The Cards left 11 runners on base against McGraw in his six innings of work and they even had the winning run thrown out at home in the ninth when Agee gunned down Curt Flood trying to score.

In the home half of the 10th, McGraw was like the legendary escape artist Houdini as he escaped from a near-impossible situation. The Cards loaded the bases with no one out, but McGraw got Dal Maxvill to bounce into a force-out at home for the first out. Cards infielder Steve Huntz struck out and McGraw ended the threat when he got Bill White to ground out.

In the bottom of the 13th, the Cards used future Hall of Fame pitcher Bob Gibson as a pinch-hitter with two men on but he lined out to first. Mike Shannon followed with an infield single that loaded the bases, but McGraw ended that rally when he got Cards catcher Tim McCarver to pop out to shortstop.

RP Tug McGraw

A free-spirited and fiery competitor, Tug McGraw provided leadership on the mound and was a driving force in the clubhouse.

The California native is best known for coining the phrase, "Ya Gotta Believe," which became the Mets' rallying cry for their improbable run to the National League pennant in 1973. McGraw saved 25 games that season as the franchise captured its second pennant.

The outgoing left-hander featured a screwball as his out pitch and had a signature tapping of his glove on his leg when he would close out a game.

After his Mets tenure, McGraw went on to win another World Championship and was on the mound when the Philadelphia Phillies closed out the 1980 World Series against the Kansas City Royals.

Strawberry, Knight Sew Up Come-From-Behind Win over Houston

Darryl Strawberry hit two game-tying home runs and Ray Knight ended it with a walk-off solo shot as the Mets came from behind twice to beat the Houston Astros 6–5 before 48,839 at Shea Stadium.

Houston took a 5–3 lead in the top of the 10th as pinch-hitter Phil Garner hit a two-run homer off Mets reliever Jesse Orosco.

In the home half of the 10th, Len Dykstra walked against Astros pitcher Frank Di Pino to start the rally.

Strawberry's second game-tying home run was a blast that cleared the 410-foot sign in center field.

DiPino got the next two outs, but Knight sent Mets fans home happy when he blasted the game-winner into the empty bleachers—it was fireworks night and the bleacher crowd was cleared out because of the impending show.

"Losing is a word we don't think of," Knight said after the game. "Things looked bleak, then Darryl hits a home run. It felt good, especially after not making much contact over the course of the night."

At a Glance

WP: Orosco (4–4)

HR: Hearn (3), Strawberry 2 (11,12), Knight (9)

Mets starter Ron Darling got a no-decision but pitched well as he allowed three runs on five hits with nine strikeouts in nine innings pitched.

The Mets trailed 3–1 with two outs in the fifth inning when Kevin Mitchell walked and Strawberry hit his first game-tying blast off Astros left-hander Jim Deshaies.

Houston's southpaw settled down to retire the last seven Mets that he faced.

The Houston Astros traded Knight to the Mets in August 1984. The versatile infielder would play the next two years in Queens, capping his Mets career with the 1986 World Series Most Valuable Player Award.

It Was Fireworks Night All Right in Atlanta

This one goes right to the top of the list in the category "Greatest Wins in Mets History."

In a game that ended at 3:55 AM Eastern time, the Mets outlasted the Atlanta Braves 16–13 in a 19-inning marathon at Atlanta-Fulton County Stadium.

The first pitch was thrown at 9:04 PM, an hour and 24 minutes late because of a rain delay. Add on a second rain delay of 41 minutes in the bottom of the third inning and the game was not over until eight hours and 15 minutes after the scheduled first pitch.

It was fireworks night in Atlanta, so a crowd of 44,947 fans showed up to see the game and the postgame show. By the time it ended, approximately 8,000 fans were left and yes, the fireworks were shot off, even at that "ungodly" hour—approximately 4:01 AM.

Wayne Minshew, the Braves' director of public relations and promotions said, "As long as there were people at the game, we were obligated to fire 'em (the fireworks) off."

"We got about 30 calls (complaints) here, and the police precinct told me they got several," Minshew said.

A total of 14 pitchers gave up 29 runs on 46 hits with 22 walks and 23 strikeouts.

The Mets set a single-game franchise record for the most hits in an extra-inning game with 28.

Catcher Gary Carter, who was behind the plate for all 19 innings, went 5-for-9, while second baseman Wally Backman and first baseman Keith Hernandez had four hits apiece.

Hernandez became the fourth Met to hit for the cycle when he singled in the 12th.

"I saw everything tonight," Hernandez said. "I saw things I'd never seen in my career before."

Mets third baseman Ray Knight left 11 runners on base before providing a key run-scoring double in the 19th.

The field was a "quagmire" as evidenced by what went on in the Mets' half of the fourth. With runners on first and second and one out, Backman singled to right, where the ball hit a puddle and stopped. Later, Hernandez had a two-run triple when Braves right fielder Claudell Washington slipped trying to field the ball.

The Mets had a 7–4 lead in the eighth inning, but reliever Jesse Orosco walked three batters to spark a four-run rally for the Braves, who took an 8–7 lead into the ninth.

Len Dykstra's RBI single tied the game in the ninth and the Mets had the go-ahead run on third with two outs, but Hernandez flied out to left.

After three scoreless innings, the Mets took a 10–8 lead in the top of the 13th on a two-run home run from Howard Johnson off Terry Forster. Atlanta came right back to tie it on Terry Harper's two-strike, two-out, two-run home run off the left-field foul pole against Mets left-hander Tom Gorman.

The Mets regained the lead in the top of the 18th on Dykstra's sacrifice fly, but the most shocking event of the game took place in the bottom half of the inning.

With two outs and no one on, the Braves were out of players, so pitcher Rick Camp, who was hitting .060 for his career, had to bat.

Gorman got the first two strikes, but Camp unloaded on a 0–2 pitch for his first career home run to tie the game 11–11.

"It's not like pitchers don't hit home runs," Gorman said, "they do, but, in that situation, with two strikes and no balls and you give a guy a pitch he can hit out, it's embarrassing."

So embarrassing that there is a classic picture of Mets left fielder Danny Heep putting both his hands (one with the glove) on his head in frustration.

Knight's double in the 19th snapped the 11–11 tie and gave the Mets a one-run lead. After Johnson was intentionally walked, Heep drilled a two-run single and a third run scored on Washington's throwing error.

Backman completed the scoring with an RBI single, as the Mets would need just about every one of those five runs.

Mets	AB	R	H	RBI
Dykstra cf	9	1	3	2
Backman 2b	10	2	4	2
Hernandez 1b	10	3	4	3
Carter c	9	1	5	2
Strawberry rf	7	0	3	1
Christensen rf	0	0	0	0
Foster lf	2	0	0	0
Orosco p	0	0	0	0
Sisk p	1	0	0	0
Chapman ph	1	0	0	0
Gorman p	2	0	0	0
Staub ph	0	1	0	0
Darling p	0	0	0	0
Knight 3b	10	2	3	1
Santana ss	4	1	1	0
Johnson ph-ss	5	4	3	2
Gooden p	1	0	0	0
McDowell p	0	0	0	0
Hurdle ph	1	0	0	0
Leach p	2	0	0	0
Heep lf	6	1	2	2
Totals	**80**	**16**	**28**	**15**

Braves	AB	R	H	RBI
Washington rf	8	3	3	0
Ramirez ss	9	2	3	2
Murphy cf	8	1	1	3
Horner 1b	4	1	1	0
Perry 1b	4	0	0	0
Harper lf	10	3	5	4
Oberkfell 3b	6	1	3	2
Camp p	2	1	1	1
Cerone c	4	1	1	1
Hall pr	0	0	0	0
Benedict c	2	0	0	0
Hubbard 2b	3	0	0	0
Shields p	0	0	0	0
Komminsk ph	1	0	0	0
Sutter p	0	0	0	0
Chambliss ph	1	0	0	0
Forster p	1	0	0	0
Garber p	1	0	0	0
Runge ph-3b	2	0	0	0
Mahler p	1	0	0	0
Dedmon p	1	0	0	0
Zuvella 2b	7	0	0	0
Totals	**75**	**13**	**18**	**13**

NYM 1 0 0 4 0 1 0 1 1 0 0 0 2 0 0 0 0 1 5 - 16 28 2
ATL 1 0 2 0 1 0 0 4 0 0 0 0 2 0 0 0 0 1 2 - 13 18 3

Mets	IP	H	R	ER	BB	SO
Gooden	2.1	2	2	2	4	3
McDowell	0.2	2	1	1	0	1
Leach	4	4	1	1	0	3
Orosco	0.2	1	4	4	3	1
Sisk	4.1	3	0	0	1	0
Gorman W (4-3)	6	5	3	3	2	2
Darling	1	1	2	0	2	1
Totals	**19**	**18**	**13**	**11**	**12**	**11**

Braves	IP	H	R	ER	BB	SO
Mahler	3.1	6	3	3	4	2
Dedmon	2	5	3	3	0	1
Shields	2.2	4	1	1	1	1
Sutter	1	3	1	1	0	1
Forster	4	3	2	2	1	3
Garber	3	1	0	0	2	2
Camp L (2-4)	3	6	6	5	2	2
Totals	**19**	**28**	**16**	**15**	**10**	**12**

E—New York Hernandez, Johnson; Atlanta Washington, Camp, Ramirez. DP—New York; Atlanta 3. 2B—New York Knight, Hernandez; Atlanta Murphy, Harper, Oberkfell. 3B—New York Hernandez; Atlanta Washington. HR—New York Hernandez (5), Johnson (3); Atlanta Camp (1), Harper (8). SH—New York Backman, Christensen. SF—New York Dykstra. LOB—New York 20; Atlanta 17. SB—New York Backman, Strawberry. Attendance: 44,947.

Mets 16, Braves 13 (19 innings)

Pitcher Ron Darling (who was making his first relief appearance since he pitched at Yale) was brought on as the Mets were out of relievers. With one out, Washington reached on a rare error by Hernandez.

With two outs, Dale Murphy and Gerald Perry walked to load the bases.

Harper singled in two runs to cut the lead to 16–13, but Darling ended a long "night's journey into day" when he fanned Camp for the final out.

The Braves' pitcher put the game in perspective.

"I couldn't care less about the home run," he said. "If they have to rely on me to hit home runs, we're in a lot of trouble."

"We should've won the game twice," Gorman said. "I could have easily picked up the save. I could have lost the game. Instead, I won it. It was the weirdest thing I've ever seen."

After the game, Darling reflected on a memorable evening.

"It was a game everyone on this team will remember, I'm just glad I got my name in the box score."

Did You Know?

Mets infielder Ted Schreiber was the final batter at the Polo Grounds. On Sept. 18, 1963, Schreiber, who played only one season in the major leagues, grounded into a game-ending double play in the final game ever played at the ol' ballpark in upper Manhattan.

Mets Crank Out Five Home Runs vs. Braves

The Mets blasted five home runs and powered their way to a 9–8 victory over the Braves at Atlanta-Fulton County Stadium before a crowd of 34,312.

"It seemed like there was a home run every inning," said Mets reliever Wally Whitehurst, who picked up his first major league win.

Darryl Strawberry had the "loudest" and most important home run as his three-run shot in the seventh gave the Mets an 8–7 lead.

Strawberry drilled a 1–1 fastball from Braves reliever Joe Hesketh and drove it over the wall in left-center field for the Mets' first lead of the game.

"The harder we play, the more successful we get," Strawberry said. "I like being in those types of situations. The key has always been just having the opportunity."

Mark Carreon, Dave Magadan, Orlando Mercado and Kevin Elster had the other Met home runs.

Ron Gant put a scare into the Mets as he smacked his second home run of the game in the ninth inning to make it a one-run game, but Jim Presley struck out against John Franco, who picked up the save.

Mets starter Bob Ojeda was roughed up for four runs in 1 ⅓ innings. Whitehurst relieved the left-hander in the second and gave up three runs in 4 ⅔ innings, but was the beneficiary of the power display.

At a Glance

WP: Whitehurst (1–0)

HR: Carreon (9), Magadan (3), Mercado (3), Strawberry (21), Elster (7)

Key stat: Strawberry 2-for-5, HR, 3 RBIs

Kanehl Goes Down in History with Mets' First Grand Slam

Rod Kanehl became the first Met to hit a grand slam and Gil Hodges moved ahead of Ralph Kiner on the all-time home run list as the Mets pummeled the St. Louis Cardinals 10–3 at the Polo Grounds.

A crowd of 14,515 was on hand to see Hodges move past Kiner into 10th place on the all-time home run list when he went deep against future Met Ray Sadecki in the second inning for a solo homer. Hodges' 370th home run, and the final one of his career, gave the Mets a 1–0 lead.

The Mets added two runs in the third inning, and Charlie Neal hit a solo homer in the fifth for a 4–0 bulge.

The Mets broke the game open with six runs in the eighth. Third baseman Felix Mantilla, who was 4-for-4, singled to open the inning. The Cards made two errors, including a throwing error by pitcher Bobby Shantz, which keyed the Mets' rally.

Kanehl took advantage of the Cardinals' mistakes when he blasted a Shantz pitch into the upper deck in left field for the first slam in franchise history.

Things went so well for the "young" Mets that they even scored a run on an intentional walk.

In the third inning, the Mets had runners at second and third with two outs and Hodges at the plate. The Cards elected to intentionally walk Hodges, who had homered in his previous at-bat against Sadecki, but the St. Louis left-hander threw a wild pitch on ball three and the Mets scored a run. The future Mets manager drew an intentional base on balls.

Roger Craig benefited from the offensive outburst as he went the distance for the victory.

Kanehl hit six career home runs during a three-year major league career, all with the Mets, but none bigger than his only career slam.

At a Glance

WP: Craig (5–11)

HR: Hodges (9), Neal (7), Kanehl (2)

Key stat: Kanehl 1-for-1, HR, 4 RBIs

Jacome's Second Start Comes Complete with 'Comfort Zone'

Jason Jacome, a 23-year-old left-hander, made his second major league start a memorable one, as he tossed a complete game six-hit shutout to lead the Mets to a 3–0 win over the Los Angeles Dodgers at Dodger Stadium.

At a Glance

WP: Jacome (1–1)

HR: Hundley (13)

Key stat: Jacome CG 6-hitter, 0 BB

Mets manager Dallas Green was certainly appreciative of the effort by his young hurler.

"It was a gem," said the skipper, "that's the kind of pitching I love to see. He's a young kid, second start, and he battled a pretty good team, tooth and nail."

Jacome got enough run support, thanks to his catcher, Todd Hundley, who smacked a 3–1 pitch from knuckleballer Tom Candiotti over the wall in right field for a 1–0 lead in the fourth.

The Mets added two more runs on a run-scoring fielder's choice and a sacrifice fly by Ryan Thompson that scored Jeff Kent with the bases loaded.

Dodgers left fielder Cory Snyder had to make a great catch on Thompson's fly or else the Mets' center fielder would've had a grand slam.

July 7, 1964

National League Takes All-Star Game at Shea

A crowd of 50,850 poured into Shea Stadium to see baseball's brightest and biggest stars. Johnny Callison stole the show as he slammed a walk-off three-run home run in the bottom of the ninth inning to give the National League a 7–4 win over the American League in the All-Star Game.

There was one representative of the local team and it was second baseman Ron Hunt, who became the first Met to start an All-Star Game.

Comeback vs. Cubs Only a Sign of Things to Come

A crowd of 55,096 watched the Mets rally with three runs in the bottom of the ninth to stun the Chicago Cubs 4–3 at Shea Stadium.

Through eight innings, the Mets could only garner one hit against future Hall of Famer Ferguson Jenkins, and that was Ed Kranepool's solo home run in the fifth.

Home runs by future Hall of Famer Ernie Banks and former Met Jim Hickman staked the Cubs and Jenkins to a 3–1 lead entering the bottom of the ninth.

Pinch-hitter Ken Boswell began the rally with a bloop double to center. Tommie Agee fouled out, but pinch-hitter Donn Clendenon lined a ball that went off the glove of Cubs center fielder Don Young for a double. Boswell had to hold up so he could only make it to third base.

With runners at second and third and one out, the Cubs elected to pitch to the National League's leading hitter, Mets left fielder Cleon Jones.

Jones lined a 1–0 curveball into left field for a two-run double that tied the game 3–3.

"He made some good pitches to me," Jones said. "He was bound to make a mistake sooner or later. That's the way this game goes. I knew we'd get some breaks sooner or later."

With the winning run at second and one out, Jenkins intentionally walked Art Shamsky. Wayne Garrett grounded out, moving the runners to second and third. Kranepool was up next.

The Mets' first baseman had been taking some heat from the hometown fans and when he got behind in the count, 1–2, they booed him. But he wasn't going to be denied.

Kranepool said, "I knew I wasn't going to see a strike."

The next pitch was on the outside corner, but Kranepool reached out and hit it over Cubs short-

Cubs	AB	R	H	RBI
Kessinger ss	4	0	1	0
Beckert 2b	4	0	2	1
Williams lf	4	0	1	0
Santo 3b	3	0	0	0
Banks 1b	4	1	1	1
Hundley c	2	0	0	0
Hickman rf	4	1	2	1
Young cf	4	0	0	0
Jenkins p	3	1	1	0
Totals	32	3	8	3

Mets	AB	R	H	RBI
Agee cf	4	0	0	0
Pfeil 3b	3	0	0	0
Clendenon ph	1	1	1	0
Jones lf	4	1	1	2
Shamsky rf	3	0	0	0
Garrett 2b	4	0	0	0
Kranepool 1b	4	1	2	2
Martin c	3	0	0	0
Weis ss	3	0	0	0
Koosman p	2	0	0	0
Boswell ph	1	1	1	0
Totals	32	4	5	4

CHI	0	0	0	0	0	1	1	1	0	-	3	8	1
NYM	0	0	0	0	1	0	0	0	3	-	4	5	0

Cubs	IP	H	R	ER	BB	SO
Jenkins L (11-6)	8.2	5	4	4	1	8
Totals	8.2	5	4	4	1	8

Mets	IP	H	R	ER	BB	SO
Koosman W (6-5)	9	8	3	3	4	6
Totals	9	8	3	3	4	6

E—Chicago Jenkins. DP—New York. 2B—New York Clendenon, Boswell, Jones. HR—Chicago Banks (14), Hickman (4); New York Kranepool (8). SH—Chicago Beckert, Kessinger. LOB—Chicago 8; New York 3. Attendance: 55,096.

stop Don Kessinger and into left field. Jones scored and the rest of the Mets, along with the crowd, were delirious.

The 1969 Chicago Cubs featured a roster with three future Hall of Famers: Billy Williams, Ernie Banks and Jenkins. The Mets had two future Hall of Famers in pitchers Tom Seaver and Nolan Ryan, so the "star power" was there to fuel a great rivalry.

Earlier in the 1969 season, the Mets lost five of eight games to the NL East-favored Cubs, but this win signified a turn. Including this game, the Mets went on to win seven of their last 10 meetings en route to winning the division and eventually the World Series.

It was also a prelude to the next night and what would be one of the most memorable games in the history of the New York Mets.

LF Cleon Jones

Cleon Joseph Jones is best known for catching the final out of the 1969 World Series, but the former All-Star outfielder had a solid Mets career.

Jones was signed as an amateur free agent in 1963 and spent 12 years in Flushing.

His best year was 1969, when he finished third in the National League with a .340 batting average.

Jones is second in franchise history with 1,188 hits and second in multi-hit games with 334.

The popular Met was inducted into the club's Hall of Fame in 1991 and is a member of the Alabama Sports Hall of Fame and the Mobile (Ala.) Sports Hall of Fame.

Seaver Flirts with Mets' First No-Hitter

A New York Mets pitcher has never thrown a no-hitter, but Hall of Famer Tom Seaver came oh, so close to "baseball immortality" when he tossed a complete game one-hitter to lead the Mets past the Cubs 4–0 at an "electric" Shea Stadium.

A crowd of 59,083, the largest in Shea Stadium history, watched Cubs rookie outfielder Jimmy Qualls spoil Seaver's bid for baseball's 11th perfect game when he singled to center with one out in the ninth inning.

Seaver was literally "unhittable" as he struck out 11 Cubs going into the ninth, including the side (Ron Santo, Ernie Banks and Al Spangler) in the second inning.

In the ninth, Randy Hundley led off trying to bunt his way on, but he couldn't get it past Seaver, who threw him out at first base. That attempt didn't sit well with the fans at Shea, who booed the Cubs' catcher.

In his two previous at-bats, Qualls flied out to deep right-center field and grounded to first base.

"We didn't know how to pitch Qualls since we hadn't seen him at all this year," Mets catcher Jerry Grote said.

Seaver threw 99 pitches in, arguably, the best game he ever pitched, but only one was a mistake.

After the game, Seaver seemed resigned to the fact that he had come so close.

At a Glance
WP: Seaver (14-3)
HR: Jones (10)
Key stat: Seaver complete game 1-hitter, 11 Ks

"I just got my breaks," the 24-year old said. "I just needed one more break."

The right-hander got two strikeouts in the first inning and the Mets rewarded him with a 1–0 lead in the bottom half of the first. Tommie Agee led off with a triple and scored on Bobby Pfeil's double.

The Mets made it 3–0 in the second inning thanks to some uncharacteristic Cubs errors by third baseman Ron Santo and shortstop Don Kessinger on consecutive batters. Seaver cashed in with an RBI single and scored on Agee's RBI double.

A solo home run by Cleon Jones in the seventh inning completed the scoring and then it was left up to "Tom Terrific."

In the Cubs' eighth, Seaver ended the inning with his second strikeout of Banks and his third "punch-out" of Spangler.

The "star of the show" was scheduled to hit third in the bottom of the eighth. With one out, Al Weis singled and Seaver stepped to the plate to a thunderous and long standing ovation. It was so lengthy that Seaver had to delay getting into the batter's box.

During an interview, Seaver admitted that he used the crowd's energy to "fuel" himself to pitch the ninth.

"You can't ignore it, you also realize what's going on," Seaver said.

Seaver bunted Weis to second base and went back to the dugout to get ready for the ninth.

Qualls' historic hit eluded Jones in left and Agee in center.

"I was just hoping that Cleon (Jones) had a chance to catch the ball," Agee said, "because I know I had no chance for it."

"I thought it was going to be a no-hitter from the first pitch," Grote said.

Even though they won, the Mets' postgame clubhouse wreaked with disappointment.

"We all wanted to save his one-hitter, he's a first class guy," said Mets first baseman Donn Clendenon, who didn't have a problem with Hundley bunting in the ninth.

"I don't think Hundley was thinking about the no-hitter either, he was just trying to start a rally," said Clendenon, who would go on to win the 1969 World Series Most Valuable Player Award.

Qualls became an "instant villain" because of the hit.

"I was just doing my job," the 22-year old said. "If you don't do your job, you don't stay long in the big leagues."

The next night, Qualls was booed mercilessly but he took it well.

"The booing didn't bother me at all," he said. "I know the New York fans wanted a perfect game, but I was glad I got the hit."

Seaver was asked if that game was the best one that he ever pitched.

"Gotta be 1, 2 or 3," he said.

Franco Delivers Against Rivera in a Pinch

Matt Franco's two-out, pinch-hit, two-run single off Yankees closer Mariano Rivera gave the Mets their most exciting win in the history of the regular-season "Subway Series" as they beat their "cousins" from the Bronx, 9–8.

With the bases loaded and the Mets down to their final out, Mets manager Bobby Valentine elected to have the left-handed hitting Franco bat for the right-handed hitting Melvin Mora.

Franco had an idea of what was coming from the man who has been referred to as "the greatest closer of all time."

"Bobby (Valentine) said, 'Be ready for that cutter, it's the same one I (Valentine) throw in batting practice,'" Franco said.

On the first pitch of the memorable at-bat, Franco fouled back a pitch that he thought was very hittable.

"I had to take a step out," he said. "I was really mad at myself."

Franco swung and missed the second pitch so he was in an 0–2 hole against Rivera.

The Mets' pinch-hitter took the third pitch for ball one. Home-plate umpire Jeff Kellogg called it low and Franco got a break on a close pitch.

"It felt down," Franco said. "Right when I took it, my heart kind of skipped a beat. I've been rung up on that pitch before."

> ## At a Glance
>
> **WP:** Mahomes (3-0)
>
> **HR:** Piazza (19)
>
> **Key stat:** Piazza 2-for-3, 4 RBIs, 2 intentional walks; Henderson 3-for-3, 3 runs

Maybe that was an omen because Franco lined the next pitch into right field for a single. Rickey Henderson scored the tying run from third and Edgardo Alfonzo slid home with the winning run, just ahead of right fielder Paul O'Neill's throw.

A crowd of 53,792 watched the Mets pour out of their dugout to mob Franco after one of the most memorable pinch-hits in the history of Shea Stadium. "Without a doubt, this is biggest moment of my career so far," the 29-year-old bench player said. "To get the game-winning hit at Shea Stadium, playing the Yankees with 53,000 people in the stands, bases loaded, down a run, in the bottom of the ninth, I don't know how it's going to get any better than that. It's a dream come true."

The game itself had been memorable, even before the ninth-inning heroics. The lead changed hands four other times.

The Mets had a 4–2 lead in the fifth inning, but back-to-back home runs by Ricky Ledee and Jorge Posada tied the game 4–4.

Two more solo home runs—from O'Neill in the sixth inning and Chuck Knoblauch in the seventh—gave the Yankees a 6–4 lead, but the Mets rallied for three runs in the seventh to regain the lead.

With two on and two outs, Mike Piazza unloaded a mammoth three-run homer off Yankees reliever Ramiro Mendoza that cleared the bullpen in left field for a 7–6 lead.

Posada's second home run of the game—a two-run shot and the Yankees' sixth of the game—gave the "Bronx Bombers" an 8–7 lead in the eighth.

Left-hander Mike Stanton set the Mets down in order in the eighth and things looked bleak with Rivera on the horizon.

With one out in the ninth, Henderson walked. Alfonzo hit a long fly ball to left-center field, but center fielder Bernie Williams had it go off his glove. The play was ruled a double and the Mets had the tying and winning runs in scoring position.

John Olerud failed to at least tie the game as he bounced out to first base and the runners had to hold.

The Yankees intentionally walked Piazza to load the bases, bringing up Franco.

The rest, as they say, is history.

Fernandez, Carter Chalk Up Gems in Wild Win

Sid Fernandez was absolutely brilliant as the left-hander went the distance on a two-hit shutout, Gary Carter set a career high with seven RBIs and there was even a "beanball war" as the Mets dominated the Atlanta Braves 11–0 before 39,924 fans at Shea Stadium.

The game featured a bench-clearing brawl in the first inning.

Carter hit a three-run homer off Braves pitcher David Palmer and received a curtain call from the Shea faithful. Palmer did not take too kindly to that display, so on the next pitch he hit Darryl Strawberry in the back. The dugouts emptied when Strawberry charged the mound.

"I know David," Carter said. "I was his catcher for six years in Montreal. He was frustrated and he took it out on Darryl."

As Strawberry got near Palmer, the Braves pitcher threw his glove at him, then moved away as catcher Ozzie Virgil tackled the Mets' slugger.

> ### At a Glance
>
> **WP:** Fernandez (12–2)
>
> **HR:** Carter 2 (15,16)
>
> **Key stat:** Carter 2-for-5, 2 HR, 7 RBIs; Fernandez CG 2-hitter, 9 Ks

Order was restored and there were no ejections.

In the second inning, Carter hit a grand slam off Palmer on a 0–2 pitch and "The Kid" had seven RBIs by the time the second inning was complete.

Fernandez was just as dominant on the mound.

The 23-year-old native Hawaiian limited Atlanta to a Terry Harper single in the second inning and an Andres Thomas double in the third. Fernandez did not give up a hit over the final six innings and was just as good at the plate, where he had three hits, an RBI and two runs scored.

Eight Runs Out of the Gate Propel Mets

The Mets used a club-record eight-run first-inning surge and coasted to a 12–5 win over the Los Angeles Dodgers at Shea Stadium.

Thanks to the help of two Dodger errors, the Mets scored eight unearned runs. Joel Youngblood started things off with a single to center off Dodgers starter and loser Burt Hooton.

Los Angeles shortstop Bill Russell made the first error by bobbling Frank Taveras' potential double-play grounder.

Two consecutive ground-outs led to one run, but the Mets kept things going as Willie Montanez drew a two-out walk, putting runners at first and third.

Singles by John Stearns and Steve Henderson scored two more runs. Consecutive walks to Elliott Maddox and Mets starting pitcher Dock Ellis produced a fourth run and Hooton was done.

The Dodgers brought in right-handed pitcher Dennis Lewallyn. Youngblood, who was batting for the second time in the inning, hit a liner to left, but Dodgers left fielder Von Joshua dropped the ball, which allowed two more runs to score.

Taveras provided a two-run double to complete the scoring. Lee Mazzilli ended the inning with a ground-out to second.

The Mets added a run in the third inning, two in the fifth and one more in the sixth as they kept up the pressure on Lewallyn, who lasted 5 1/3 innings.

> ## At a Glance
>
> **WP:** Ellis (1–2)
>
> **Key stat:** Youngblood 3-for-5, 2 RBIs, 3 runs; Henderson 3-for-5, 2 RBIs, 2 runs

A crowd of 13,218 at Shea watched Ellis keep the Dodgers off the board until the seventh inning, when he gave up his first run. After running the bases in the bottom of the seventh, the right-hander ran out of gas.

"If he doesn't run the bases, Ellis would have stayed in there the whole game," Mets manager Joe Torre said.

In the eighth inning, the Dodgers got to Ellis for four runs, three on a home run by Steve Garvey.

Neil Allen pitched the final 1 2/3 to seal the win.

Mets Topple Seaver for First Time Since Trade

For the first time since the infamous trade of June 15, 1977, the Mets beat Tom Seaver.

Left-hander Jerry Koosman hooked up against his old pal and went 6 ^{2}/$_3$ innings as the Mets scored a 4–2 victory over the Reds at Cincinnati's Riverfront Stadium before a crowd of 35,226.

A little more than two months after he was traded in 1977, Seaver had beaten the Mets and Koosman in a dramatic return to Shea.

"Beating Tom Seaver was the last thing on my mind," Koosman said.

At a Glance
WP: Koosman (3–9)
HR: Youngblood (2)
Key stat: Mazzilli 2-for-4

The Mets' southpaw allowed two runs on seven hits. Seaver gave up three runs, (one earned) in seven innings pitched.

The Mets took a 2–0 lead against their former ace in the second.

With one out, John Stearns singled and stole second. Future Hall of Famer Johnny Bench's throw sailed into center field and Stearns took third.

With the infield in, Reds shortstop Dave Concepcion booted Steve Henderson's sharp grounder and a run scored.

A sacrifice fly by Doug Flynn plated the second run.

The Reds scored their first run off Koosman in the third inning, but the Mets added a run in the fifth on Lenny Randle's sacrifice fly.

It was 3–2 in the eighth when Joel Youngblood greeted Reds reliever Manny Sarmiento with a solo home run to make it a two-run game.

Skip Lockwood relieved Koosman in the seventh and pitched scoreless ball over the final 2 ^{1}/$_3$.

Seaver made 11 starts against his former team and was 5–3 with a 2.28 ERA.

Piazza's 2 Homers Help Mets Drop Red Sox

Mike Piazza hit two home runs to power the Mets to a 6–4 victory over the Boston Red Sox at Fenway Park before a crowd of 33,293.

In the fourth inning, Piazza tied the game 1–1 with a solo home run against former Mets pitcher Pete Schourek.

The Mets took a 3–1 lead in the fifth on a two-run homer by Melvin Mora, but Boston scored three in the seventh to take a one-run lead.

Mets reliever Dennis Cook came on to face Boston's Brian Daubach with one out and the tying run in scoring position in the seventh.

Red Sox manager Jimy Williams tried to play "head games" with Cook. After the left-hander got out in front of Daubach with an 0–2 count, Williams came out to argue about the way Cook was rubbing the baseball between pitches.

Cook said, "I've been rubbing the ball for 15 years the same way and the only teams that seem to have a problem with it are the Braves and the Red Sox."

Cook stepped off the mound and Daubach stepped out of the batter's box in an unusual game of "baseball chicken."

Mets catcher Todd Pratt had words for Daubach and the two nearly came to blows as both benches emptied.

At a Glance

WP: Mahomes (3–1)

HR: Piazza 2 (25,26), Mora (6)

Key stat: Piazza 2-for-4, 2 HR, 3 RBIs

"He told me to save it," Pratt said. "I just said, 'Who are you to tell me to 'save it?' I couldn't believe a guy who's got one year in is telling me to save it. I told him how I felt about it."

After order was restored and both benches were warned, Daubach lined a single to left to tie the game 3–3, but was thrown out trying for second.

Cook walked the next batter—Nomar Garciaparra—and then hit Carl Everett with a pitch, putting runners on first and second.

Cook felt Everett was out of the batter's box but umpire Marty Foster was having none of that and he ejected the Mets' reliever.

Southpaw Rich Rodriguez relieved Cook and gave up a run-scoring single to Troy O'Leary as the Red Sox took the lead.

In the eighth inning, Piazza drove a pitch from Derek Lowe over the "Green Monster" and off a "giant cola bottle" above the left-field wall for a 5–4 lead. Mora's single in the ninth drove in the final run.

Franco's Record 108th Save Staves Off Padres

John Franco set a club record with his 108th save as the Mets nipped the San Diego Padres at Shea Stadium 5–4.

Franco entered the game in the ninth inning with a 5–2 lead, but he gave up two runs on four hits to put a scare into the crowd of 23,897.

The left-hander finally ended it when he struck out Eddie Williams looking.

"It wasn't pretty but I got it done," Franco said afterward. "It was maybe the first one all year of all my saves where I really struggled. I made a couple of bad pitches but I got the out when I needed to."

At a Glance

WP: Jacome (2–1)

Key stat: Franco sets club record 108th save

The Mets used three hits and a key error to score three times in the first inning for a 3–0 lead.

San Diego came back with two runs in the sixth inning off Mets winner Jason Jacome, but Fernando Vina's RBI single in the home half made it a 4–2 game.

Franco's save moved him past Jesse Orosco for first place on the club's all-time list.

The 5-foot-10 southpaw from St. John's University in New York pitched 14 seasons for the Mets, recording 276 saves. He had his best season in Queens in 1998, when he garnered 38 saves, but also went 0–8. In 1999, he had 19 saves before Armando Benitez replaced him as closer and helped the Mets earn the National League wild-card spot.

John Franco set a franchise record with his 108th save on July 16, 1994, against the Padres. He spent 14 seasons with the Mets and accumulated 276 saves.

Two-Run Homer by Hicks Sends Larsen, Giants Packing

A crowd of 26,574 at the Polo Grounds watched Joe Hicks hit a walk-off, two-run home run in the bottom of the 11th inning to give the Mets a thrilling 9–7 win over the defending National League champion San Francisco Giants.

Joe Christopher singled off Giants reliever Don Larsen to start the inning. Hicks followed with his first home run in a Mets uniform—a game-winning, two-run shot.

The Mets trailed 7–6 in the bottom of the ninth but Duke Snider singled and pinch runner Rod Kanehl scored the tying run on Frank Thomas' RBI double.

The game went back and forth. Christopher's home run in the fourth gave the Mets a 5–3 lead, but Mets right-hander Tracy Stallard gave up a solo home run to future Hall of Famer Willie McCovey in the fifth to make it a one-run game.

> ### At a Glance
>
> **WP:** Cisco (6–7)
>
> **HR:** Gonder (6), Christopher (1), Hicks (2)
>
> **Key stat:** Christopher 3-for-5, 3 runs; Gonder 3 RBIs; Thomas 3-for-5

McCovey had singled in his first at-bat to extend his hitting streak to 22 straight games.

Run-scoring singles by future Hall of Famer Orlando Cepeda, Chuck Hiller and Jose Pagan in the eighth had given San Francisco a 7–6 lead.

Galen Cisco tossed three scoreless innings in relief to earn the win while Larsen took the loss.

Hicks was acquired from the Washington Senators for cash in December 1962 and played one season for the Mets. The left-handed hitting outfielder played in 56 games in 1963, when he hit five home runs and had 22 RBIs.

Gallagher's Grand Slam in 9th Shuts Down Giants

Jeff Kent hit two home runs and Dave Gallagher added a grand slam to power the Mets to a 12–6 win over the San Francisco Giants before 53,210 fans at Candlestick Park.

Gallagher's slam keyed a six-run rally in the ninth inning that blew the game wide open.

San Francisco got the early lead with three runs in the first inning against Mets starter Pete Schourek.

With a runner on first and two outs, Barry Bonds slammed a two-run homer. Three straight singles followed to produce a third run against the left-hander, but Schourek settled down from there and did not give up another run, as he lasted six innings.

"I was thinking I was one pitch away from being out of the game," Schourek said, "from going two-thirds of an inning and heading to the showers."

The Giants had to use an emergency starter in right-hander Greg Brummett and the Mets took advantage.

Future Hall of Famer Eddie Murray hit a two-run homer off Brummett in the third inning to put the Mets back in the game.

At a Glance

WP: Schourek (3–10)

HR: Murray (12), Kent 2 (8,9), Gallagher (3)

Key stat: Gallagher HR, 4 RBIs; Murray 3 RBIs; Coleman 3 runs

Kent's first home run tied the game in the fourth, and the Mets took their first lead on a RBI single by Vince Coleman in the fifth.

In the seventh, Bobby Bonilla's two-run double made it a 6–3 game.

The Mets loaded the bases for Gallagher, who had his "moment in the sun" when he took Giants reliever Michael Jackson deep for a memorable blast.

The versatile outfielder had not seen many at-bats and was feeling a "lack of confidence," so the slam was a welcome sight.

Kent went back-to-back with his second home run of the game to complete the scoring. It was the first time in his career that Kent hit two home runs in a game.

Gallagher came to the Mets from the California Angels in December 1991 for outfielder Hubie Brooks. Gallagher played two seasons with the Mets until he was traded to the Braves in November 1993 for right-handed pitcher Pete Smith.

Strawberry's Grand Slam, 7 RBIs Highlight Win over Braves

It was a record-setting game for Darryl Strawberry, who hit two home runs—including a grand slam—and drove in a career-high seven runs to lead the Mets to a 16–4 annihilation of the Atlanta Braves at Shea Stadium.

A crowd of 35,650 saw a remarkable performance because Strawberry was dealing with a thumb injury.

"My thumb still hurts and it will for the rest of the season," Straw said.

"Doc" Gooden went six innings, giving up a run on two hits for the win, but it was the offense that carried the load.

"With the lead we had, I thought it was a great move to take me out," said Gooden, who would go on to win the 1985 National League Cy Young Award.

Len Dykstra had three hits out of the leadoff spot and scored three runs, while Strawberry and Howard Johnson also had three hits apiece.

Strawberry's slam came in the bottom of the first. The bases were loaded after two walks and an error. Steve Bedrosian fed Strawberry a 2–2 slider on the inner part of the plate and the Mets' slugger drove it high over the fence in right-center field for a 4–0 lead.

Strawberry's second home run capped a five-run rally in the fourth inning. With a run in and two on, Strawberry took Braves pitcher Len Barker deep and the Mets had a 10–1 lead. Danny Heep followed with a solo home run and it was 11–1.

Strawberry had a previous single-game high of five RBIs, which he had done twice. In June 1983, Strawberry drove in five against the Cardinals in a 10–1 win at Busch Stadium in the first game of a doubleheader. The other time was in September 1984 at Wrigley Field in a 9–3 win over the Cubs.

At a Glance

WP: Gooden (14–3)

HR: Strawberry 2 (9,10), Johnson (5), Heep (6), Hurdle (3)

Key stat: Strawberry 2 HR, 7 RBIs, 3 runs

Jackson Shuts Down Powerful Pirates with 2-Hit Shutout

Al Jackson came within five outs of a no-hitter and settled for a two-hit shutout as the Mets blanked the Pittsburgh Pirates 1–0 before 22,670 at Forbes Field.

Jackson dazzled a Pirates lineup that included future Hall of Famers Willie Stargell, Roberto Clemente and Bill Mazeroski.

With one out in the eighth, Stargell got the first Bucs hit when he lined a single to left.

The only other Pittsburgh hit was a leadoff single by Ozzie Virgil in the ninth inning. Virgil took second on a throwing error by Mets third baseman Charley Smith.

Jackson pounced on Bob Bailey's sacrifice attempt for the first out. Manny Mota struck out for the second out and the Mets' diminutive left-hander induced Clemente to ground out to second to end the gem.

The only threats before Stargell's hit came in the fourth inning, when Mets second baseman Chuck Hiller committed an error with two outs to allow the first Pirate base runner. Future Met Donn Clendenon grounded out to end the inning.

In the seventh, Jackson walked Clemente with one out but got out of it when Clendenon hit into a 5–4–3 double play.

At a Glance

WP: Jackson (5–12)

Key stat: Jackson CG 2-hitter, 4 Ks

The Mets got their the only run of the game in the fifth inning. With two outs and a runner on second, Hiller scored on an error by Mazeroski. The ball went right between his legs for an unearned run.

On June 22, 1962, Jackson pitched the first one-hitter in franchise history when he blanked the Houston Colt .45s in the first game of a doubleheader at the Polo Grounds.

When Push Comes to Shove, HoJo's Homer Does in Reds

Howard Johnson's three-run homer in the top of the 14th inning led the Mets to a gutty 6–3 win over Cincinnati at Riverfront Stadium in a game that featured a bench-clearing brawl and some brilliant managerial maneuvering by Dave Johnson.

In the 10th inning, Reds pinch runner Eric Davis took off for second while Eddie Milner was going down on strikes against Mets reliever Jesse Orosco. Davis tried for third on the strikeout, but when he got there safely, he pushed Mets third baseman Ray Knight.

The two shoved each other and then Knight threw a punch that appeared to graze Davis.

Howard Johnson, right, joined teammates, from left, Tim Teufel and Kevin Mitchell, with rally caps and towels during Game 5 of the National League Championship Series in 1986. HoJo's three-run homer lifted the Mets to a win over the Reds in 14 innings on July 22, 1986.

"When he elbowed me," Knight said, "I said to him, 'What's your problem?' He said, 'You pushed me.' We had hit each other solidly, but I knew he had the base. I'm at peace with myself about it. I don't like to fight with anybody, but I felt threatened."

Davis blew off reporters after the game, but his teammate, Dave Parker, offered some support.

"It was triggered by Knight," said Parker, who would make a key mistake in this game. "He pushed Davis off the base."

That's when the benches emptied. When order was restored, four players had been ejected, including Knight, Davis, Mets outfielder Kevin Mitchell and Reds pitcher Mario Soto, who wasn't pitching.

The Mets were trailing 3–1 and were down to their final out in the ninth inning when Len Dykstra walked. Tim Teufel's double put the tying runs in scoring position.

Reds closer and future Met John Franco was brought on to save it and he got Keith Hernandez to hit a fly ball to right field. Parker settled under the ball but dropped it. The crowd of 23,707 was stunned as Teufel touched the plate with the tying run.

At a Glance

WP: McDowell (8–4)

HR: Johnson (6)

Key stat: Johnson 3-run homer in 13th

Darryl Strawberry had already been thrown out of the game in the sixth for arguing a called third strike. The ejections really left the Mets in dire straits, so Mets manager Johnson courageously decided to manipulate his pitchers by placing them alternately in the field in order to keep them in the game.

In the bottom of the 10th, Roger McDowell was brought on to pitch and Dave Johnson moved Orosco to right field. In the 11th, Johnson maneuvered the pitchers once again. With two outs and a runner on second, and the left-handed hitting Max Venable due up, Johnson put McDowell into right field and brought Orosco back in to pitch. Reds skipper Pete Rose protested the fact that Orosco got eight warm-up pitches when he returned to the mound. The left-hander ended the inning by striking out Venable.

In the 13th, the pitchers switched again and Orosco registered a putout in right field when he caught a fly ball from future Hall of Famer Tony Perez.

The winning rally began against Reds losing pitcher Carl Willis. A double

July 22, 1986
Mets 6, Reds 3 (14 innings)

Darryl Strawberry is arguably the greatest position player ever produced by the Mets organization.

Strawberry was selected number one overall in the 1980 draft and made quite a splash when he debuted in 1983. Strawberry was named the National League's Rookie of the Year that year, when he 26 home runs and had 74 RBIs.

The 6-foot-6 outfielder had a "sweet left-handed swing," was built like an "Adonis" and could hit some monster home runs.

During his eight-year career with the Mets, Strawberry became the club's all-time leader in home runs (252), extra-base hits (469), RBIs (733) and runs scored (662).

Strawberry became a member of the Mets Hall of Fame in 2010.

by Ed Hearn and a walk to Orosco put runners on first and second with no one out.

Ted Power relieved Willis and struck out McDowell.

Howard Johnson did not start the game and was already 0-for-3, but he sure helped finish it as he blasted a 2–2 breaking ball from Power over the wall in right field for a three-run lead.

After the game, "Ho Jo" was modest about his big hit.

"I'm not supposed to hit those (breaking pitches)," he said. "If I could bottle that swing and put it in my back pocket, I could make a million. I just didn't want to get fooled with a curve."

Johnson couldn't have been more proud of his team.

"There's so much pride in this team," he said. "People call us one of the cockiest teams in the league, and other people talk about how arrogant we are. They're always looking for a chance to retaliate, but we enjoy fighting, and if that's what it takes, then we'll fight. We won't be pushed around."

Orosco put his outfield experience in perspective.

"It was fun, I was laughing out there but I'd better stay on the pitcher's mound. I'm less nervous out there," he said.

Emergencies Galore Before Stephenson Comes Through

John Stephenson's pinch-hit RBI single in the bottom of the 10th inning led the Mets past the Philadephia Phillies 3–2 at Shea Stadium in a game that saw four Phils players end up in the hospital following a series of nasty collisions on the field.

Johnny Callison, Cookie Rojas (a future Mets coach), John Briggs and Tony Taylor all went to Roosevelt Hospital in New York for x-rays.

The worst collision occurred in the bottom of the eighth inning. Mets catcher Chris Cannizzaro lifted a pop fly into short right-center field. Phillies right fielder Callison, center fielder Briggs and second baseman Taylor all converged on the ball.

The three collided as Taylor made a sensational catch, but the Phils' second baseman and Briggs had to leave the game with injuries. Taylor was carried off on a stretcher with cuts under his left eye. Briggs was helped off the field with cuts above and below his right eye. Callison remained in the game after being treated for scratches on his cheek.

An inning later, the same three defensive positions were involved in a second collision.

Mets shortstop Roy McMillan hit a pop fly into the same area where the ball was hit the previous inning. This time, Taylor's replacement, Rojas, made the catch as he ran into Briggs' replacement in center, Tony Gonzalez, and Callison from right.

The uncanny occurrence of multiple collisions in the same game almost added another. With two outs in the ninth, Ron Swoboda hit a pop-up on the left side of the infield. Gonzalez, left fielder Alex Johnson and shorstop Ruben Amaro came together, but Johnson had the putout.

With one out and none on in the 10th, Ed Kranepool singled and took third on Chuck Hiller's pinch-hit single.

With the right-handed hitting Cannizzaro due up, Mets manager Casey Stengel used the left-handed hitting Stephenson against righty Jack Baldschun. Stephenson lined a single to right for the game-winning hit.

At a Glance

WP: Fisher (7–11)

HR: Hickman (8)

Key stat: Fisher 10 IP, 5 H, 2 R

Agee Steals Home, and Mets Walk Away a Winner over Dodgers

Tommie Agee provided one of the most unique "walk-off" wins in club history as he stole home in the bottom of the 10th inning to give the Mets a 2–1 win over the Los Angeles Dodgers before 53,657 fans at Shea Stadium.

Mets reliever Tug McGraw singled to lead off the inning. Agee's sacrifice attempt was too hard, but when Dodgers first baseman Wes Parker threw to second for the force, shortstop Billy Grabarkewitz dropped the throw to put two runners on.

Al Weis ran for McGraw and was immediately picked off second.

With one out, Agee stole second and moved to third on a wild pitch by Dodgers losing pitcher Jim Brewer.

After Bud Harrelson fanned for the second out, Los Angeles elected to load the bases by walking Ken Singleton and Donn Clendenon.

Cleon Jones was the batter and, with a 1–1 count, Agee broke for home. Agee was not to be denied as he ran into Dodgers catcher Tom Haller and home-plate umpire Shag Crawford, who called him safe.

> ### At a Glance
> **WP:** McGraw (2–3)
> **Key stat:** Agee steals home in 10th

The Dodgers took a 1–0 lead in the fourth inning on a RBI single by Ted Sizemore, but the Mets came back to tie it in the sixth on an RBI double by Jones.

Mets starting pitcher Jerry Koosman allowed a run on six hits in nine innings pitched. Dodgers starter Bill Singer was just as good. He went nine innings, allowing a run on five hits.

Throughout the course of franchise history, the Mets have stolen home a total of 27 times.

It's Stallard's Time to Shine in First Career Shutout

Tracy Stallard pitched the first complete game shutout of his career as the Mets blasted the Milwaukee Braves 10–0 at Shea Stadium.

Stallard allowed three hits while walking two and striking out seven as he stole the show in front of 28,097 fans who were also on hand for the annual Old Timers' Day celebration.

Tim Harkness keyed the lineup with four hits and three runs scored from the leadoff spot.

Joe Christopher and George Altman added home runs to back the pitching of Stallard, who faced 29 batters and allowed only one hit to the outfield.

Harkness led off the first inning with a single and scored on Christopher's home run off Milwaukee starter and loser Tony Cloninger.

The Mets blew the game open in the fifth inning by scoring six runs with two outs. Two-run singles by Jesse Gonder and Roy McMillan keyed the rally to knock Cloninger out of the game.

Altman's two-run home run in the sixth inning closed out the scoring.

Stallard is famous for giving up Roger Maris' 61st home run in 1961 and he was the losing pitcher in Jim Bunning's perfect game against the Mets earlier in the year.

At a Glance

WP: Stallard (6–13)

HR: Christopher (10), Altman (4)

Key stat: Stallard CG 3-hitter, 7 Ks; Harkness 4-for-5, 3 runs

---

The Mets acquired the 26-year-old right-hander from Boston, along with infielder Pumpsie Green, in exchange for infielder Felix Mantilla. Stallard pitched two seasons with the Mets and in 1964 he was a 20-game loser.

Mookie's Walk-Off Blast Aids Torrez

Mookie Wilson hit a walk-off home run in the bottom of the 10th inning and Mike Torrez went the distance on a four-hitter as the Mets scored a 2–1 win over the Atlanta Braves at Shea Stadium before a crowd of 13,380.

The game featured a bench-clearing brawl in the sixth inning that actually began when Braves pitcher Rick Camp hit Wilson with a pitch in the fifth.

When the Mets' switch-hitter came to the plate in the 10th, did he have revenge on his mind?

"My job was to go up there and get a base hit," Wilson said. "It was a breaking pitch, but definitely down."

Camp was an emergency replacement for former Met Pete Falcone, who was scratched with a pulled muscle in his right side. When Camp came to bat in the sixth inning, Torrez had Wilson's back.

The Mets starting and winning pitcher hit Camp in the hip. The Braves' hurler glared at Torrez and started to first base, but halfway down the line, Camp charged Torrez on the mound.

> ## At a Glance
>
> **WP:** Torrez (6–12)
>
> **HR:** Wilson (3)
>
> **Key stat:** Torrez 10 IP, 1 R, 4 H; Wilson 2-for-4, HR

Both benches emptied, but no one was hurt and no one was ejected. Mets manager Frank Howard would have liked to have seen Camp get tossed.

"The umpires told me that if Camp goes, Torrez also must go," Howard said. "They handled it properly."

The Braves grabbed a 1–0 lead in the fourth inning on a solo home run by former Met Claudell Washington, but the Mets tied the game in the sixth.

With two outs, Darryl Strawberry walked, stole second and scored the tying run on Bob Bailor's RBI single.

Torrez faced some trouble in the top of the 10th as Atlanta had runners on first and third with two outs, but he got Brett Butler to ground into a force-out that kept the Braves from gaining the lead.

Torrez allowed a run on four hits in his 10-inning, complete game effort.

The 36-year-old right-hander pitched one-and-a-half seasons in a Mets uniform and compiled an 11–22 record with a 4.47 ERA.

Sasser, Boston Get Their Licks In Early for Viola

The Mets pounded out 14 hits and Frank Viola allowed just three hits over eight innings in a 10–1 rout of the St. Louis Cardinals at Shea Stadium.

A crowd of 43,184 was on hand to see the Mets put up a five-spot in the first inning thanks to a two-run single by Mackey Sasser and a two-run triple by Daryl Boston.

Except for one inning, Viola cruised through the lineup. The offensive outburst certainly didn't hurt.

"Ten runs is 10 runs," Viola said, "put those ingredients together and it's no problem."

"Offense, offense, offense," said Mets manager Bud Harrelson.

The Mets got to Cardinals starter and loser Bryn Smith for seven runs on eight hits in two innings pitched.

Dave Magadan's three-run triple keyed a four-run third inning that gave the Mets a 10–1 lead.

During the game, the Mets unloaded an unhappy player as they dealt outfielder Mike Marshall to the Boston Red Sox for two minor leaguers and a player to be named later.

In his 53-game tenure as a member of the Mets, Marshall hit .239 with six home runs and 27 RBIs.

Viola was dealt to the Mets in July 1989 as part of a five-player deal with the Minnesota Twins at the trade deadline. The former American League Cy Young Award winner would win 20 games for the Mets in 1990. The left-hander finished third in the National League Cy Young voting that season.

At a Glance

WP: Viola (14–5)

Key stat: Magadan 3-for-5, 4 RBIs, 2 runs; O'Malley 3-for-4

Elster's Solo Blast Provides All the Support Ojeda Needs

Bob Ojeda went the distance on a three-hitter and Kevin Elster provided the offense with a solo home run as the Mets beat the Pittsburgh Pirates and nemesis John Smiley 1-0 at Shea Stadium.

Smiley had retired 19 straight hitters when Elster came up to bat with one out in the eighth inning. Elster saw change-ups in his previous two at-bats against the Pirates' left-hander, so he knew what to expect.

"I went up there looking for it," Elster said. "He (Smiley) likes to get ahead with his change-up. I had broken my bat the last time up. It turned out to be fortunate because I got a heavier bat and stayed back on the change-up."

After he hit the ball, Elster wasn't sure he had a home run.

"That's as hard as I can hit it," he said.

Pirates left fielder Barry Bonds went back on the ball but ran out of room as it just cleared the wall in left field.

"It barely went out but that's all I had," Elster said.

Ojeda was brilliant as he struck out six and walked only one. He retired 11 of the last 12 hitters (the only batter to reach base during that stretch did so on an error by Mets first baseman Dave Magadan).

> ### At a Glance
> **WP:** Ojeda (8–8)
>
> **HR:** Elster (7)
>
> **Key stat:** Ojeda CG 3-hitter, 6 Ks

"Who would have thought one run would hold up?" Mets manager Dave Johnson said.

A crowd of 49,584 watched both pitchers work quickly and efficiently as reflected by the game time of two hours and seven minutes.

Jones Goes the Distance; Trammell Goes Yard

Bobby J. Jones went the distance on a four-hitter and Bubba Trammell hit a home run in his first at-bat with the Mets as they topped the St. Louis Cardinals 4–2 at Shea Stadium.

Jones walked one and fanned nine. After the game, the right-hander was pleased with the way he threw the ball and how the fans in a crowd of 45,733 lauded him.

"Sure, it's special," he said. "I'm just glad I showed them the good Bobby Jones."

Trammell, who was acquired from Tampa Bay two days earlier, unloaded on an 0–2 fastball from Cards pitcher Garrett Stephenson and drove it over the wall in left field for a three-run homer and a 4–0 lead.

> ### At a Glance
> **WP:** Bobby J. Jones (5–5)
> **HR:** Agbayani (8), Trammell (1)
> **Key stat:** Trammell 3 RBIs

With that home run, Trammell became the seventh Met to homer in his first at-bat.

In 1974, Benny Ayala became the first player to hit a home run in his first at-bat when he homered in his first Mets at-bat. Since Trammell's home run, two other Mets have accomplished the feat—Kaz Matsui in 2004 and Mike Jacobs in 2005. Both of these were in their first big-league at-bats.

The Cards got one back in the sixth inning and added one more in the ninth on Ray Lankford's home run, but Jones got future Met Fernando Tatis on a strikeout to end it.

Trammell would finish the 2000 season with the Mets but was traded to San Diego in the off-season.

Jones went 74–56 during his eight-year tenure, but his Mets career is best known for one of the greatest, postseason pitching performances in team history.

On Oct. 8, 2000, Jones tossed a complete game one-hitter to beat the San Francisco Giants 4–0 in Game 4 of the National League Division Series. (see: 10/8/2000 in the postseason section)

July 30, 1969

Hodges Puts His Foot Down as Mets are Swept and Embarrassed by Astros

The Astros put a whuppin' on the Mets by sweeping a doubleheader at Shea Stadium by a combined score of 27–8, but they may have helped shape the fateful journey that was yet to come.

In the opening game, Houston's Denis Menke and Jimmy Wynn both hit grand slams in the ninth inning and the Astros scored 11 runs to earn a 16–3 win.

Three innings into the second game, the Astros scored 10 more, but there was much more than just a run-scoring barrage.

Manager Gil Hodges, certainly miffed at what he was seeing on the field, did not like the fact that Cleon Jones seemed to be "dogging it" on a RBI double by Astros catcher Johnny Edwards.

A crowd of 28,922 watched Hodges walk to left field, where he spoke a few words with Jones and then pulled him from the game. Despite hitting .346, Jones was not in the lineup for the next game.

Jones claimed he had a bad leg, but many felt this was the "turning point" of the 1969 season.

Orosco Claims Victories on Both Ends of Doubleheader

Jesse Orosco became the third pitcher in Mets history to win both ends of a doubleheader as the Mets swept a pair from the Pittsburgh Pirates, 7-6 and 1-0, at Shea Stadium.

Both games went 12 innings and both were decided on "walk-off" hits.

In the opener, Bob Bailor's single with the bases loaded off Pirates losing

Jesse Orosco earned a place in Mets history when he became the third pitcher in franchise annals to win both games of a doubleheader on July 31, 1983.

Mets 7, Pirates 6 (12 innings); Mets 1, Pirates 0 (12 innings)

pitcher Jim Bibby gave the Mets a 7–6 win. Orosco got the win by tossing four scoreless innings in relief.

Mets starter Walt Terrell did not record an out as he gave up four runs in the first inning, but the bullpen combined for more than 11 innings of scoreless relief, led by Orosco.

In the nightcap, Mets starter Mike Torrez pitched 11 scoreless innings, but Pirates rookie pitcher Jose DeLeon, who was making only his third big-league start, was just as stingy as he pitched nine scoreless with 11 strikeouts. The 22-year-old DeLeon held the Mets hitless until Hubie Brooks singled with one out in the ninth inning.

Brooks was impressed.

"Through eight innings, he (DeLeon) was perfect," Brooks said. "The key was his control down low, everything just above the knees. In the ninth, he made a mistake."

Mookie Wilson led off the 12th inning with a single. With runners on first and second and one out, George Foster bounced to second baseman Johnny Ray, who flipped to Dale Berra for the force.

Wilson already had his mind made up that he would try to score on a ground ball.

"Before the pitch, I checked with (third base coach) Bobby (Valentine)," Wilson said. "He signaled that if it was a ground ball, go all the way."

The speedy Mets outfielder did just that, as the throw home was a little late.

Orosco joined Craig Anderson (see: May 12, 1962) and Willard Hunter (Aug. 23, 1964) as the only Met pitchers to win both ends of a twinbill.

At a Glance

Game 1

WP: Orosco (6–5)

HR: Hernandez (9), Foster (17)

Key stat: Wilson 3-for-5, Giles 3-for-5; Orosco 4 IP

Game 2

WP: Orosco (7–5)

Key stat: Torrez 11 IP, 0 runs

AUGUST

Dwight Gooden, left, and Gary Carter joined forces for the Mets beginning in 1985. Carter was traded in the offseason to the Mets from Montreal. Gooden chalked up 24 wins, 268 strikeouts and a 1.53 earned-run average in 1985 as Carter continued his Hall-of-Fame career.

Leiter Notches 15 Ks, but Mahomes Adds Spark

Mets left-hander Al Leiter struck out a career-high 15 batters, but it was reliever Pat Mahomes who played the hero in a crazy 13-inning, 5–4 win over the Chicago Cubs at Wrigley Field before 39,222 fans.

Mahomes was a one-man gang. Not only did he retire the Cubs in the bottom of the 13th inning to preserve his victory, but he also drove in the go-ahead run in the top of the inning.

With runners at first and second and two outs, Mahomes blooped a single off Cubs reliever Scott Sanders into short left-center field to score Roger Cedeno with the lead run.

Mahomes got the first two outs in the 13th, but Sanders (who was hitting because the Cubs were out of position players) doubled off the left-field wall.

The Mets appealed, claiming Sanders missed first, but the umps ruled he touched the bag.

Mahomes struck out Jeff Reed on a 2–2 pitch and exhaled with a hollar.

"I worked so hard to get back, and it seems like it's all paying off," Mahomes said in an excited clubhouse.

Leiter was in line for the win with seven superb innings. The Toms River, N.J., native had it all working.

"I had a great curveball," Leiter said in an interview. "Fastball, curveball was good. I had the right-handed hitters locked out."

The Mets' southpaw threw 135 pitches in seven innings, but that was actually a result of how good his stuff was.

"My ball was moving so much, guys weren't getting good swings," Leiter said. "The ball actually hit bats with two strikes, which extended the counts."

Leiter's final line read: 7 IP, 2 hits, 2 runs (both earned), 2 walks, 15 strikeouts.

The Mets were leading 3–2 when Leiter left the game, so he was in line for the win, but closer Armando Benitez gave up a leadoff home run to the Cubs' Henry Rodriguez to start the ninth inning. Leiter ended up with a no-decision and the game went to extra innings.

The Mets took a 4–3 lead in the 10th on Edgardo Alfonzo's sacrifice fly, but the Cubs came right back with a run in the bottom of the inning.

Two walks by Benitez enabled Chicago to load the bases. The Cubs tied the game on a rare error by Mets first baseman John Olerud, which allowed the tying run to score.

Four Mets pitchers followed Benitez with three scoreless innings in relief, while the Mets were able to push a run across in the 13th.

Roger Cedeno led off with a double to left. After Todd Pratt lined out to center field and Rey Ordonez popped out, the Cubs intentionally walked Benny Agbayani to load the bases for Mahomes.

The hit gave Mahomes a .400 average (4-for-10) in the National League, his first since he spent the first part of his career in the American League.

"Granted, I haven't hit for nine years, but I've always been able to hit pretty well," Mahomes said. "I knew I wasn't going to strike out."

Mahomes pitched in 92 games as a member of the Mets. In 1999, he went 8–0 and finished his Mets career with a 13–3 record.

Mets	AB	R	H	RBI
Henderson lf	3	2	0	0
Mora lf	0	0	0	0
Piazza ph	1	0	0	0
McElroy p	0	0	0	0
Mahomes p	1	0	1	1
Alfonzo 2b	4	1	0	1
Olerud 1b	5	0	2	2
Ventura 3b	5	0	2	0
Hamilton cf	5	0	2	1
Cedeno rf	5	1	1	0
Pratt c	6	0	1	0
Ordonez ss	5	1	1	0
Leiter p	2	0	0	0
Wendell p	0	0	0	0
Franco ph	1	0	0	0
Benitez p	0	0	0	0
Taylor p	0	0	0	0
Cook p	0	0	0	0
Agbayani ph-lf	0	0	0	0
Totals	43	5	10	5

Cubs	AB	R	H	RBI
Morandini 2b	6	1	1	0
Alexander ss	5	2	2	1
Grace 1b	5	0	3	1
Sosa cf	6	0	0	0
Hill rf	5	0	1	0
Rodriguez lf	5	1	1	2
Gaetti 3b	3	0	0	0
Adams p	0	0	0	0
Nieves ph	1	0	0	0
King p	0	0	0	0
Sanders p	1	0	1	0
Santiago c	3	0	0	0
Reed ph-c	3	0	1	0
Farnsworth p	1	0	0	0
Blauser ph	1	0	0	0
Beck p	0	0	0	0
Heredia p	0	0	0	0
Goodwin ph	1	0	0	0
Serafini p	0	0	0	0
Rain p	0	0	0	0
Houston ph-3b	2	0	0	0
Totals	48	4	10	4

NYM 0 0 0 0 3 0 0 0 1 0 0 1 - 5 10 1
CHI 0 0 0 2 0 0 0 1 1 0 0 0 - 4 10 2

Mets	IP	H	R	ER	BB	SO
Leiter	7	7	2	2	2	15
Wendell	1	0	0	0	0	2
Benitez	1	2	2	2	2	1
Taylor	0.1	0	0	0	1	0
Cook	0.2	0	0	0	0	0
McElroy	1.2	0	0	0	0	1
Mahomes W (5-0)	1.1	1	0	0	0	1
Totals	13	10	4	4	5	20

Cubs	IP	H	R	ER	BB	SO
Farnsworth	5	2	0	0	1	4
Beck	0.1	1	3	3	2	0
Heredia	1.2	2	0	0	1	2
Serafini	1	1	0	0	0	0
Rain	1	0	0	0	0	0
Adams	1	1	1	1	2	1
King	2	1	0	0	1	1
Sanders L (4-5)	1	2	1	1	1	0
Totals	13	10	5	5	8	8

E—New York Olerud; Chicago Reed, Morandini. DP—New York 2; Chicago. 2B—New York Olerud, Cedeno; Chicago Grace, Sanders. 3B—Chicago Morandini. HR—Chicago Rodriguez (19). SH—New York Ordonez, Leiter. SF—New York Alfonzo. HBP—New York Agbayani. LOB—New York 11; Chicago 10. SB—New York Henderson; Chicago Alexander. Attendance:39,222.

Cleon Jones Reaches Magical Mark with 1,000 Career Hits

Mets first baseman Willie Mays used two infield hits to key the Mets' offense and Cleon Jones became the first player in franchise history to reach 1,000 career hits as the Mets rocked the Pittsburgh Pirates 5–1 at Shea Stadium.

With runners at first and third and one out in the third inning, Mays hit a chopper that went high in the air toward the third-base line. By the time it came down, Don Hahn scored from third and Mays reached second on the infield single when Pirates pitcher Jim Rooker threw the ball past first base.

Jones was the next batter and he lined a double down the right-field line for a 3–0 lead. The hit allowed Jones to become the first Met in franchise history to reach the coveted milestone of 1,000 career hits.

Mays' savvy helped produce two more runs in the eighth inning.

With Felix Millan on the run from first base, Mays laid down a beautiful bunt between the mound and the third-base line. Pirates pitcher John Lamb threw to an uncovered first base and the ball sailed into right field to allow Millan to score and the future Hall of Famer to reach second.

Mays scored the Mets' fifth run on a suicide squeeze bunt by catcher Jerry Grote.

A crowd of 13,429 saw Mets starter Ray Sadecki blank the Pirates through eight innings, but when the Bucs put the first two runners on in the ninth, Mets manager Yogi Berra went to the bullpen for closer Tug Mc-Graw.

At a Glance

WP: Sadecki (2–1)

Key stat: Mays 2-for-4, 2 runs

Richie Zisk singled in a run but McGraw fanned Bob Robertson for the first out.

With runners at first and second, Mays made a nice stop on Richie Hebner's hard ground ball for the second out as the runners moved up.

McGraw walked Dal Maxvill to load the bases, but he ended the suspense by striking out Dave Cash to end it.

Grote's Walk-Off Homer Caps Five-Run Comeback Win over Braves

The Mets overcame a five-run deficit to beat the Atlanta Braves 6–5 in 11 innings on Jerry Grote's walk-off home run.

A crowd of 34,696 was ecstatic when the Mets tied the game in the sixth inning with a five-run rally.

Wayne Garrett's RBI single put the Mets on the board to make it 5–1.

Braves reliever Cecil Upshaw replaced the starter, Milt Pappas, but pinch-hitter Art Shamsky singled and Rod Gaspar reached on a bunt single to load the bases.

An error by future Met second baseman Felix Millan allowed a second run to score and the bases to remain loaded.

Mets manager Gil Hodges went to Cleon Jones to bat for pitcher Don Cardwell and Jones delivered with a two-run single to make it a one-run game.

Mets shortstop Bud Harrelson greeted Braves reliever Paul Doyle with a sacrifice fly to tie the game 5–5.

The Mets had a chance in the ninth with two on and one out, but Ed Kranepool lined into an inning-ending double play.

Cardwell, Jack DiLauro and Ron Taylor gave the Mets six innings of shutout relief.

Losing pitcher Claude Raymond breezed through the 10th, but Grote led off the 11th by jumping on a 2–0 pitch and driving it over the right-field fence for a satisfying win.

At a Glance

WP: Taylor (6–2)

HR: Grote (4)

Key stat: Grote 2-for-4, 2 runs; Mets bullpen provides 6 scoreless innings

Swoboda Provides the Excitement with 3-Run Homer in 9th Inning

Ron Swoboda hit a pinch-hit, three-run home run in the bottom of the ninth inning to stun the San Francisco Giants 8-6 at Shea Stadium before a crowd of 41,038.

The Mets trailed future Hall of Famer Juan Marichal and the Giants 6–1 going into the bottom of the eighth. Marichal set down the first 17 Mets before Mets pitcher Dennis Ribant singled to break up the no-hit bid.

Pinch-hitter John Stephenson hit a two-run homer off of Marichal to make it a 6–3 game. Singles by Chuck Hiller, Al Luplow and Larry Elliot produced one more run to make it a 6–4 deficit.

In the ninth inning, Marichal gave up a leadoff home run to Ken Boyer to make it 6–5 and was pulled for Lindy McDaniel.

Ed Bressoud singled and with one out, Stephenson singled, putting runners at first and second base.

The Giants went to left-hander Bill Henry to pitch to the left-handed hitting Hiller, but Mets manager Wes Westrum countered with the right-handed hitting Swoboda.

> ## At a Glance
>
> **WP:** Hamilton (6–11)
>
> **HR:** Stephenson (1), Boyer (11), Swoboda (8)
>
> **Key stat:** Swoboda 1-for-1, HR, 3 RBIs

Swoboda later admitted that he had to keep telling himself to "stay loose," but on the first pitch from Henry, he swung at a high pitch that likely would have been ball one.

The second pitch was low and in for a ball, but Swoboda drove the 1–1 pitch from Henry over the wall in left field for a three-run, walk-off home run.

The 22-year-old outfielder described his magical trot around the bases as "elation — the epitome, my greatest thrill."

Swoboda played six seasons with the Mets but was best known for one of the greatest catches in World Series history when he made an "all out" dive to snag Brooks Robinson's liner in Game 4. Many observers feel that play was the turning point of the Mets' World Series victory in 1969.

Eight Runs in Final Two Innings More Than Enough for Victory

The Mets took advantage of mistakes to score eight runs in the final two innings as they cruised to a 10–3 win over the St. Louis Cardinals at Shea Stadium.

St. Louis had a 3–2 lead going to the bottom of the seventh inning, but the Mets tied the game when Cardinals right fielder Bernie Carbo misplayed John Milner's line drive into a run-scoring double.

Cleon Jones was intentionally walked to load the bases and set up a potential double play, but Wayne Garrett foiled that strategy with a two-run single to left to give the Mets a 5–3 lead.

The Mets broke the game open with five runs in the eighth inning. With the bases loaded and one out, Cards second baseman Dave Campbell booted Garrett's grounder, allowing two runs to score for a 7–3 advantage.

Winning pitcher and former Cardinal Harry Parker singled in a run and Don Hahn's sacrifice fly completed the scoring.

Parker relieved Mets starter George Stone and tossed three scoreless innings to pick up the victory.

A crowd of 21,845 was on hand for what seemed like just a routine Mets win, but little did they know what was to come, as this was the beginning of a memorable run to the National League's East Division title.

Going into the game, the Mets were 11.5 games behind the first-place Cards with 54 games to play.

The Mets would go 34–19 the rest of the way to finish at 82–79 and win the National League East crown.

At a Glance

WP: Parker (7–2)

Key stat: Garrett 3-for-5, 3 runs

In the National League Championship Series, the Mets knocked off the favored Cincinnati Reds in five games, but lost the World Series in seven to the Oakland A's.

Parker pitched three seasons for the Mets after being acquired from St. Louis in an eight-player trade. The Mets got Parker and Jim Beauchamp plus two other players for outfielder Art Shamsky and pitchers Jim Bibby, Rich Folkers and Charlie Hudson.

Parker compiled a 14–19 record, including a 4–12 mark in 1974.

Add Another First as Hickman Hits for the Cycle

A crowd of 20,649 at the Polo Grounds watched Jim Hickman become the first Met to hit for the cycle in a 7–3 win over the St. Louis Cardinals.

Hickman not only had a single, double, triple, and a home run in the same game; he did it in that order.

The Mets' third baseman singled to lead off the first inning and doubled in the second after the Mets had already plated two runs for a 2–0 lead.

In the fourth, Hickman's RBI triple scored winning pitcher Tracy Stallard. The Mets knocked out Cards losing pitcher Ernie Broglio when Duke Snider singled in two more for a 5–1 lead.

In the sixth inning, Hickman batted against Cards knuckleballer Barney Schultz and completed the cycle with a home run into the upper deck in left field.

Stallard went the distance, giving up three runs on six hits. The righty ran into trouble in the seventh, when the Cards loaded the bases with no one out. Stallard got Bill White, who earlier in the game had hit a two-run single off him, to pop out. Stallard ended the threat when he induced Ken Boyer to hit into an inning-ending, 6–4–3 double play.

Nine Mets have hit for the cycle in franchise history, including Keith Hernandez in 1985 (see: July 4, 1985) and Jose Reyes, who was the last to do it. The Mets' switch-hitting shortstop accomplished the feat on June 21, 2006, in a 6–5 loss to the Cincinnati Reds at Shea Stadium.

Broglio usually pitched well against the Mets, but in this game the Cardinals' right-hander gave up six runs in 3 $\frac{2}{3}$ innings pitched.

> ## At a Glance
>
> **WP:** Stallard (5–10)
>
> **HR:** Hickman (10)
>
> **Key stat:** Hickman hits for the "natural" cycle

Charles, Bob Johnson Help the Mets Steal a Victory

Bob Johnson's solo home run in the bottom of the 11th inning lifted the Mets past the Atlanta Braves 3–2 at Shea Stadium.

A crowd of 21,280 saw Braves left-hander Denny Lemaster dominate the Mets to the tune of one hit through seven shutout innings. At one point, the Atlanta southpaw set down 16 straight batters.

In the eighth, the Mets left the bases loaded and went into the ninth trailing 2–0.

Johnson singled with one out. Pinch-hitter Ed Kranepool lined a ball into the left-center field gap to score Johnson and it was 2–1.

Ron Swoboda hit a ball to center field that looked like it was going to be an extra-base hit to tie the game, but Braves center fielder and future manager Felipe Alou raced back to the fence to make a one-handed catch for the second out.

At a Glance

WP: Taylor (3–3)

HR: Johnson (4)

Key stat: Johnson 2-for-5, HR, 2 runs

Down to a last out and a final strike, Ed Charles delivered a two-out RBI single off Braves reliever Cecil Upshaw to tie the game 2–2.

Johnson led off the 11th inning and drove the first pitch from Braves losing pitcher Jay Ritchie over the wall for the win.

The Mets purchased Johnson from the Baltimore Orioles in May 1967. The 5-foot-10 right-handed hitter from Omaha, Neb., played 90 games for the Mets before he was traded to the Cincinnati Reds in November 1967 in exchange for left-handed hitting outfielder Art Shamsky.

How Does Hickman Top the Cycle? With a Grand Slam

Jim Hickman hit a walk-off grand slam to lead the Mets over the Chicago Cubs 7–3 before a crowd of 12,116 at the Polo Grounds. Two days earlier, Hickman had become the first Met to hit for the cycle.

With the game tied 3–3, Joe Hicks got the winning rally started with a one-out single.

Choo Choo Coleman struck out, but Al Moran doubled into the left-field corner to put runners at second and third.

The Cubs went to the bullpen for reliever Lindy McDaniel, but he walked pinch-hitter Tim Harkness to load the bases for Hickman.

The count went to 3–2 and Hickman ended the game with a slam that banged off the scoreboard in left field.

The Mets took a 1–0 lead in the fourth inning on a solo home run by Frank Thomas, but in the ensuing inning Chicago scored twice to take the lead.

Solo home runs by Andre Rodgers and Lou Brock off Roger Craig gave the Cubs a 2–1 lead.

The Mets rallied for two runs in their half of the fifth to take a 3–2 lead in this "topsy-turvy" game, but the Cubs tied it once again in the top of the eighth on a sacrifice fly by Ron Santo.

At a Glance

WP: Craig (3–20)

HR: Thomas (11), Hickman (11)

Key stat: Craig CG 8-hitter, 8 Ks; Hickman HR, 4 RBIs

Craig went the distance, giving up three runs on eight hits to earn the win.

The veteran right-hander and future manager, who was an "original" Met, ended a personal 18-game losing streak. Craig, who would pitch two seasons in Queens, went 5–22 in 1963 and was 15–46 in his career with the Mets.

McGraw Comes Up Big for Win in Relief

Tug McGraw was brilliant in relief as he struck out nine in four scoreless innings to preserve the Mets' 6–4 win over the San Diego Padres at San Diego Stadium.

Mets starter Gary Gentry set down the first nine Padres hitters and was given a four-run lead but he couldn't hold it, mainly because of back problems.

Tommie Agee's RBI single scored the first run and Ken Singleton's two-run double made it a 4–0 lead, but Gentry struggled in the bottom of the fourth and gave up two runs to see the lead cut in half.

In the fifth, Dave Campbell's RBI double cut it to 4–3 and Gentry was done. After the game, the right-hander complained of back pain.

Ray Sadecki was brought on to get the final out and he did so when Cito Gaston flied out to center.

The Mets added a run in the sixth to make it a 5–3 game and McGraw was brought on to start the sixth.

The energetic left-hander immediately gave up a home run to Nate Colbert, but that was all the Padres would get in front of a sparse crowd of 6,542.

At a Glance
WP: McGraw (8–3)
Key stat: McGraw 4 IP, 9 Ks

The Mets added a run in the eighth on Jerry Grote's RBI single. McGraw proceeded to post two stretches of four consecutive strikeouts, including fanning the side in the ninth to end the game.

McGraw was one of the most popular figures ever to put on a Met uniform.

The California native was signed by the Mets in June 1964 and played nine years in Queens.

McGraw saved 86 games in his Mets career but was best known for coining the phrase, "You Gotta Believe," which became the rallying cry for the remarkable run to the 1973 National League pennant.

McGraw was on the mound for the final out of the 1973 National League Championship Series, when the Mets beat the Cincinnati Reds in five games.

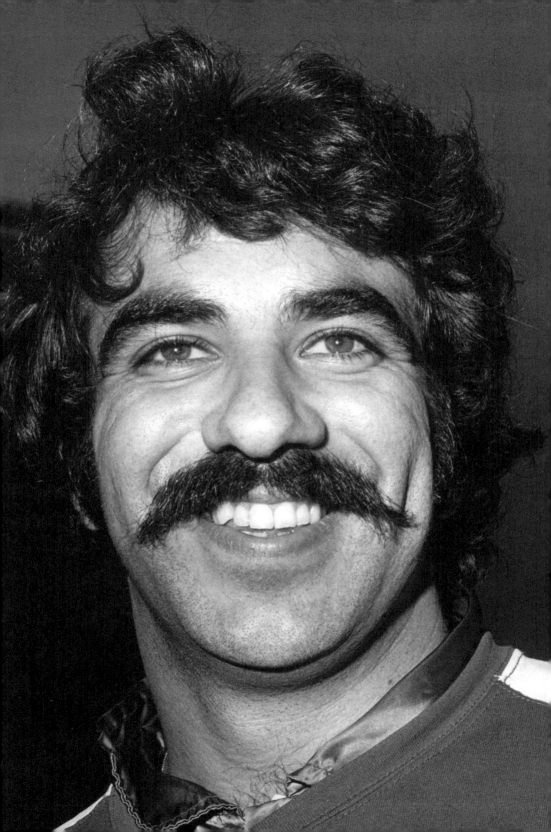

Danny Frisella, Please Report to Your Gate Immediately

How about winning your first major league game, and then you're not even at the ballpark to savor the moment?

That's what happened to Mets pitcher Danny Frisella, who won his first big-league game in the Mets' 3–2 win over the Pittsburgh Pirates at Shea Stadium. Afterward, he had to get on a plane and fly to California for National Guard duty.

Frisella was battling the clock as well as the Pirates.

The 21-year-old righty, who was promoted two weeks earlier, was booked on an 11:30 PM flight to San Francisco, so the Mets imposed a "personal" curfew of 10:15 PM for Frisella, who had a car waiting to take him to Kennedy Airport.

The Mets gave Frisella a 1–0 lead in the first inning on Larry Stahl's RBI single.

At a Glance
WP: Frisella (1–1)
Key stat: Frisella 1-for-2, run, RBI

In the third, Frisella added his first major league hit, a run-scoring double to make it 2–0. The pitcher scored the third run on a passed ball.

Pittsburgh got one back in the fifth and then added another run in the seventh. Manny Mota tripled and scored on Jose Pagan's ground-out. After May walked, Mets manager Wes Westrum took Frisella out and replaced him with reliever Don Shaw as the clock read 9:51 PM. Frisella got an ovation from the 29,202 on hand.

Shaw sat the side down in order in the eighth inning as Frisella headed for the airport.

In the ninth, the Pirates rallied and had the tying and winning runs on base, with the .344 hitting Roberto Clemente due up as a pinch-hitter.

Clemente swung and the ball trickled in front of the plate, where catcher Jerry Grote fielded it and threw to first to preserve Frisella's first win, even as he sat at Kennedy Airport waiting for his flight to take off.

Twenty-one-year-old Danny Frisella put together an interesting day on Aug. 11, 1967, when he earned his first win in the majors. Before the game ended, he had to leave Shea Stadium early to board a plane and report to National Guard duty.

For Milner, 475-foot Blast a Sight to be Seen

John Milner hit one of the longest home runs in the history of Shea Stadium as the Mets scored a 3–1 win over the Los Angeles Dodgers before a crowd of 33,431.

Milner's majestic home run came in the bottom of the sixth inning off Dodgers losing pitcher Andy Messersmith. It was a shot that hit the scoreboard in right field and was reportedly measured at 475 feet, which would make it the longest home run in Shea history.

Harry Parker outpitched Messersmith as he gave up a run on nine hits in going the distance.

The Mets took a 2–0 lead in the first inning. Rusty Staub had an RBI single and then the Mets pulled off a double steal with Milner taking third and "Le Grand Orange" taking second with one of his six career steals as a Met.

Ed Kranepool's sacrifice fly plated Milner from third with the second run.

Parker was able to stay out of trouble, even though the Dodgers had at least one man on base in every inning until the seventh.

Los Angeles hit the right-hander pretty hard in the fifth inning, but the Dodgers were only able to score one run.

Bill Russell led off with a single but was erased on a line drive to Mets third baseman Wayne Garrett, who turned it into a 5–5–3 double play.

Messersmith doubled with two out and scored on Davey Lopes RBI single to make it a 2–1 game before Bill Buckner put a scare into the crowd with a long drive to the wall in right field that was hauled in by Staub.

Parker finished the game in style as he struck out Dodgers catcher Steve Yeager on three pitches.

> ## At a Glance
>
> **WP:** Parker (4–10)
>
> **HR:** Milner (18)
>
> **Key stat:** Parker CG 9-hitter, 1 R; Milner 2-for-4, HR, 2 runs, RBI

Bogar's Career Day Makes Jones a First-Time Winner

Mets infielder Tim Bogar had a career game as he went 4-for-5 with two home runs and Bobby J. Jones won his big-league debut to lead the Mets over the Philadelphia Phiillies 9-5 at Veterans Stadium.

Bogar's first home run, a three-run shot that pushed the Mets' lead to 8-4, was your conventional "over the wall job," but it was his second home run in the top of the ninth that was more memorable.

Bogar was facing Phillies reliever Bobby Thigpen when he smacked a ball that caromed off the top of the wall in the deepest part of left-center field.

The 26-year-old took the cue and raced around the bases.

"Got it in gear," Bogar said.

When he reached home plate, Bogar dove face-first to complete his inside-the-park home run.

Bogar acted like a judge after the game when he rated his "dive."

"On a scale of 1 to 10, a '3.' A face plant," he said.

In addition to the two home runs, Bogar also had two doubles, which gave him 12 total bases. (At the time, that was one shy of the club record.)

The game also marked the major league debut of 23-year-old right-hander Jones, who pitched six innings in front of 46,393 at the Vet. Jones gave up five runs, one earned, on seven hits, while walking one and striking out three. He wasn't fazed despite a porous defense behind him that committed four errors.

"Good pitchers have a chance of getting good

Mets	AB	R	H	RBI
Thompson cf	4	1	0	0
Bogar 2b	5	4	4	4
Murray 1b	5	0	1	0
Bonilla 3b	5	1	0	0
Gallagher lf	3	2	2	1
O'Brien c	4	0	2	2
Burnitz rf	4	0	0	1
Baez ss	3	1	1	0
Jones p	2	0	0	0
Telgheder p	0	0	0	0
McKnight ph	1	0	0	0
Schourek p	0	0	0	0
Innis p	0	0	0	0
Totals	**36**	**9**	**10**	**8**

Phillies	AB	R	H	RBI
Dykstra cf	4	0	0	0
Duncan 2b	4	1	3	0
Kruk 1b	4	0	1	2
Daulton c	3	0	1	0
Eisenreich rf	4	1	1	0
Thompson lf	3	0	0	0
Mason p	0	0	0	0
Chamberlain ph	1	0	0	0
Thigpen p	0	0	0	0
Batiste 3b	4	1	2	1
Stocker ss	4	2	2	0
Jackson p	1	0	0	1
Jordan ph	1	0	0	0
Williams p	0	0	0	0
Incaviglia lf	2	0	0	0
Totals	**35**	**5**	**10**	**4**

											R	H	E
NYM	0	1	3	0	1	3	0	0	1	-	9	10	4
PHI	0	0	1	0	3	1	0	0	0	-	5	10	1

Mets	IP	H	R	ER	BB	SO
Jones W (1-0)	6	7	5	1	1	3
Telgheder	1	1	0	0	0	0
Schourek	0.1	1	0	0	0	1
Innis S (2)	1.2	1	0	0	0	0
Totals	**9**	**10**	**5**	**1**	**1**	**4**

Phillies	IP	H	R	ER	BB	SO
Jackson L (9-9)	5	8	5	2	1	1
Williams	1	1	3	3	2	0
Mason	2	0	0	0	0	1
Thigpen	1	1	1	1	0	0
Totals	**9**	**10**	**9**	**6**	**3**	**2**

E—New York Baez, Burnitz, Bonilla 2; Philadelphia Jackson. DP—New York 2. 2B—New York O'Brien, Bogar, Baez; Philadelphia Kruk, Duncan, Eisenreich, Stocker. HR—New York Bogar 2 (2,3). SH—New York Jones. LOB—New York 4; Philadelphia 4. Attendance: 46,393.

hitters out," Jones said afterward.

Manager Dallas Green was impressed.

"He held his composure, pitched us through," Green said. "He gave us what he had."

Bogar doubled and scored on an error and catcher Charlie O'Brien doubled home two more runs to give the Mets a 4–0 lead in the third.

The Phillies added four unearned runs combined in the third and fifth innings to cut the Mets' lead to 5–4 before Bogar's first home run opened some daylight between the teams.

The Mets selected Bogar in the eighth round of the 1987 draft. He played four seasons in New York before being dealt to the Houston Astros in March 1997.

Jones would go on to win 74 games with the Mets, good for ninth place on the club's all-time list.

Did You Know?

David Wright recorded the first Met hit and first Met home run at Citi Field in 2009. Luis Castillo had the team's first RBI at Citi Field.

Trio of First-Inning Homers Puts Mets on Their Way

Tom Paciorek, Gary Carter and Ray Knight all went deep in the first inning off ex-Mets left-hander Jerry Koosman and the Mets outslugged the Philadelphia Phillies 10–7 at Shea Stadium before a crowd of 36,663.

It was the first time in 11 years that the Mets had smacked three home runs in one inning. The previous time was July 20, 1974, when George Theodore, Rusty Staub and Cleon Jones did it against the Padres in San Diego.

The Phillies scored a run in the top of the first inning on future Hall of Famer Mike Schmidt's RBI single.

At a Glance

WP: Orosco (4–4)

HR: Paciorek (1), Carter (17), Knight (5)

Key stat: Backman 3 runs

Wally Backman led off with a walk and scored when Paciorek hit a 2–1 pitch from Koosman for a two-run homer and a 2–1 lead.

After Darryl Strawberry flied out, Carter drilled a home run over the wall in left field.

George Foster walked with two outs and Knight completed the first-inning "trifecta" with a two-run blast that went over the right-field wall.

Unfortunately for the Mets, Dwight Gooden was not having one of his better games as he gave up five runs on eight hits in only five innings pitched.

Schmidt and Rick Schu roughed up Gooden with long balls before he departed after five innings.

The Phils tied the game 6–6 in the top of the seventh inning when short-stop Rafael Santana made an error with the bases loaded.

The Mets regained the lead in the bottom of the seventh on a RBI ground-out, but the Phils tied it once again in the eighth on Ozzie Virgil's pinch-hit RBI single.

The Mets took charge of the game in the bottom of the eighth against noted Met killer Don Carman. With one out, Ronn Reynolds singled. After a sacrifice and an intentional walk to Backman, Len Dykstra lined a double that bounced over the fence as the Mets took an 8–7 lead. Two more runs scored when Von Hayes misplayed a pop-up.

Stout Pitching Limits Padres to 1 Run in Sweep of Twinbill

Mets pitching held San Diego to a total of one run on eight hits in a double-header sweep of the Padres—2–0 in the opener and 2–1 in the nightcap.

Tom Seaver and Ron Taylor combined to blank the "Pads" in the first game.

Coming into this start, the eventual 1969 National League Cy Young Award winner had been experiencing arm problems, but Seaver still tossed eight shutout innings.

"In the eighth, I started to get tired," Seaver said. "I felt some of the tenderness in my shoulder."

The future Hall of Famer ran into trouble in the second inning but worked out of it thanks to some help from his defense, as two Padre runners were eliminated on the bases. The first was a pickoff of Al Ferrara at second base on a throw from Mets catcher Jerry Grote. Ivan Murrell was then caught stealing in a rundown to end the inning.

The Mets scored a run in the fifth inning on a RBI single by Tommie Agee and added their second run in the seventh when Bobby Pfeil singled in a run.

Taylor came on for the ninth and tossed a 1–2–3 inning for the save.

In the nightcap, Grote's pinch-hit RBI single in the seventh inning snapped a 1–1 tie and the Mets went on to sweep the twinbill with a 2–1 win.

A crowd of 19,940 turned out for the doubleheader that lasted just under five hours.

At a Glance
Game 1
WP: Seaver (17–7)
Key stat: Seaver 8 IP, 4H
Game 2
WP: McAndrew (4–5)
HR: Jones (12)
Key stat: Jones 2-for-3, HR

Jim McAndrew gave up a run on three hits in seven innings pitched to keep the Mets in a game that was tied 1–1.

Former Met Larry Stahl homered in the second off McAndrew for a 1–0 lead, but Cleon Jones tied the game with a solo home run in the fourth.

In the seventh inning, managers Preston Gomez for San Diego and the Mets' Gil Hodges matched wits and strategy.

A throwing error by Padres pitcher Gary Ross put Ron Swoboda at third base with no one out. Ross got past pinch-hitters Wayne Garrett and Ed Kranepool without a run being scored.

After Bud Harrelson was walked to load the bases, Hodges sent up left-handed hitting Art Shamsky to bat for McAndrew, but Gomez countered with left-hander Dave Roberts.

Hodges had the last move and he used it by sending up the right-handed hitting Grote for Shamsky and the veteran catcher came through with an RBI single that broke the tie.

Tug McGraw was brought on and he pitched scoreless ball over the final two innings to preserve the win and the sweep of the doubleheader.

Simply the greatest Met to ever wear the uniform, Hall of Famer Tom Seaver became the face of the franchise and one of the most dominant pitchers in major league history.

Seaver holds the club's all-time record for wins (198), ERA (2.57) and strikeouts (2,541).

"The Franchise" won the first of his three Cy Young Awards in 1969 when he led the league with 25 wins and led the Mets on their remarkable run to the World Championship. That same season, Seaver finished second in the MVP voting.

In 1992, Seaver was elected to the National Baseball Hall of Fame with the highest percentage (98.84 percent) ever recorded.

Seaver's number 41 is one of three numbers retired by the Mets and he was inducted into the club's Hall of Fame in 1988.

Seaver, Koosman Prove to be Too Much for Giants

Tom Seaver and Jerry Koosman combined on a four-hitter in blanking the San Francisco Giants 3-0 at Shea Stadium.

Mets manager Roy McMillan decided to move the veteran left-hander Koosman into the bullpen and he picked up his second major league save in preserving the win for Seaver.

Seaver tossed three-hit ball over 7 ⅓ innings. The future Hall of Famer ran into trouble in the top of the eighth inning when the Giants had two on and one out.

A crowd of 30,593 watched Koosman get the call and he did the job as he retired Von Joshua and Derrel Thomas on force-outs.

McMillan stressed that Koosman was not being demoted and the 32-year-old southpaw played team player in accepting the move.

"Roy called me into his office before the game and asked me if I'd mind going to the bullpen," Koosman said. "In a way it's very demoralizing, but physically and mentally, I'm ready for relief pitching."

> ## At a Glance
>
> **WP:** Seaver (17–7)
>
> **Key stat:** Seaver and Koosman combine on 4-hit shutout

The Mets took a 1–0 lead in the third inning on Del Unser's RBI double. They added two more runs in the fifth inning. Mike Phillips' ball to right-center turned into a triple when Joshua fell. An RBI single by Seaver scored Phillips from third and a sacrifice fly by Rusty Staub later in the inning made it 3–0.

The "dynamic duo," who combined to lead the Mets to a World Championship in 1969 and a National League pennant in 1973, playfully jabbed each other after the game.

"Seaver told me once that if he ever saw me coming in to relieve him, he'd never leave the mound. He was gone by the time I got there and I'm just as glad he was," Koosman said.

Seaver was a little more serious.

"I was done, it was time to go," the right-hander said. "I'd lost the pop on my fastball and one or two pitches and it might have been a tie."

Agee's Homer Hands Marichal Rare Loss

Tommie Agee's home run off future Hall of Famer Juan Marichal in the bottom of the 14th inning broke up a scoreless tie and the Mets beat the San Francisco Giants 1-0 at Shea Stadium before 48,968 fans.

The Mets' center fielder had struck out in three previous at-bats against the Giants' right-hander, but Agee lined a 1–0 pitch from Marichal over the left-field fence for a dramatic win.

Marichal was magnificent as he walked one and struck out 13 Mets before Agee's blast ended quite a pitchers' duel.

Gary Gentry threw 157 pitches as he matched Marichal for 10 scoreless innings while reliever Tug McGraw got the win with four scoreless innings of one-hit relief.

The Mets nearly won the game in the 12th inning but the Giants' defense kept the game alive.

Cleon Jones opened the inning with an infield single. McGraw laid down a sacrifice bunt that Marichal fielded and threw to first. The throw went to second baseman and former Met Ron Hunt, who was covering first, but McGraw knocked the ball loose in a collision between the two players.

The ball rolled down the right-field line as Jones, who went to second base on the bunt, tried to score all the way from first.

Despite being shaken up, Hunt recovered enough to retrieve the ball and throw it home to catcher Jack Hiatt.

Jones slammed into Hiatt but was tagged for the second out. The inning ended with McGraw at third when Wayne Garrett flew out.

In the top of the 13th inning, the Mets' defense preserved the tie. With two outs and no one on, McGraw faced future Hall of Famer Willie McCovey, who was hitting .320 with 36 home runs.

Mets manager Gil Hodges employed a four-

Giants	AB	R	H	RBI
Bonds rf	6	0	0	0
Hunt 2b	6	0	0	0
Mays cf	6	0	0	0
McCovey 1b	5	0	0	0
Burda lf	4	0	1	0
Etheridge 3b	3	0	0	0
Hiatt c	1	0	0	0
Barton c	3	0	1	0
Marshall ph	0	0	0	0
Mason ss	2	0	0	0
Lanier ss	3	0	2	0
Davenport ph-3b	2	0	0	0
Marichal p	4	0	1	0
Totals	45	0	5	0

Mets	AB	R	H	RBI
Agee cf	6	1	1	1
Pfeil 3b	5	0	1	0
Jones lf	5	0	3	0
Shamsky rf	3	0	0	0
McGraw p	1	0	1	0
Garrett 2b	5	0	0	0
Kranepool 1b	4	0	0	0
Harrelson ss	5	0	0	0
Dyer c	5	0	1	0
Gentry p	3	0	0	0
Gaspar rf	2	0	0	0
Totals	44	1	6	1

```
SF  0 0 0 0 0 0 0 0 0 0 0 0 0 0 - 0 5 1
NYM 0 0 0 0 0 0 0 0 0 0 0 0 0 1 - 1 6 0
```

Giants	IP	H	R	ER	BB	SO
Marichal L (14-9)	13.1	6	1	1	1	13
Totals	13.1	6	1	1	1	13

Mets	IP	H	R	ER	BB	SO
Gentry	10	4	0	0	4	5
McGraw W (6-2)	4	1	0	0	1	0
Totals	14	5	0	0	5	5

E—San Francisco Marichal. SH—New York Shamsky. LOB—San Francisco 10; New York 5. SB—New York Jones 2. Attendance: 48,968.

August 19, 1969

Mets 1, Giants 0 (14 innings)

CF Tommie Agee

In December 1967, the Mets acquired outfielder Tommie Agee and Al Weis from the Chicago White Sox in a six-player swap that included Tommy Davis and Jack Fisher going back to Chicago.

It turned out to be one of the better deals in Mets history.

Agee was one of the sparkplugs of the 1969 World Championship team and capped it with two magnificent catches in Game 3 of the World Series.

In the fourth inning, Agee made a tremendous backhand, running catch in the gap in left-center field to rob Elrod Hendricks of a sure extra base hit that would've scored two runs.

In the seventh inning, Baltimore had the bases loaded and two outs. With Nolan Ryan pitching, Paul Blair lifted a ball toward the gap in right-center field, but Agee was there again to make a diving grab and deny the Orioles again.

The former American League Rookie of the Year hit one of the longest home runs in Shea Stadium history. On April 10, 1969, Agee hit the only ball that ever landed fair in the left-field upper deck for a monstrous homerun.

Agee was inducted into the Mets Hall of Fame in 2002. The Mobile (Ala.) Sports Hall of Fame inducted him in 1993.

man outfield. Third baseman Bobby Pfeil moved to the left-field corner. Jones covered left-center field, while Agee and Rod Gaspar patrolled the right side.

The entire left side of the infield was bare, with three infielders on the right side of second base.

McCovey lined McGraw's first pitch deep into left-center field for what appeared to be the go-ahead run, but Jones made a spectacular catch to end the inning.

Jones leaped and bounced off the fence, hitting the warning track dirt. He clutched the ball with an acrobatic catch that saved the game.

The Giants had a chance to break the scoreless deadlock in the ninth. With two outs and two on, pinch-hitter Jim Davenport grounded out.

In his fabulous career, Juan Marichal made 40 starts against the Mets. He completed 26 games, threw nine shutouts and was 26–8 with a 2.13 ERA against the "Amazins."

This game was one of Marichal's best against the Mets, yet it turned into one of his eight losses.

Gooden's 16 Ks Puts Him on Path to Cy Young

Dwight Gooden continued to roll along to the 1985 National League Cy Young Award as he went the distance on a seven-hit shutout and tied a career high with 16 strikeouts in blanking the San Francisco Giants 3–0 at Shea Stadium.

"You're looking at something special," Mets manager Dave Johnson said.

To say Gooden was dominant was understating the fact.

"Doc" threw 143 pitches, with 101 of those being strikes. From the last out of the first inning through the fifth inning, he faced 15 batters and struck out 11 of them.

With 11 Ks through five innings, there were some in the crowd of 31,758 who thought Gooden would have a shot at the all-time, single-game record of 19 (which has since been broken), but the Mets' 20-year-old was realistic about the pursuit.

"A couple of guys mentioned the strikeouts to me between innings," Gooden said. "You know, go for 20, but it takes a lot of luck. I can't try to strike everybody out because the fans are cheering."

At a Glance

WP: Gooden (19–3)

Key stat: Gooden CG 7-hitter, 16 Ks

The Giants had their best—and really, their only—chance at getting to Gooden in the first inning.

Brad Wellman looped a one-out single to right-center field. Chili Davis lined a single to right for one of his three hits, and Wellman took third base when Darryl Strawberry bobbled the ball for an error.

The Giants ran themselves out of an inning as Davis was caught stealing second while Wellman remained at third.

Gooden walked Dan Driessen and Chris Brown to load the bases, but he struck out former Met Joel Youngblood to snuff out the rally.

"He was getting everything over," Youngblood said. "He's outstanding."

The Mets took a 2–0 lead in the second inning on RBI singles from Rafael Santana and Len Dykstra. They added one more run in the fifth inning on Gary Carter's RBI single.

From there, it was the "Doc" Gooden show.

The Giants got four more hits off Gooden but could do nothing with them.

Staub Makes It Official as Mets' Best Pinch-Hitter

Rusty Staub set a club record for pinch-hit RBIs, and Jose Oquendo hit his first major league home run to lead the Mets to a 4–3 win over the San Francisco Giants before a crowd of 12,020 at Candlestick Park.

Ed Kranepool held the previous club record for pinch-hit RBIs with 17. That mark fell in the eighth inning. The Mets had runners on first and third when Staub was sent up to bat for Brian Giles.

"Le Grand Orange" lined a double to the gap in right-center field to score George Foster and Darryl Strawberry. They were the 17th and 18th pinch-hit RBIs for the season, setting a new club standard.

Oquendo's first big-league clout came off Giants reliever Gary La Lavelle in the seventh inning. After 248 at-bats in the majors, Oquendo hit a ball over the left-field fence to give the Mets a 2–0 lead.

"I was surprised," Oquendo said. "I never expected to hit a homer. I just got lucky."

Mike Torrez had tossed eight scoreless innings but he faltered in the ninth as the Giants staged a last-gasp rally.

Run-scoring singles by Bob Brenly and Steve Nicosia made it a 4–2 game.

Mets closer Jesse Orosco entered the game with runners at first and third base and one out.

The Mets traded a run for an out as Johnnie LeMaster grounded into a force play, scoring Brenly from third to make it a one-run game.

Orosco ended the game when he got pinch-hitter John Rabb looking at a called third strike on a 3–2 pitch.

Mets	AB	R	H	RBI
Bradley cf	4	0	2	0
Brooks 3b	3	0	0	0
Hernandez 1b	5	0	1	0
Foster lf	5	2	1	1
Orosco p	0	0	0	0
Strawberry rf	3	1	1	0
Giles 2b	3	0	0	0
Staub ph	1	0	1	2
Bailor pr-2b-ss	0	0	0	0
Ortiz c	4	0	1	0
Oquendo ss	3	1	2	1
Ashford 2b	0	0	0	0
Torrez p	4	0	0	0
Heep lf	0	0	0	0
Totals	35	4	9	4

Giants	AB	R	H	RBI
LeMaster ss	5	0	0	1
Bergman 1b	4	0	0	0
Rabb ph	1	0	0	0
Clark rf	3	0	1	0
Evans 3b	3	0	0	0
Leonard lf	4	1	1	0
Davis cf	3	0	1	0
Youngblood 2b	2	1	0	0
Brenly c	3	1	1	1
Hammaker p	2	0	0	0
Lavelle p	0	0	0	0
Venable ph	0	0	0	0
Barr p	0	0	0	0
Nicosia ph	1	0	1	1
Pettini pr	0	0	0	0
Totals	31	3	5	3

```
NYM  0 0 0 0 0 1 1 2 0 - 4 9 0
SF   0 0 0 0 0 0 0 0 3 - 3 5 1
```

Mets	IP	H	R	ER	BB	SO
Torrez W (7-14)	8.1	5	3	3	7	4
Orosco S (14)	0.2	0	0	0	0	1
Totals	9	5	3	3	7	5

Giants	IP	H	R	ER	BB	SO
Hammaker L (10-6)	6	3	1	1	4	4
Lavelle	1	1	1	1	0	2
Barr	2	5	2	0	1	1
Totals	9	9	4	2	5	7

E—San Francisco Evans. DP—New York; San Francisco. 2B—New York Staub, Ortiz; San Francisco Leonard. HR—New York Foster (22), Oquendo (1). LOB—New York 9; San Francisco 8. SB—New York Bradley; San Francisco Clark. Attendance: 12,020.

Three Hits, 4 RBIs Make a Career Day for Beauchamp

Jim Beauchamp had a rather "nondescript" major league career, but he had a day with the Mets as he combined with Tom Seaver for "top billing" in a 4–2 win over the Houston Astros at Shea Stadium.

The 33-year-old journeyman tied a career high with three hits and set a career high by driving in all four runs for the Mets. One night earlier, Beauchamp had hit two home runs, including the ninth-inning game-winner, on his 33rd birthday.

Seaver, who went the distance and struck out 10, found himself trailing 1–0 in the first inning courtesy of an unearned run.

The Mets tied the game in the second. Tommie Agee walked and Duffy Dyer singled to put runners at first and second base.

After John Milner's ground-out to first base moved up the runners, Beauchamp's first RBI tied the game. He beat out a chopper behind the bag at third base that allowed Agee to score.

Astros left fielder Bob Watson homered off Seaver in the fourth inning to give Houston a 2–1 lead, but Beauchamp answered in the home half with a home run into the left-field bullpen off Dave Roberts.

> ## At a Glance
> **WP:** Seaver (15–9)
>
> **HR:** Beauchamp (3)
>
> **Key stat:** Beauchamp 3-for-4 4, 4 RBIs

"I was as surprised as anyone," Beauchamp said after the game. "It was an off-speed pitch, a knuckleball, and I didn't think it had a chance of going out. I thought I was just running out a fly ball but the crowd noise kept getting louder."

Beauchamp's final act came in the eighth.

With the bases loaded, two outs and 30,368 fans cheering, Beauchamp delivered a tie-breaking, two-run single over the shortstop to close out the scoring.

Seaver kept the Astros at bay in the ninth with an easy 1–2–3 inning.

Beauchamp played the final two seasons of his 10-year career with the Mets.

Chris Jones Gives Mets a Lift with Clutch Hit

Chris Jones' pinch-hit RBI single with two outs in the bottom of the ninth inning gave the Mets a 5–4, come-from-behind win over the San Diego Padres at Shea Stadium.

Jones singled through the right side of the infield on a 0–1 pitch from Padres pitcher Doug Bochtler, who relieved San Diego closer and losing pitcher Trevor Hoffman.

The Mets trailed 4–2 entering the ninth inning, but Carl Everett got things going with a leadoff single.

With one out, Rico Brogna singled, sending Everett to third base.

With Ryan Thompson at the plate, Hoffman uncorked a wild pitch to score Everett and cut the deficit to 4–3.

Thompson singled to score Tim Bogar with the tying run, and moved to second on an error by left fielder Bip Roberts. Bogar was pinch running for Brogna.

Bill Spiers was intentionally walked to put runners on first and second base. The Padres brought on Bochtler to relieve Hoffman and he struck out Kelly Stinnett for the second out.

Jones took a strike and then lined Bochtler's fastball into right field to score Thompson with the winning run.

At a Glance

WP: Florence (2–0)

HR: Kent (14)

Key stat: Everett 2-for-4, run; Brogna 2-for-4, run

"We won the game and I got the winning hit," said a satisfied Jones after the game that drew 14,705 fans.

Don Florence got the win in relief for the Mets, but starter Dave Mlicki pitched very well and probably deserved a better fate.

Mlicki pitched 7 $^2/_3$ innings but it was a two-run double by Jody Reed in the eighth inning that ended his outing.

Jones spent two seasons of his nine-year big-league career with the Mets.

Youngest Pitcher to Win 20 Games Just What Doc Ordered

At the age of 20 years, nine months and nine days, Dwight "Doc" Gooden became the youngest pitcher in the history of Major League Baseball to win 20 games as the Mets stomped on the San Diego Padres 9–3 at Shea Stadium.

A crowd of 37,350 saw Gooden give up three runs (two earned) on five hits in six innings pitched.

Gooden surpassed Hall of Famer and former Cleveland Indians great Bob Feller, who was 20 years, 10 months and five days old when he won his 20th game in 1939. (The National League mark was previously held by Christy Mathewson, who won his 20th at the age of 21 years, one month and nine days back in 1901 as a member of the New York Giants.)

Gooden became the third Mets pitcher to win 20 games, joining Tom Seaver (who did it four times) and Jerry Koosman.

Offensively, Darryl Strawberry had a big game with three hits, three runs scored and four RBIs, including a monstrous home run over the fence in center field off Padres starter Eric Show.

Catcher Gary Carter also had three hits, but he got more of a thrill catching the young phenom.

"We're all just fortunate to be a part of Dwight's little world," Carter said.

The score is not indicative of how difficult it was for the Mets' ace in this one. Rain delayed the start of the game and there was a mist throughout, which made gripping the ball more difficult than usual. And it showed. Gooden threw two wild pitches in the third inning and also committed a throwing error that led to two San Diego runs.

With a runner on second and no one out, the right-hander fielded a bunt by Show and tried for the runner at third, but he threw the ball away and that allowed a run to score.

Carter went out to the mound to calm down his pitcher. "I was trying to pump him up a little. I was afraid it might affect his concentration when he threw the ball away. He takes pride in his fielding," Carter said.

> ### At a Glance
>
> **WP:** Gooden (20-3)
>
> **HR:** Strawberry (20)
>
> **Key stat:** Gooden, McDowell combine for 6-hitter; Strawberry 3-for-3, 4 RBIs, HR, 2B

In the sixth, "Doc" gave up a run on a ground-out, but he had thrown 94 pitches to that point so manager Dave Johnson felt it was time to go to the bullpen.

Gooden indicated after the game that he "didn't have his best stuff."

"The rain was drizzling and all," he said. "I just couldn't find my rhythm. The ball wasn't rubbed up enough."

"It's too bad he couldn't finish," Johnson said, "but evidently the ball was slipping.

He threw 140 the last time out (see: Aug. 20, 1985) when he struck out 16 and I didn't want to drain him. He's done it all by himself all year, so it's only fitting that we helped him out on his big day."

Led by Strawberry and Carter, the Mets pounded out 16 hits. Six Mets had two or more hits, while Strawberry and Keith Hernandez each scored three runs.

Gooden would go on to capture the 1985 National League Cy Young Award with the one of the more remarkable pitching seasons in major league history.

The 20-year-old would post a National League-best 24–4 record with a 1.53 ERA. He led the league with a career-high 276 $^2/_3$ innings while recording 268 strikeouts.

Gooden had 16 complete games (he pitched eight innings seven times) and eight shutouts. He also had 11 games with double-digit strikeout totals. Of his 35 starts, he pitched less than seven innings only seven times.

Gooden received all 24 first-place votes from the Baseball Writers Association of America to capture the Cy Young Award, easily outdistancing the second-place finisher, St. Louis left-hander John Tudor.

Mr. Koufax, Meet Mr. McGraw—He's Only 20

Whenever you hear the name "Sandy Koufax," you think of one of the greatest pitchers in baseball history.

The New York Mets knew that all too well as the Dodgers' left-hander dominated them since they entered the league in 1962. So it came as quite a surprise when they finally beat him for the first time.

The Mets downed Koufax and the Dodgers 5–2 before a roaring and "electric" crowd at Shea Stadium that included New York City Mayor Robert Wagner and his wife.

Mets left-hander Tug McGraw, four days short of his 21st birthday, stymied the Dodgers for 7 1/3 innings in picking up the win, while his teammates did the rest.

Coming into the game, Koufax's career numbers against the Mets were mind-boggling. The Brooklyn-born southpaw made 14 starts against the Mets, posting a 13–0 record. He completed 10 of those starts, tossed five shutouts and struck out 130 batters in 117 innings while compiling a 1.15 ERA.

It seemed like the same old story as the Dodgers scored a run in the top of the first inning off McGraw to take a 1–0 lead. Leadoff batter Maury Wills, who was 4-for-4, singled and took second base on a sacrifice bunt. After Junior Gilliam struck out, Lou Johnson doubled home Wills with the first run.

> ### At a Glance
>
> **WP:** McGraw (2-2)
>
> **HR:** Swoboda (19), Christopher (4)
>
> **Key stat:** Swoboda, Christopher homers in 8th top Koufax

The Mets answered right back and more in the bottom of the first. Ron Hunt walked on five pitches to lead off the inning and Roy McMillan tied the game with a RBI double into the left-field corner.

Joe Christopher sacrificed McMillan to third base, and after Ron Swoboda popped out to second, Jim Hickman singled to score the go-ahead run. The Mets had a 2–1 lead against the mighty Koufax.

The Hall of Famer settled down to retire 17 of the next 18 batters, but McGraw was nearly as good.

The young Mets hurler took the lead and ran with it as he allowed four hits over the next six scoreless innings.

The Mets pushed their lead to 3–1 in the seventh inning thanks to some shoddy defense by the Dodgers. With one out, Ed Kranepool doubled down the right-field line. Chris Cannizzaro was walked intentionally and pinch-hitter Bobby Klaus forced him at second, putting runners on first and third with two outs.

Koufax induced his counterpart, McGraw, to hit what looked like a routine grounder to third. But Don LeJohn's throw to first base pulled Wes Parker off the bag for an error as Kranepool scored the Mets' third run.

With the Dodgers down by two runs in the eighth inning, Koufax had to be lifted for pinch-hitter Dick Tracewski, who walked with one out.

Wills' fourth hit, a single to left-center, sent Tracewski to third, but the Dodgers' shortstop was cut down at second base as he was trying to stretch the hit into a double. Hickman found second baseman Ron Hunt perfectly as Hunt applied the tag on Wills for the second out.

Ironically, Parker followed with a triple to right-center that scored the second run and most certainly would have plated the third run if Wills had still been on base.

After the triple, Jack Fisher replaced McGraw, who got a huge standing ovation from the 45,950 fans who were on hand for this memorable game.

In the eighth inning, Christopher and Swoboda put the "icing on the cake" with solo home runs off Dodgers reliever Johnny Podres for a 5–2 lead entering the ninth inning.

Fisher pitched a stress-free ninth inning to earn the save.

Koufax would go on to make five more starts against the Mets during his final season in 1966. The fabulous southpaw finished with a career mark of 17–2 and a 1.44 ERA against the Mets. He lost his final game to the Mets in August 1966, when he allowed six runs (five earned) in two innings of a 10–4 win at Shea.

During his 19-year career, McGraw would go 10–7 against the Dodgers.

Double Play Starts at Home, Ends at Third, and Leads to a Win

This game ended with a different kind of "walk-off"—a win for the road team.

The Mets stunned the 19,747 fans at Jack Murphy Stadium by turning a spectacular 8–2–5 double play in the bottom of the 11th inning to preserve a 6–5 victory over the San Diego Padres.

The Mets snapped a 5–5 tie in the top of the 11th. One-out singles by Len Dykstra and Wally Backman put runners at first and third base and Keith Hernandez drove home the go-ahead run with a long fly to left-center.

With Doug Sisk on the hill for the Mets, Garry Templeton smoked a lead-off double.

After Padres pitcher Craig Lefferts struck out as a pinch-hitter, Tim Flannery lined a single to center as the Mets' defense took over and closed the game.

Mets center fielder Len Dykstra grabbed the hit on one bounce and fired to home plate, where catcher John Gibbons was waiting for the ball and a collision with Templeton.

After the two collided, Gibbons held onto the ball for the out. Meanwhile, Flannery had taken second base and was looking to go to third while Gibbons was temporarily stunned from the rough play at the plate. Or was he?

Gibbons, who had a reputation as a "tough cookie," had enough of his senses to realize what Flannery was doing, so he fired to third baseman Howard Johnson, who applied the tag to end the game.

The Mets roughed up Padres starter Ed Whitson for five runs and a 5–0 lead, but San Diego chipped back with a run in the sixth inning and then tied the game with a four-run rally in the eighth.

Mets reliever Roger McDowell began the eighth inning but clearly did not have it as he faced four batters and they all reached base.

With the bases loaded and no one out, Steve Garvey's sharp ground ball to second kicked off Wally Backman's glove as two runs scored.

Jesse Orosco relieved McDowell and struck out Bruce Bochy, but pinch-hitter Carmelo Martinez singled to center to score future Met Kevin McReynolds to make it a 5–4 lead.

Templeton's RBI single fell in front of Strawberry and tied the game, but

Orosco ended the inning by striking out pinch-hitter Marvell Wynne and getting Flannery on a ground-out to second.

The Mets took a 3–0 lead in the first inning, keyed by a two-run single by Darryl Strawberry. They added two more runs in the third when Strawberry hit a mammoth two-run homer that went over the right-field fence for a 5–0 lead. The clout was Strawberry's 100th career home run.

The Mets were not the only ones "flashing the leather" on defense. Padres right fielder Tony Gwynn had three assists, which was one short of the major league record for a single game.

The future Hall of Famer threw out Strawberry at home in the first inning. He also threw out Rafael Santana trying to stretch a single into a double in the second inning, and he chucked out Hernandez, who was going for a double in the fifth inning.

Mets	AB	R	H	RBI
Dykstra cf	5	2	2	0
Backman 2b	5	1	2	0
Hernandez 1b	4	2	2	1
Strawberry rf	4	1	2	4
Heep lf	4	0	0	0
Wilson lf	1	0	0	0
Knight 3b	5	0	0	1
Sisk p	0	0	0	0
Gibbons c	5	0	2	0
Santana ss	5	0	2	0
Gooden p	2	0	1	0
Mazzilli ph	1	0	0	0
McDowell p	0	0	0	0
Orosco p	0	0	0	0
Johnson 3b	1	0	0	0
Totals	**42**	**6**	**13**	**6**

Padres	AB	R	H	RBI
Flannery 2b-3b	6	0	1	0
Gwynn rf	5	1	3	0
Kruk lf	4	2	2	0
McReynolds cf	4	1	0	0
Garvey 1b	5	1	1	2
Nettles 3b	3	0	0	0
Bochy ph-c	2	0	0	0
Kennedy c	3	0	0	0
Martinez ph	1	0	1	1
Roberts pr-2b	1	0	0	0
Templeton ss	5	0	3	1
Whitson p	1	0	1	0
Iorg ph	1	0	0	0
Hawkins p	0	0	0	0
Royster ph	1	0	1	0
McCullers p	0	0	0	0
Wynne ph	1	0	0	0
Gossage p	0	0	0	0
Lefferts ph	1	0	0	0
Totals	**44**	**5**	**13**	**4**

NYM 3 0 2 0 0 0 0 0 1 - 6 13 1
SD 0 0 0 0 0 1 0 4 0 0 0 - 5 13 2

Mets	IP	H	R	ER	BB	SO
Gooden	7	7	1	1	1	7
McDowell	0	2	4	3	1	0
Orosco	2	2	0	0	0	2
Sisk W (3-2)	2	2	0	0	0	1
Totals	**11**	**13**	**5**	**4**	**2**	**10**

Padres	IP	H	R	ER	BB	SO
Whitson	5	6	5	4	3	4
Hawkins	2	2	0	0	1	2
McCullers	1	1	0	0	0	0
Gossage L (5-7)	3	4	1	1	0	3
Totals	**11**	**13**	**6**	**5**	**4**	**9**

E—New York Backman; San Diego Whitson, Templeton. DP—New York; San Diego. 2B—New York Hernandez; San Diego Kruk, Garvey, Templeton. HR—New York Strawberry (19). SH—New York Backman. SF—New York Hernandez. LOB—New York 10; San Diego 8. SB—New York Strawberry; San Diego Gwynn 2. Attendance: 19,747.

It's Sweet Music as Viola Tops Hershiser in Cy Young Showcase

This pitchers' duel lived up to its advance billing and more.

In a first-time meeting of reigning Cy Young Award winners, the Mets' Frank Viola outpitched the Dodgers' Orel Hershiser in a 1–0 nailbiter before 38,820 at Dodger Stadium.

Viola won the 1988 American League Cy Young Award with the Minnesota Twins before being dealt to the Mets at the trade deadline as part of a blockbuster, five-for-one deal. Hershiser was the reigning National League Cy Young winner.

The Mets scored the only run of the game in the third inning. Gregg Jefferies singled and scored from second base on a two-out single by Howard Johnson.

Viola lived up to his Cy Young form by going the distance on a three-hitter. Viola did not walk a batter and struck out five.

He was never really threatened as the Dodgers never put two runners on base in an inning. He put his stamp on this masterpiece by retiring the last 15 batters.

> ### At a Glance
> **WP:** Viola (2–3)
> **Key stat:** Viola CG 3-hitter, 5 Ks

On July 31, 1989, the Mets acquired Viola from the Twins in exchange for pitchers Rick Aguilera, David West, Kevin Tapani and Tim Drummond along with a player to be named later, who was pitcher Jack Savage.

Viola pitched parts of three seasons with the Mets. He had his best year in 1990, when he went 20–12 with a 2.67 ERA and a National League-leading 249 $^2/_3$ innings pitched.

The left-hander finished third in the voting for the 1990 National League Cy Young Award behind Pirates pitcher Doug Drabek and Dodgers pitcher Ramon Martinez (brother of future Met Pedro Martinez).

Coming off the 1988 American League Cy Young Award while he was with the Minnesota Twins, Frank Viola was nearly as impressive in 1990, when he finished third in voting for the National League Cy Young Award.

Another Near-Miss for Mets as Cone Throws 1-Hitter

David Cone pitched the 17th one-hitter in Mets history as he dominated the San Diego Padres at Shea Stadium with a 6-0 win.

Only a fourth-inning double by future Hall of Famer Tony Gwynn would spoil Cone's bid to become the first Met to toss a no-hitter.

"I have no regrets about Gwynn," Cone said. "He missed a fastball. He took a forkball for a strike. I threw another forkball, down and away, exactly where I wanted, and he just hit it over first base."

The 25-year-old right-hander walked two and faced 30 batters, three over the minimum.

· Rookie Gregg Jefferies provided the offensive fireworks. He had three hits, including his first big-league home run, and finished a single short of the cycle.

Rain kept the crowd down, but 16,444 fans saw a mild protest to begin the game. The Mets announced the delayed starting time of the game to be 7:45 PM, 10 minutes after the scheduled first pitch. When managers Jack McKeon of San Diego and Dave Johnson of the Mets brought out the lineup cards, Cone was not ready to pitch. McKeon played the game under protest after he stated that he did not receive any notice of a later starting time.

"We weren't notified of any delay," McKeon said to Johnson at the lineup exchange.

"I'm notifying you," Johnson answered.

It turned into a "nothing protest" as Cone showed from the start that he was going to be tough to score on, even if he had to use his shin to get an out. Leadoff hitter Stanley Jefferson lined a ball off of Cone's right shin, but it bounded to Keith Hernandez at first base, where he stepped on the bag for the out.

Cone remained in the game to toss a masterpiece.

At a Glance
WP: Cone (14–3)
HR: Jefferies (1)
Key stat: Cone CG 1-hitter, 8 Ks; Jefferies 3-for-4, 2 runs, 2 RBIs

Alfonzo Blasts Record-Tying 3 Homers, 5 RBIs

To say Edgardo Alfonzo had a record-setting night would be a gross understatement.

The Mets' second baseman set a club record with six hits—including a club record-tying three home runs—and scored a club-record six runs to lead a 21-hit attack in a 17–1 demolition of the Houston Astros at the Astrodome. Alfonzo also drove in five runs.

With his three home runs, Alfonzo set a club record for the most home runs by a second baseman in a single season. His 16 total bases also set Mets record, breaking the old mark set by Darryl Strawberry in 1985.

Edgardo Alfonzo watches the flight of his ninth-inning double against the Houston Astros on Aug. 30, 1999. Alfonzo went 6-for-6 with three homers and 5 RBIs in a 17–1 victory.

For those who watched, it was a memorable game. But for the humble Alfonzo, team goals mattered more than his historic performance, as evidenced by his reaction to the question about his favorite moment of the game.

"The last out, because we won the game," he said. "I don't think it's going to be good if you have the numbers but you lose the game."

The 26-year-old native of Venezuela got things going in the first inning with a one-out home run off Astros starter and loser Shane Reynolds.

The Mets blew the game open with six runs on six hits in the second inning off Reynolds. Darryl Hamilton smacked a leadoff home run for a 2–0 lead.

Alfonzo singled for his second hit of the game and scored on John Olerud's two-run double. Mike Piazza completed the scoring and made it a 7–0 lead with a two-run homer.

In the fourth inning, Alfonzo had his third hit and his second home run, a two-run blast that pushed the lead to 9–0.

The Mets scored one run in the fifth inning and added two in the sixth as Alfonzo smashed his third home run.

Alfonzo was already 4-for-4 when he led off the eighth inning with a single, moved to second base on Olerud's walk and scored his fifth run on Shawon Dunston's RBI single.

Alfonzo would get one more at-bat to tie the all-time major league record for home runs in a single game, but he settled for a single off Trever Miller.

Manager Bobby Valentine could do nothing but be awed by the performance of his second baseman.

> ## At a Glance
> **WP:** Yoshii (9–8)
>
> **HR:** Alfonzo 3 (21,22,23), Hamilton (7), Piazza (32)
>
> **Key stat:** Alfonzo 6-for-6, 5R, 5 RBIs

"He has very high expectations for his play and he keeps striving to be better," Valentine said. "That's why he isn't settling for being a .300 hitter and hitting to right field and taking a pitch on a 3–1 count. Edgardo knows he's good but he doesn't quite know how good he is."

Left unnoticed were six shutout innings by Mets starter and winner Masato Yoshii. The native of Japan walked one and struck out eight. Yoshii left the game because he felt tightness in his calf and was replaced by a troika of Jeff Tam, Billy Taylor and Chuck McElroy, who combined to allow one run over the final three innings.

Alfonzo played eight seasons with the Mets and had a promising career cut short by a back injury.

SEPTEMBER/ OCTOBER

Tommie Agee made two of the greatest catches in World Series history to help the Mets claim the 1969 World Championship. His grabs in Game 3 helped the Mets hold on

History from Japan, and a Display from Jackson

The Mets beat the San Francisco Giants 4–1, but the crowd of 39,379 at Shea Stadium witnessed the first appearance by a Japanese-born player in the major leagues.

In the eighth inning, Japanese-born left-hander Masanori Murakami entered the game for the Giants and made baseball history, but it was Mets left-hander Al Jackson who really stole the show.

Jackson went the distance and nearly pitched a shutout against a formidable Giants lineup that featured future Hall of Famers Willie Mays and Orlando Cepeda.

Jackson allowed six hits (all singles) and one walk. He held the Giants scoreless until two outs in the ninth inning, when Cepeda's single drove in the only San Francisco run.

The Mets got the jump on starter and loser Bob Hendley in the first inning on Ron Hunt's solo home run into the lower grandstand in left field.

In the seventh inning, the Mets gave Jackson some breathing room. Ed Kranepool and Roy McMillan opened the inning with singles. With one out, Bobby Klaus singled to score Kranepool. On the play, Mays made a rare error when his throw home bounced past Giants catcher Del Crandall, so the runners moved up to second and third.

The Giants changed pitchers but strangely enough, they chose to have the reliever, John Pregenzer, walk Hunt to load the bases.

> ## At a Glance
>
> **WP:** Jackson (9–13)
>
> **HR:** Hunt (6)
>
> **Key stat:** Jackson CG 6-hitter; Christopher 2-for-4, 2 RBIs; Giants' Murakami becomes first Japanese-born player in major leagues

Joe Christopher took advantage of the unusual strategy employed by Giants manager Alvin Dark by lining a two-run double into the right-field corner for a 4–0 lead.

The first batter that Murakami faced was Charley Smith and he struck him out.

Chris Cannizzaro singled to center, but Kranepool struck out and McMillan was retired on a ground-out to shortstop.

In the ninth inning the Giants put two runners on base with no one out, but Jackson got Jim Ray Hart to hit into a 6–4–3 double play that killed the rally.

Hickman Adds to History Books with 3 Homers

Jim Hickman became the first player in franchise history to hit three home runs in a game as the Mets dumped the St. Louis Cardinals 6–3 before a crowd of 13,774 at Busch Stadium.

All three home runs came off future Met and Cards left-hander Ray Sadecki, and there wasn't a "cheap" one in the bunch.

Hickman's first home run gave the Mets a 1–0 lead in the second inning and was estimated at more than 400 feet into the seats in center field.

The Mets added a run in the third inning on Roy McMillan's RBI single.

Hickman's second home run in the fourth inning gave the Mets a 3–0 lead. This one landed in the left-field bleachers.

At a Glance

WP: Selma (1–0)

HR: Hickman 3 (10,11,12)

Key stat: Hickman 4-for-5, 3 HR, 3 runs, 4 RBIs

The Cards got two runs back on a two-run homer by Bill White off winning pitcher Dick Selma, but Hickman's third home run, a two-run shot in the sixth inning, made it a 5–2 game. The record-setting blast reportedly slammed into a concession stand in the rear of the seats in left field.

Selma, who was making his first big-league start, allowed three runs on six hits in more than five innings of work.

Gordon Richardson, who was acquired from the Cardinals in a trade during the off-season, pitched four hitless and scoreless innings to earn the save.

Murray's 17th Grand Slam Helps Mets Surge Past Reds

Future Hall of Famer Eddie Murray hit his 17th career grand slam to power the Mets to a 5–2 win over the Cincinnati Reds at Riverfront Stadium.

With one out in the sixth inning, Murray smoked an 0–1 fastball from pitcher Tim Belcher into the second tier of seats in right-center field to snap a 1–1 tie and give the Mets a 5–1 lead.

The 36-year-old first baseman joined Hall of Famers Jimmie Foxx and Ted Williams for third place on the all-time grand slam list.

Todd Hundley got the sixth inning going with a double to right. With one out, Vince Coleman singled to left. An error on a sacrifice fly tied the game 1–1.

Chico Walker drew a walk to load the bases and Murray made a winner of Sid Fernandez with his milestone-setting blast.

"El Sid" gave up a run on four hits in 7 ⅓ innings. The portly left-hander walked three and struck out two.

Murray signed with the Mets as a free agent and spent two very productive years in New York. The slugging switch-hitter hit 43 home runs and drove in 193 runs during his two-year tenure.

The Hawaiian-born Fernandez pitched 10 seasons for the Mets. He had his best season in 1986, when he went 16–6 with a 3.52 ERA. During his Mets career, Fernandez was 98–78.

> ### At a Glance
>
> **WP:** Fernandez (12–9)
>
> **HR:** Murray (14)
>
> **Key stat:** Murray HR, 4 RBIs; Fernandez 7 ⅓ IP, 4H, 1R

Sadecki and McGraw Team Up for 4-Hitter

Ray Sadecki and Tug McGraw combined on a four-hitter as the Mets blanked the Philadelphia Phillies 4–0.

Starter Sadecki gave up three hits in 5 ^{2}/$_3$ innings while walking five and striking out six. McGraw entered the game with two outs and two on in the sixth. After walking Billy Grabarkewitz, McGraw ended the inning by retiring pinch-hitter Cesar Tovar on a harmless fly to right.

Sadecki encountered trouble in the fourth inning when Philadelphia had the bases loaded with two outs, but Phillies pitcher Wayne Twitchell was called out on strikes.

A crowd of 12,563 at Shea Stadium saw Rusty Staub hit a two-out, two-strike home run in the first inning for a 1–0 lead.

The Mets added a second run in the fifth inning. Wayne Garrett walked with one out, and took second on an error by future Hall of Famer Mike Schmidt. After John Milner walked to load the bases, Twitchell uncorked a wild pitch that got past Phillies catcher Bob Boone for a 2–0 lead.

The Mets completed the scoring off of Phillies reliever George Culver in the sixth.

Jerry Grote walked and with one out, Bud Harrelson singled. After McGraw struck out, Wayne Garrett plated two more runs with a triple off the right-field wall.

At a Glance

WP: Sadecki (4–3)

HR: Staub (12)

Key stat: Garrett 1-for-4, 2 RBIs

McGraw gave up one hit—Schmidt's single to lead off the ninth inning—but he struck out Grabarkewitz and Craig Robinson then got the final out on a force-out at second base.

Lone Infield Hit Keeps Gooden Out of the Record Books

Dwight Gooden came within an infield hit of throwing the Mets' first no-hitter as he went the distance on a one-hitter in blanking the Chicago Cubs 10–0 before a crowd of 46,301 at Shea Stadium.

Keith Moreland's infield single in the fifth inning was the only hit Gooden allowed. "Doc" walked four and struck out 11.

"Tonight was one of my better games," Gooden said. "I felt great going into the game and I felt strong at the end."

The Mets made it easy for Gooden as they took a 1–0 lead in the first inning on a sacrifice fly by Mookie Wilson and then broke the game open in the third with five runs against losing pitcher Dick Ruthven.

Wilson doubled home a run while George Foster's three-run homer keyed the offensive barrage.

The Mets added another run in the fourth inning to give "Doc" a 7–0 lead.

Gooden got seven of his strikeouts through the first four innings.

In the fifth, Moreland swung at a 1–2 pitch from Gooden and hit a slow grounder toward third. Mets third baseman Ray Knight, who was playing back, had no chance to make a play.

> ## At a Glance
>
> **WP:** Gooden (15–8)
>
> **HR:** Foster (20), Strawberry (21)
>
> **Key stat:** Gooden CG 1-hitter, 11 Ks; Wilson 2-for-4, 3 RBIs

"I was playing back and off the line," Knight said. "Nobody had been pulling Doc, and Moreland goes the other way and he doesn't run well. I came in at such a sharp angle, I had to catch the ball and throw it all at once. But I never got the ball out of my hand. My momentum was carrying me toward their dugout and there was no way I could throw the ball."

Moreland never got past first base. In fact, Bob Dernier, who walked and stole second in the first inning, was the only Cubs base runner to reach second.

Gooden's 11 strikeouts gave him 235 on the season to break the National League record for rookies, previously set by Grover Cleveland Alexander (227). Gooden also tied Tom Seaver's single-season club record of 13 games with 10 or more strikeouts.

More Amazin' Antics En Route to the Pennant

Tommie Agee provided the offense while Jerry Koosman handled the pitching chores and they led the Mets to a 3–2 win over the Chicago Cubs before a crowd of 43,274 at Shea Stadium.

The win moved the Mets to within 1.5 games of the National League East-leading Cubs.

Agee's two-run homer came in the third inning off starter Bill Hands to give the Mets a 2–0 lead.

The Cubs scored twice in the sixth inning to tie the game 2–2. After Don Kessinger and Glenn Beckert singled, future Hall of Famer Billy Williams singled in the first run. Chicago tied it on a sacrifice fly to left field by Ron Santo.

Agee started the home half of the sixth inning with a shot that got past Santo at third base and then used his savvy to get into scoring position.

Rain fell throughout the game. Not enough to stop play, but enough to make the field a little "dicey," and Agee took advantage of that. The Mets' center fielder knew he could hustle into second base because the wet grass would slow the ball down.

Wayne Garrett followed with a single to right and Agee was able to score when Jim Hickman's throw went up the third-base line.

At a Glance

WP: Koosman (13–9)

HR: Agee (26)

Key stat: Agee 2-for-3, 2 runs, 2 RBIs

After getting the lead, Koosman buckled down to finish strong.

The 25-year-old lefty gave up three hits and struck out six over the final three innings to nail down a very big win.

Black Cat Brings More Amazin' Results for Mets

A crowd of 51,448 fans saw the Mets sweep a two-game series from the Chicago Cubs with what became known as the "Black Cat" game.

With the Cubs' history of futility, many superstitious fans believed this game was an omen of things to come for the beleaguered franchise.

The "sign" came with two outs in the top of the first inning.

A black cat wandered onto the field, walked past the mound in front of Mets pitcher Tom Seaver, then made its way toward the Cubs' dugout.

Ron Santo was in the on-deck circle as the cat seemed to pause and stare at him, and then the players, as it strolled near the steps of the dugout. Cubs manager Leo Durocher, in particular, caught the feline's eye.

In a matchup of future Hall of Famers, Tom Seaver outpitched Ferguson Jenkins in a 7–1 Mets win that left them a half-game behind the Cubs in the National League East.

Seaver went the distance, giving up a run on five hits while the Mets got to Jenkins for seven runs (five earned) in seven innings of work.

Throughout the game, the large crowd at Shea was in a frenzy as they were waving handkerchiefs and serenading Durocher with chants of "Goodbye Leo."

Before 1969, the Mets never had a winning season—much less a chance at postseason play—so the fans were caught up in a wave of excitement.

Jenkins was working on two days' rest and it showed in the first inning as Tommie Agee drew a leadoff walk. With one out, Cleon Jones walked to put runners at first and second base.

> ## At a Glance
>
> **WP:** Seaver (21-7)
>
> **HR:** Clendenon (13), Shamsky (13)
>
> **Key stat:** Seaver complete game 5-hit shutout; Clendenon 2-run HR

Jenkins retired Art Shamsky on a comebacker to the mound and looked to be primed to end the inning, but Ken Boswell lined a ball into the gap in right-center field for a two-run double and a 2–0 lead.

Chicago's defensive lapse led to two more runs in the third inning. With one out, Shamsky was nearly picked off at first base, but during the rundown, Cubs second baseman Glenn Beckert dropped the throw. Boswell then struck out but Donn Clendenon struck a crushing blow. The Mets' first baseman hit a 2–0 pitch over the fence in right-center field for a two-run homer and a 4–0 lead.

Seaver gave up a run in the fourth inning on Santo's RBI single, but he helped get that one back with his bat. Leading off the fourth inning, the 25-year-old right-hander doubled off the left-field fence as he reached second base with a daring head-first slide. Seaver went to third base on a ground-out and scored on Wayne Garrett's sacrifice fly to center.

Shamsky homered to open the fifth inning and Jerry Grote completed the scoring in the seventh inning with an RBI double.

Mets shortstop Bud Harrelson spoke for many of his teammates when he put the win in perspective.

"I remember back in 1966, we'd get to the seventh inning and I was scared, scared they'd hit the ball to me, scared we'd lose, and everyone else felt the same way, that's why we lost," Harrelson said. "If we won, it was like winning the World Series. Instead of being disappointed if we lost, if we won, champagne flowed. As a ninth-place ballclub, you can't think you're going to win the pennant, but now everything's fallen into place and we're just as good as anyone in the league."

To some extent, the success of the team even exceeded manager Gil Hodges' expectations.

"I knew we'd have an improved team but I didn't really anticipate we'd develop quite so quickly," Hodges said. "A lot of that, of course, has to do with the personality of certain men, it rubs off on the other players."

In the postgame clubhouse, Seaver was relaxed but not yet satisfied.

"When I came here, there was still an attitude of futility and I couldn't accept it," he said. "But it's altogether different now, we know we can win and that's a contagious type of feeling. I think it grows."

Sweep Moves Mets into First Place for First Time

For the first time in franchise history, the New York Mets were a first-place team. It was reportedly 10:13 PM when 23,512 fans at Shea Stadium began a chant of "We're Number One! We're Number One!"

In the opener, Mets starter Jim McAndrew gave up leadoff triples in each of the first two innings to Ty Cline and Mack Jones.

Cline scored on an error and Jones came home on a poor throw by Mets first baseman Donn Clendenon at the end of the play.

McAndrew settled down and allowed only one more hit over nine scoreless innings.

Like his counterpart, Expos starter Mike Wegener also pitched 11 innings. The 22-year-old righty gave up two unearned runs on five hits with 15 strikeouts.

The Mets scored a run in the first inning on a walk to Tommie Agee, a passed ball and an RBI single by Art Shamsky.

With two outs in the fifth inning, Agee reached on a throwing error by Expos third baseman Coco Laboy. Wayne Garrett singled Agee to third and Cleon Jones walked to load the bases.

Wegener balked to allow Agee to score the tying run before he fanned Shamsky to end the inning.

The Expos had a golden opportunity to break the 2–2 tie in the seventh inning with the bases loaded and one out, but Ron Fairly bounced into an inning-ending 6–6–3 double play.

There was another chance for Montreal in the top of the 12th. Ron Taylor relieved McAndrew and gave up singles to Angel Hermoso and Kevin Collins.

When Agee's throw to third bounced away, Hermoso tried to score but Taylor retrieved the ball and threw out the potential go-ahead run at the plate.

> ### At a Glance
> **Game 1**
>
> **WP:** Taylor (8-4)
>
> **Key stat:** McAndrew 4-hitter in 11 innings pitched; Jones 2-for-5
>
> **Game 2**
>
> **WP:** Ryan (6-1)
>
> **Key stat:** Ryan complete game 3-hitter, 11 Ks

Cleon Jones batted .340 and started the All-Star Game in left field during the 1969 run to the World Series title by the Amazin' Mets.

Bill Stoneman relieved Wegener and got the first two outs, but Jones singled and Rod Gaspar walked.

Ken Boswell ended the game with an RBI single to center and the crowd went crazy. The moment Jones crossed the plate with the winning run, the Mets were, at least temporarily, in first place in the National League East.

Future Hall of Famer Nolan Ryan pitched the nightcap and went the distance in a 7–1 victory.

Ryan allowed a run on three hits with 11 strikeouts.

The Mets blew the game open by scoring six runs in the third inning. Jerry Grote doubled and went to third on a single by Bud Harrelson. Grote was thrown out at home on Ryan's grounder, but Agee was hit to load the bases. A wild pitch by losing pitcher Howie Reed tied the score and Garrett's RBI single gave the Mets a 2–1 lead. A two-run single by Jones made it 4–1. The Mets added a run on Boswell's RBI single and a RBI ground-out by Clendenon.

When the inning ended, the result of the Cubs' game was posted on the scoreboard, and an additional message was posted.

"Look Who's No. 1"

EAST	WON	LOST	PCT
METS	83	57	.593
CUBS	84	58	.592

That said it all.

After the doubleheader, a team that was not yet satisfied was popping champagne. A number of Mets had visited a Brooklyn winery the day before the twinbill and brought some bottles to the ballpark with them.

Seaver hinted that this team had not yet reached its full potential.

"I think being in first place will just make us tougher and help us," he said. "We always did believe in ourselves, but each time you win the belief grows."

"We're happy, but we've been happy all year," Jerry Koosman said. "It just isn't a strange idea to us that we should win, we think we should. I said in spring training that we had a chance to win the pennant, and I meant it, whether people believed me or not."

The rivalry between the Mets and Cubs took on a new tone after Koosman admitted to hitting Ron Santo in retaliation for a Bill Hands pitch that knocked down Agee in the opening game of the two-game series.

Cubs pitcher Ken Holtzman responded to the admission.

"Koosman and Seaver are good pitchers," Holtzman said, "but they act like they run the league. They think they can intimidate our guys. But they're not the only guys in the league who can throw hard at somebody."

Holtzman was just warming up.

"I'll say one thing. If it's this close when they come into Chicago, I better not hear anyone popping off. I can speak for Fergie (Jenkins) and Hands, too. If they start coming close to our big hitters in Chicago, their whole team better watch out. If the Mets win, fine. If they deserve to win, they deserve to win. But they will not intimidate us."

September 11, 1974

Mets Lose to Cardinals In Record-Setting 25-Inning Marathon

A game that began at 8:09 PM Eastern ended seven hours and four minutes later at 3:13 in the morning when the St. Louis Cardinals edged the Mets 4–3 in a 25-inning epic at Shea Stadium in front of 13,460.

Time-wise, the game fell short of the record seven hours and 23 minutes between the Mets and San Francisco Giants that was the nightcap of a doubleheader on May 31, 1964.

The innings total set a Mets record, breaking the previous mark of 24 innings in Houston in 1968.

A total of 50 players were used, including nine who played the entire game. There were 202 at-bats, approximately 15 dozen baseballs used and three separate seventh-inning stretches were conducted.

In an uncanny twist of fate, the home-plate umpire was Ed Sudol.

"Why does it always happen to me," moaned Sudol after the game.

At 1:30 AM, Sudol tossed Mets manager Yogi Berra, who came out of the dugout to argue a checked swing in the Mets' half of the 20th inning.

The veteran arbiter was behind the plate for not only this record-setting nightcap, but also for the Mets' 24-inning loss in Houston.

Doc K-O's Rookie Strikeout Record

It was a record-setting game for 19-year-old Dwight Gooden, who struck out 16 in the Mets' 2-0 win over the Pittsburgh Pirates at Shea Stadium.

Gooden struck out former Met Marvell Wynne in the sixth inning for his 11th strikeout of the game and 246th of the season. That broke Herb Score's Naitonal League rookie record that had stood for 29 years.

A crowd of 12,876 fans saw "Doc" break Nolan Ryan's club record of 14 strikeouts by a rookie in a single game, and it was the 14th time he had 10 or more strikeouts in a game. That set a new club record, breaking the mark Tom Seaver set in 1971.

Gooden brought his "A" game as he threw 120 pitches, 92 for strikes.

Pirates starter John Tudor matched Gooden for three innings, but the Mets broke through in the fourth. Keith Hernandez led off with a single and Hubie Brooks followed with a two-run homer for all the scoring in the game.

Gooden recorded his strikeouts in seven of the nine innings. He didn't strike out a batter in the first and ninth innings, but he struck out two batters each in the second, third, fourth, sixth and seventh. In the fifth and the eighth, Gooden fanned the side. He struck out four in a row twice and at one point, Doc struck out six straight hitters.

Darryl Strawberry could do nothing but admire his teammate.

"He should win Rookie of the Year hands up," Strawberry said. "I can't see anybody close to him." (Gooden would go on to win the 1984 National League Rookie of the Year Award with 23 of the 24 first-place votes.)

Pirates	AB	R	H	RBI
Wynne cf	4	0	0	0
Lacy lf	4	0	1	0
Ray 2b	4	0	1	0
Thompson 1b	4	0	1	0
Pena c	4	0	0	0
Morrison 3b	3	0	0	0
Frobel rf	3	0	0	0
Gonzalez ss	3	0	0	0
Tudor p	2	0	1	0
Orsulak ph	1	0	1	0
Scurry p	0	0	0	0
Totals	**32**	**0**	**5**	**0**

Mets	AB	R	H	RBI
Wilson cf	4	0	1	0
Chapman 2b	4	0	1	0
Hernandez 1b	4	1	1	0
Foster lf	4	0	0	0
Brooks ss	3	1	1	2
Strawberry rf	3	0	0	0
Knight 3b	3	0	1	0
Fitzgerald c	3	0	2	0
Gooden p	3	0	2	0
Totals	**31**	**2**	**9**	**2**

PIT 0 0 0 0 0 0 0 0 0 - 0 5 0
NYM 0 0 0 2 0 0 0 0 X - 2 9 0

Pirates	IP	H	R	ER	BB	SO
Tudor L (9-11)	7	9	2	2	0	7
Scurry	1	0	0	0	0	1
Totals	**8**	**9**	**2**	**2**	**0**	**8**

Mets	IP	H	R	ER	BB	SO
Gooden W (16-8)	9	5	0	0	0	16
Totals	**9**	**5**	**0**	**0**	**0**	**16**

2B—Pittsburgh Lacy. HR—New York Brooks (16). LOB—Pittsburgh 5; New York 5. SB—Pittsburgh Orsulak. Attendance: 12,876.

Mets Sweep Twinbill by Identical 1-0 Scores

The Mets swept a doubleheader from the Pittsburgh Pirates at Forbes Field by identical 1–0 scores with both starting pitchers driving in the only runs before 19,303 fans.

In the opener, Jerry Koosman went the distance on a three-hitter and drove in the only run of the game in the fifth inning.

With two on and one out, Koosman, who was 3-for-69 coming into the at-bat, lined the first pitch into right field for an RBI single.

In the ninth inning, an error by former Pirates first baseman Donn Clendenon put the tying run on base, but Koosman retired future Hall of Famers Willie Stargell on an infield pop and Roberto Clemente on a ground-out.

The second game was more of the same, although starting pitcher Don Cardwell did not go the distance.

Cardwell gave up four hits in eight innings and Tug McGraw pitched a scoreless ninth for the save.

With two outs and Bud Harrelson at second base in the second inning, Cardwell drove in the only run with a single to left.

Hundley's 41st Homer Sets New Standard for Catchers

Mets catcher Todd Hundley set a major league record for catchers with his 41st home run of the season as the Mets beat the Atlanta Braves 6–5 in 12 innings.

Hundley broke Roy Campanella's 1953 mark of 40 home runs in one season by a catcher when he connected off Atlanta's Greg McMichael for a three-run shot that tied the game in the seventh inning.

Hundley was down 0–2 in the count, but he drove McMichael's change-up over the left-field fence for the record-setting blow.

"When I got it, I knew it was gone," Hundley said. "There's a click you're looking for and I got the click."

The record-setting ball bounced back onto the field, but Braves left fielder Jermaine Dye mistakenly picked it up and threw it back in the stands.

A 17-year-old eventually presented the ball to Hundley in exchange for an autographed bat.

As he triumphantly ran around the bases, the scoreboard flashed "41." When Hundley got to home plate, he was mobbed by his teammates.

The crowd of 22,857 implored the Mets catcher to come out for a "curtain call."

"I wanted it for the fans," Hundley said. "I've been through a lot with them. I've gone from being booed by 46,000 people to being cheered by the 20,000 or 30,000 that were here. It was nice to be able to get the curtain call and be able to wave to them. I wanted to just stand there for awhile but the game was going on."

Lance Johnson's single in the 12th inning brought home Matt Franco with the winning run to cap a memorable day at Shea.

"That's the way you want a game like this to end," Johnson said, "with Todd breaking Campanella's record and the team getting a 'W.'"

At a Glance

WP: Wallace (2–1)

HR: Hundley (41)

Key stat: Hundley sets single-season record for HR by a catcher

---

Todd Hundley hit his 41st home run on Sept. 14, 1996, to set a single-season record for major league catchers.

September 15, 1969

Mets 4, Cardinals 3

Swoboda Homers Trump Carlton's 19 Strikeouts

Ron Swoboda slammed a pair of two-run homers to offset a record-setting performance by St. Louis Cardinals left-hander Steve Carlton as the Mets scored a memorable 4–3 win at Busch Stadium.

A crowd of 13,086 watched Carlton set a major league record with 19 strikeouts, breaking the old mark previously held by Sandy Koufax, Bob Feller and Don Wilson.

Swoboda struck out twice but in the fourth inning, he gave the Mets a 2–1 lead with his first home run.

Donn Clendenon walked to lead off the inning and Swoboda lined an 0–2 pitch from Carlton into the mezzanine in left field.

Carlton finished that inning by striking out the side.

The Cards scored twice in the fifth inning to take a 3–2 lead. Starter Gary Gentry got the first two outs but gave up a single to future Hall of Famer Lou Brock, who stole second. Curt Flood's RBI single tied the game and St. Louis took the lead back on future Mets manager Joe Torre's RBI single.

In the eighth inning, Tommie Agee singled to center. After Clendenon was called out on strikes, Swoboda hit his second home run as he connected on a 2–2 pitch from Carlton and drove it into the same general area as his first home run.

Tug McGraw, who was already in the game, pitched one-hit ball over the final three innings to earn the win.

Carlton struck out exactly half of the 38 batters that he faced.

The 24-year-old southpaw had 16 strikeouts and would have to fan the side in the ninth if he

Mets	AB	R	H	RBI
Harrelson ss	4	0	1	0
Otis lf	5	0	0	0
Agee lf	4	1	1	0
Clendenon 1b	3	1	1	0
Swoboda rf	4	2	2	4
Charles 3b	4	0	0	0
Grote c	4	0	2	0
Weis 2b	4	0	1	0
Gentry p	2	0	0	0
Pfeil ph	1	0	1	0
Gosger pr	0	0	0	0
McGraw p	1	0	0	0
Totals	36	4	9	4

Cardinals	AB	R	H	RBI
Brock lf	4	1	2	0
Flood cf	5	2	2	1
Pinson rf	4	0	3	1
Torre 1b	4	0	1	1
McCarver c	4	0	0	0
Shannon 3b	4	0	0	0
Javier 2b	4	0	0	0
Maxvill ss	3	0	0	0
Browne ph	1	0	0	0
Carlton p	3	0	0	0
Gagliano ph	1	0	0	0
Nossek pr	0	0	0	0
Totals	37	3	8	3

											R	H	E
NYM	0	0	0	2	0	0	0	2	0	-	4	9	4
STL	0	0	1	0	2	0	0	0	0	-	3	8	1

Mets	IP	H	R	ER	BB	SO
Gentry	6	7	3	3	1	3
McGraw W (8-3)	3	1	0	0	1	3
Totals	9	8	3	3	2	6

Cardinals	IP	H	R	ER	BB	SO
Carlton L (16-10)	9	9	4	4	2	19
Totals	9	9	4	4	2	19

E—New York Harrelson, Clendenon, Charles 2; St. Louis Javier. DP—New York. HR—New York Swoboda 2 (8,9). LOB—New York 7; St. Louis 9. SB—St. Louis Pinson, Brock 2. Attendance: 13,086.

wanted to set a new mark. In the ninth, Carlton struck out McGraw and Bud Harrelson looked at strike three.

It was remarkable that Carlton was still in the game because it had been delayed twice by rain for a total of 81 minutes.

Amos Otis, who was just up from the minors and had struck out in three previous at-bats, swung and missed to give Carlton the all-time record.

"It was the best stuff I ever had," Carlton said. "I had a great fastball that kept rising and my curve was falling right off the table. When I had nine strike-outs, I decided to go all the way, but it cost me the game, because I started to challenge every hitter."

After the game, Carlton said he was sick before the game.

"I had a fever all day," Carlton said, "and I felt so bad that I slept an extra hour and didn't get to the ball park until 7 o'clock, an hour before the game was to start."

"He threw pitches to me that were worse than the home run pitches," said Swoboda. "He'd throw a pitch so good that I'd say to myself, if he throws two more like it, there's no way I can touch it."

Did You Know?

Only two Met pitchers have hit a grand slam. On July 15, 1963, Carl Willey hit a grand slam at the Polo Grounds against Houston's Ken Johnson. Nearly four years later, Jack Hamilton smacked a grand slam off former Met and Cardinals pitcher Al Jackson on May 20, 1967.

Gooden Dodges Fans as Mets Secure NL East Title

The New York Mets clinched their third National League East Division title and their first in 13 years as they knocked off the Chicago Cubs 4–2 before a crowd of 47,823 at Shea Stadium.

Cubs	AB	R	H	RBI
Walker rf	4	1	0	0
Sandberg 2b	3	0	1	0
Palmeiro lf	3	1	1	2
Moreland 3b	4	0	0	0
Durham 1b	3	0	1	0
Davis c	3	0	0	0
Dunston ss	4	0	1	0
Dernier cf	3	0	0	0
Speier ph	1	0	1	0
Martinez pr	0	0	0	0
Eckersley p	2	0	1	0
Hoffman p	0	0	0	0
Bosley ph	1	0	0	0
DiPino p	0	0	0	0
Mumphrey ph	1	0	0	0
Totals	32	2	6	2

Mets	AB	R	H	RBI
Dykstra cf	4	2	2	0
Backman 2b	3	1	1	0
Magadan 1b	4	0	3	2
Jefferson 1b	0	1	0	0
Hernandez 1b	0	0	0	0
Carter c	4	0	1	0
Strawberry rf	3	0	2	1
Wilson lf	4	0	0	0
Knight 3b	4	0	2	0
Santana ss	4	0	0	0
Gooden p	3	0	0	0
Totals	33	4	11	3

CHI	0 0 0 0 0 0 0 2 0	-	2	6	3
NYM	0 0 2 0 1 0 1 0 X	-	4	11	0

Cubs	IP	H	R	ER	BB	SO
Eckersley L (6-10)	4.1	8	3	3	0	7
Hoffman	1.2	1	0	0	2	0
DiPino	2	2	1	0	0	1
Totals	8	11	4	3	2	8

Mets	IP	H	R	ER	BB	SO
Gooden W (15-6)	9	6	2	2	5	8
Totals	9	6	2	2	5	8

E—Chicago Eckersley, Durham, Walker. DP—Chicago; New York. 2B—Chicago Dunston, Sandberg; New York Dykstra, Carter, Knight. HR—Chicago Palmeiro (2). SH—New York Backman, Gooden. LOB—Chicago 8; New York 9. SB—Chicago Sandberg. Attendance: 47,823.

Dwight Gooden went the distance, giving up two runs on six hits with eight strikeouts. Gooden got the final out when he retired future Met Chico Walker on a ground-out to second baseman Wally Backman, and the Mets were back in the playoffs.

Many in the crowd began the pour onto the field, despite the presence of uniformed guards. Mets general manager Frank Cashen was not happy with the fans' behavior as he told reporter Jack O'Connell.

"For the life of me, I can't understand what makes people think they have the right to destroy a ballpark," Cashen said. "I have been asked if this puts a pall on what we have accomplished this year, and I have to say that it does."

Approximately 8,000 fans sang and danced on the field for more than half an hour, but there were still games to be played.

Mets head groundskeeper Pete Flynn was confident they could get the field in shape to play.

"I'm putting 20 men to work through the night re-sodding it," Flynn said. "There's heavy damage everywhere. The infield is a mess. It won't be 100 percent but we'll have a game."

A frustrated Flynn told O'Connell, "We've got a first-place team and last-place fans."

Mets first baseman Dave Magadan was in the lineup for Keith Hernandez, who was battling the flu and a 102-degree fever. Magadan came through with three hits.

Hernandez got into the game as a defensive replacement and caught the final putout. After Magadan got his third hit, Hernandez reportedly kidded manager Dave Johnson by saying, "Maybe you should trade me."

In the third inning, Magadan broke the scoreless tie with an RBI single. Darryl Strawberry's RBI single made it 2–0.

Magadan and Strawberry added RBI singles in the fifth and seventh innings, respectively, to make it 4–0.

Gooden faltered in the eighth inning when he gave up a two-run homer to Cubs rookie Rafael Palmeiro, but that was all Chicago would get.

According to O'Connell, the players were just as "happy" in the clubhouse as the fans who were celebrating on the field.

Ron Darling, Bobby Ojeda, Roger McDowell, Jesse Orosco, Howard Johnson, Darryl Strawberry, Rafael Santana and Rick Aguilera stormed Mets manager Dave Johnson's office, pelted him with a shaving-cream pie, anointed him with champagne, stuffed ice down his back and carried him off to the shower.

"Not you, too, Aggie," Johnson said to Aguilera, not a regular member, as were the others, of what was known as the "Scum Bunch."

"Sorry, skip, it's tradition," Aguilera said.

Magical Rally Lifts Mets Past Bucs in 9th

An improbable ninth-inning rally gave the Mets a stunning 6–5 win over the Pittsburgh Pirates before 12,336 at Three Rivers Stadium.

The Mets were trailing 4–1, but out of nowhere came some magic that emanated from the 1973 season as a whole. With one out, Jim Beauchamp singled and Wayne Garrett doubled against Pirates pitcher Ramon Hernandez. Felix Millan scored both runners with a two-run triple to right-center field that split the outfielders to make it a 4–3 game.

After Rusty Staub walked, the managerial wheels were put in motion by both skippers. First, Mets manager Yogi Berra sent up right-handed hitting Duffy Dyer to bat for Tug McGraw, who was surprisingly inserted into the game in the seventh inning because the Mets were trailing 4–1.

Pirates manager Danny Murtaugh countered by going to the bullpen for

Felix Millan was part of an impressive group of players who signed for the 1973 season. Mets Manager Yogi Berra, center, poses in the team cart at Shea Stadium. (Back row, from left) Ed Kranepool, Berra and Tug McGraw. (Front row, from left) Millan and John Milner. Cleon Jones also signed, but was not present for the picture session.

right-hander Dave Giusti. Berra did him one better as he sent up Ron Hodges to bat for Dyer with runners on first and third base and one out. Hodges delivered with a single to right to score Millan with the tying run. Teddy Martinez ran for Hodges and after Cleon Jones walked to load the bases, Don Hahn delivered a two-out, two-run single to give the Mets a 6–4 lead.

Mets pitcher Bob Apodaca made his major league debut to begin the home half of the ninth and he promptly walked the first two hitters that he faced. Berra had to go back to the bullpen to bring in right-hander Buzz Capra.

At a Glance

WP: McGraw (5–6)

Key stat: Mets bullpen 6 IP, 1 R

A sacrifice bunt by Pirates second baseman Dave Cash moved the runners up and the Mets traded a run for an out on a ground-out by Al Oliver.

The Mets put the winning run on base by intentionally walking Willie Stargell, and it almost backfired when Richie Zisk walked, which put the winning run into scoring position.

Manny Sanguillen, who almost never walked, worked the count to 3–1 against Capra, but the 25-year-old reliever got the Pirates' catcher to fly out to left.

September 18, 1963

Final Game at the Polo Grounds

A crowd of 1,752 showed up for the final game ever played at the Polo Grounds.

The Mets were supposed to move into Shea Stadium in August 1963, but the construction of the ballpark was being delayed, so this became the last game.

At 4:21 PM Eastern, pinch-hitter Ted Schreiber grounded into a 4–6–3 double play to end an era on W. 155th Street and 8th Avenue as the Mets closed the place with a 5–1 loss to the Philadelphia Phillies.

Mays Bids Farewell Before 'Ball on the Wall Miracle'

The signature game of the 1973 season became known as the "ball on the wall miracle."

On the same day that future Hall of Famer and all-time great Willie Mays announced that 1973 would be his final season as a player, the Mets stunned the Pittsburgh Pirates with a 4–3 win in 13 innings at Shea Stadium before a crowd of 24,855.

The "ball on the wall" event in the top of the 13th inning would never have happened had it not been for Mets catcher Duffy Dyer.

The Mets trailed Pittsburgh 3–2 in the bottom of the ninth when Dyer's two-out, pinch-hit double brought home Ken Boswell with the tying run.

In the top of the 13th inning, Richie Zisk singled with one out. Manny Sanguillen flied out to right field for the second out. The next batter was Pirates center fielder Dave Augustine, who slammed a Ray Sadecki pitch and hit it deep to left field. Cleon Jones went back, but the ball looked like it was going to go over the fence for a two-run homer. Instead, the ball hit the top of the wall and bounded back to Jones.

The Mets left fielder fired a strike to the cutoff man, shortstop Wayne Garrett, who fired a strike to catcher Ron Hodges at the plate. Hodges properly blocked the plate and applied the tag on Zisk to keep the game tied.

John Milner led off the 13th with a walk. After Boswell walked, the Pirates replaced losing pitcher Luke Walker with Dave Giusti, who had failed in his previous relief appearance against the Mets (see: Sept. 18, 1973). Don Hahn failed on a sacrifice attempt as he popped out to first.

> ### At a Glance
> **WP:** Sadecki (5-4)
>
> **Key stat:** Sadecki allows 2 hits, strikes out 6 in 4 innings of shutout relief; Cash 3-for-6, RBI, 2B

Hodges came up and ended a memorable day with a line single to left-center field to score Milner with the winning run.

Both starting pitchers, Jim Rooker of the Pirates and Jerry Koosman of the Mets, were stingy in a tightly contested game. Rooker gave up two runs on five hits in eight innings pitched. Koosman matched his opposite number with eight innings, giving up two runs (one unearned) on four hits with eight strikeouts.

An rare error by shortstop Bud Harrelson allowed the Bucs to take a 1–0 lead in the fourth inning, but the Mets tied the game in the sixth on a clutch two-out single by Jones.

Future Met Richie Hebner homered off Koosman in the seventh inning to give the Pirates a 2–1 lead, but the Mets tied it a second time in the eighth inning on Felix Millan's single.

Pittsburgh took its third lead of the game in the ninth inning on a two-out RBI double by Dave Cash before the Mets sent the game into extra innings on Dyer's big hit.

Before the game, Mays announced that he was calling it quits, effective at the end of the 1973 season. Mays became emotional while making the announcement.

"Maybe I'll cry tomorrow," said the 42-year old Mays, who would play 22 years in the majors.

"It's been a wonderful 22 years," he said, "and I'm not getting out of baseball because I'm hurt. I just feel that the people of America shouldn't have to see a guy play who can't produce."

Mays was hitting just .211 in 66 games with six home runs and saw the writing on the wall.

"It was my decision alone," Mays said as he warded off any suggestions that he was being pressured to retire. "I'm not ashamed of the way things have gone the last couple of months. They didn't run me out. In San Francisco, I don't think I would have played this year. The people would have run me out of the city. In New York, they let me hit .211."

Mays played 135 games in two years with the Mets. He hit 14 of his 660 career home runs and had 44 of his 1,903 career RBIs while playing in Queens.

Hodges spent his entire 12-year big-league career with the Mets and was known for his defensive skills behind the plate. In 1983, Hodges caught a career-high 96 games and made 110 appearances.

Emotions Run Deep in Tribute to Post-9/11 America

One of the most emotional games in the history of the New York Mets began with their players hugging opposing players from the Atlanta Braves in a show of solidarity.

"I had a tear in my eye as soon as I stepped on the line," Mets reliever John Franco said. "I've been having a tear in my eye since this stuff happened."

That "stuff" that the Brooklyn-born Franco was referring to was the most horrific act on American soil in the history of the United States. It was 10 days after two planes slammed into the Twin Towers at the World Trade Center in New York City. Thousands of innocent people died and the entire country was propelled into a state of shock.

Major League Baseball shut down for a week until President George W. Bush gave Commissioner Bud Selig the go-ahead to resume the games.

Mets broadcaster Howie Rose was working TV for that game.

> ### At a Glance
> **WP:** Benitez (6-3)
>
> **HR:** Piazza (34)
>
> **Key stat:** Piazza 3-for-4, 2 RBIs, HR, 2 2B

"I had no interest in resuming the season," Rose said during an interview.

Four days earlier, the Mets resumed their schedule in Pittsburgh, but this game was the first significant sporting event in the city since the 9/11 disaster. In a matter of hours on that fateful day, lives dramatically changed. Instead of being able to enter the ballpark in a quick and easy manner, fans now had to pass through security checkpoints. Bags were now being searched and anytime a plane took off from nearby LaGuardia Airport, people immediately looked to the sky.

The Federal Aviation Administration banned any flights over the ballpark, but the ambient noise left fans a little "spooked."

On the field, there were painted ribbons of red, white and blue. The messages on top of the dugouts read "God Bless America" and "Welcome to New York City." Both were flanked by American flags.

Mike Piazza gestures to fans following the end of the Mets' 3–2 win over the Atlanta Braves on Sept. 21, 2001. The emotionally charged game at Shea Stadium—the first major sporting event in New York City since 9/11—proved to be part of the healing process in New York.

September 21, 2001
Mets 3, Braves 2

The stylized city skyline, above the scoreboard in right field at Shea, had a red, white and blue ribbon placed in front of the Twin Towers of the World Trade Center.

Before the players staged their emotional embrace, there was a stirring rendition of *God Bless America* by Diana Ross.

After a moment of silence and a 21-gun salute by the United States Marine Corps, pop star Marc Anthony sang *The Star Spangled Banner*, accompanied by 41,235 fans.

The Mets resumed the baseball season in Pittsburgh on Sept. 17. During the three-game series in Pittsburgh, the Mets wore hats during the game to honor New York City police, fire, and emergency medical services workers, many of whom gave their lives to help people during the crisis.

Mets owner Fred Wilpon asked Major League Baseball for permission for his team to wear those hats for the rest of the season, and that request was granted.

The Mets also added the infamous date (9/11/01) and an American flag on either side of their uniform sleeves.

After police, fire and rescue workers threw out the ceremonial first pitch, the game finally got underway as things seemed to be returning to normal for all who were affected by the tragedy.

Al Leiter was not scheduled to pitch, but he tried to put the return of baseball in its proper perspective.

"We knew what it meant to the world, our playing baseball again," the left-hander said.

The teams traded runs in the fourth inning, but Atlanta took a 2–1 lead in the eighth inning on Brian Jordan's RBI double.

With one out, Edgardo Alfonzo walked. Desi Relaford pinch ran for Alfonzo and Mike Piazza stepped to the plate against local product and Braves reliever Steve Karsay.

There was a buzz that encircled the crowd and filtered into the Mets dugout. "It's one of those moments everybody on the bench thinks it's going to happen," Mets first baseman Todd Zeile said. "We've got the right guy up there, got a guy on. How more fitting could this possibly be?"

Piazza drilled a 0–1 offering from Karsay and lined it off the middle tier of a three-tier camera stand in center field for a two-run homer and a 3–2 lead.

The slugging catcher got a curtain call from the fans who not only appreciated the home run, but the moment as well.

Piazza's home run was the seminal "bookmark" of the game, where it seemed all right to enjoy baseball once again.

The Mets donated their "game checks" to help those in need. Piazza's donation was more than $68,000 dollars, but you couldn't put a price on what his home run meant.

"It's not life or death," he said, "with so many thousands of people down there, (trapped in the rubble at the World Trade Center) sacrifice is life and death, baseball's not."

Armando Benitez, who was already in the game and got the win, closed it out when he induced a game-ending double play from Keith Lockhart.

After the final out, *America the Beautiful*, sung by Ray Charles, played on the loudspeakers.

Fans were standing and singing along, waving flags and holding banners. A chant of "U-S-A, U-S-A!" went up as the public address announcer read the final stats.

"I truly felt like we were just spectators tonight," Piazza said. "The way they saluted their fallen brothers and sisters, just a lot of emotion. Taking the game out of it, it was just a really, really incredible ceremony."

"We've been to the World Series," said Zeile, who wore a New York Police Department hat and a Fire Department T-shirt. "I think everyone on this field will tell you tonight's game was more important than any game in the World Series."

Darling's Gem Lifts Mets to Fourth NL East Title

The Mets beat the Philadelphia Phillies 3–1 to clinch their fourth National League East Division title before 45,274 fans at Shea Stadium.

Ron Darling was brilliant as he allowed one run on six hits in going the distance. The 28-year-old right-hander struck out Phillies catcher Lance Parrish for the final out and the celebration was underway.

The Mets stormed into their clubhouse to begin the "champagne ritual," while the fans were well behaved and enjoyed the moment from the stands, unlike two years earlier, when the field was torn to pieces by fans who stormed the field after the Mets clinched the division title.

This time there was an "army" of police officers who enveloped the field on horseback, not to mention an additional 800 on foot.

The Mets were going against their ol' nemesis in Phillies left-hander Don Carman, who had previously beaten them three times.

Philly took a 1–0 lead in the fourth inning on a sacrifice fly by Von Hayes, but the Mets tied the game with a run in the fifth.

The Mets took a 2–1 lead in the sixth inning when Carman threw a wild pitch that allowed Darryl Strawberry to score from third base.

The Mets added their third and final run in the seventh inning. With Mookie Wilson at second base, McReynolds beat out an infield hit toward third. When Phillies first baseman Ricky Jordan argued the call—without calling for time—Wilson took off and scored easily.

> ### At a Glance
> **WP:** Darling (16–9)
>
> **Key stat:** Darling CG 6-hitter; Wilson 3-for-4

The ninth inning was "electric." Darling struck out Hayes for the first out and got future Met Juan Samuel on a comebacker to the mound before Parrish struck out to end it.

In the raucous postgame celebration, Mets manager Dave Johnson (who became the first Mets skipper to win two divisional titles) said, "I think a lot of people in New York expect to see us as a super team. They expect us to win more games than we do. And it's always tougher to win when everybody expects you to win."

Harrelson's RBI Single Helps Mets Overcome Gibson, Clinch a Tie

The Mets clinched a tie for the National League East Division title as they got by the St. Louis Cardinals and future Hall of Famer (and future Mets pitching coach) Bob Gibson 3–2 in 11 innings.

Bud Harrelson's walk-off, one-out RBI single scored Ron Swoboda with the winning run.

The Mets had only beaten Gibson five times in 27 previous decisions, so they knew they'd have their hands full when the game began.

Bud Harrelson kept things Amazin' when he drove in the winning run in a 3–2 win over the St. Louis Cardinals in 11 innings on Sept. 23, 1969.

September 23, 1969
Mets 3, Cardinals 2 (11 innings)

The Mets broke through against the Cardinals' ace in the third inning on a RBI single by Wayne Garrett.

St. Louis took a 2–1 lead in the fifth inning, thanks to a pair of unearned runs off starter Jim McAndrew. Future Hall of Famer Lou Brock and Curt Flood singled with two out. Second baseman Ken Boswell booted a grounder by Vada Pinson as Brock scored the tying run. Future Mets manager Joe Torre lined a single off McAndrew's leg to tie the game 2–2.

In the eighth inning, the Cardinals had the bases loaded and two outs with Gibson, a terrific hitting pitcher, at the plate.

Gibson hit a sinking line drive into right field that seemed destined to drop in, but Swoboda made a diving catch to deny the Cardinals any more runs.

In the home half, Tommie Agee singled, was bunted to second and scored on Art Shamsky's single to right.

With one out in the 11th, Swoboda beat out an infield single to deep short.

Jerry Grote hit a ball off of Cards second baseman Julian Javier's glove to put the winning run in scoring position.

> ### At a Glance
>
> **WP:** McGraw (9–3)
>
> **Key stat:** McAndrew 7 IP, 2 runs (unearned); Swoboda 2-for-5, run

A crowd of 44,080 at Shea Stadium saw Harrelson take a 1–2 pitch from Gibson and knock it into left-center field for the game-winning hit.

Tug McGraw pitched four scoreless innings of relief to earn the win.

A win over the Cardinals the next night (see: Sept. 24, 1969) or a Cubs loss to the Expos the following afternoon would give the Mets their initial National League East Division crown.

'The game is over. The Mets are the champions.'

The New York Mets shocked the baseball world as they wrapped up their first—and the inaugural—National League East Division title with their 6–0 whitewashing of the St. Louis Cardinals before 54,928 excited fans at Shea Stadium.

Rookie right-hander Gary Gentry went the distance on a four-hitter and was on the mound when future Mets manager Joe Torre bounced into a game-ending 6–4–3 double play.

"It was unbelievable," Gentry said. "I couldn't tell you how excited I was before the game."

Mets TV announcer Lindsey Nelson was at the mic when the final out was recorded.

"Ground ball to short, this could be it. There's one, there's two, the game is over. The Mets are the champions. At 9:07 on Sept. 24, the Mets have won the championship of the East Division of the National League."

The fans stormed the field, while the players retreated to the clubhouse to begin the ceremonial champagne-filled celebration.

The game was hardly in doubt as the Mets put up five runs in the bottom of the first inning.

Donn Clendenon hit the first of his two home runs—a three-run shot—and Ed Charles added a two-run blow to make it 5–0 against losing pitcher and future Hall of Famer Steve Carlton.

> ## At a Glance
>
> **WP:** Gentry (12-12)
>
> **HR:** Clendenon 2 (14,15), Charles (3)
>
> **Key stat:** Gentry complete game 4-hitter; Clendenon 2-for-3, 4 RBIs, HR; Charles 2-for-4, 2 RBIs, HR

Clendenon took a curveball from Carlton and put it over 410-foot mark in center field.

"I knew I got it all. I didn't think any ballpark in the world would hold that one," the first baseman said after the game.

Clendenon's second home run of the game put the icing on the cake.

In the postgame locker room celebration, Mets manager Gil Hodges, who had been part of a World Championship team with the Brooklyn Dodgers, said this was his "biggest thrill in baseball."

"Because of the way these boys had been coming on, and held lightly regarded that the opening of the season, they're startin to hit their way around,

around the last part of May and comin on and doin the job, it was just great," Hodges said.

Mets second baseman Ken Boswell didn't mind the celebration.

"I'm glad we won it here in New York," Boswell said. "I think they deserve it more then we do almost."

The aftermath of the celebration by the fans made the Shea Stadium field look like it was hit by a tornado. Chunks of the field (estimates ranged from 1,000 to 1,500 square feet of sod) were torn up and taken by fans for souvenirs.

The flag in center field was stolen, while one fan put up a banner after climbing a light tower.

The field was littered with papers, programs, ice cream containers and beer cans.

Three wheels on the batting cage were broken and the netting was stripped, while the "coup de grace" came in the theft of home plate.

Head groundskeeper John McCarthy summed it up best.

"It usually takes us four hours to clean up," he said. "This time it'll take us four days."

The Mets were 100–1 longshots to win the World Championship, so this first step was a huge surprise in itself. The Mets went on to beat the Atlanta Braves in the National League Championship Series and the heavily favored Baltimore Orioles in the World Series.

Future Hall of Famer Tom Seaver recently reflected on the division clincher, where he intimated that the long odds did not reflect the attitude of the team.

"Everybody was on the same page," Seaver said. "That's kinda of a dream come true for everybody. There's a 'little boy' in all of us."

Aspromonte's Pinch Single Scores Foli for Game-Winner

Bob Aspromonte's pinch-hit single scored Tim Foli with the winning run in the bottom of the 15th inning as the Mets "walked off" with a 2–1 win over the Pittsburgh Pirates at Shea Stadium.

Most of the 29,965 fans remained throughout the three hour and 50 minute marathon to see Foli start the winning rally with a single to left off left-hander and losing pitcher Ramon Hernandez.

Winning pitcher Danny Frisella laid down a perfect sacrifice bunt to move Foli to second base, but Bud Harrelson flied out to center for the second out.

The Pirates elected to intentionally walk Leroy Stanton and pitch to the left-handed hitting Dave Marshall.

Mets manager Gil Hodges sent up the right-handed hitting Aspromonte. He picked on Hernandez's first pitch and lined a ball just past second base.

The throw from Pirates center fielder Gene Clines appeared to beat Foli to the plate, but the 20-year-old second baseman cleverly slid under the tag of catcher Manny Sanguillen as home-plate umpire Billy Williams signaled safe.

The Mets took a 1–0 lead in the third inning. Harrelson doubled and scored on Cleon Jones' one-out sacrifice fly.

Pittsburgh tied it in the fourth as Carl Taylor tripled and scored on a wild pitch by starter Jon Matlack.

Both starters were on top of their games. Left-hander Bob Johnson gave up a run on four hits in nine innings. Matlack tossed eight innings and gave up a run on five hits.

The bullpens were just as good. Bob Veale and John Lamb held the Mets down for five innings, while Tug McGraw and Frisella kept the Pirates in check for seven scoreless innings.

At a Glance

WP: Frisella (8–5)

Key stat: Matlack 8 IP, 1 run; Agee 2-for-5

Santana Shows His Brilliance in 3-Hitter

Johan Santana was brilliant as he went the distance on a three-hit shutout in beating the Florida Marlins 2–0.

A crowd of 54,920 turned out for what was the penultimate game ever played at Shea Stadium.

What made Santana's game even more remarkable, it was later discovered, was that he was pitching with a bad knee. Five days after tossing his gem, Santana underwent arthroscopic surgery to repair a torn meniscus in his left knee.

"What Santana did that day was take the Mets club on his back and willed his way to victory," said Mets radio broadcaster Wayne Hagin, who worked the game. "It was a stunning exhibit of tenacity, guile, and talent."

Johan Santana delivers a pitch during his three-hitter against the Marlins on Sept. 27, 2008. It was the second-to-last game ever at Shea Stadium. Santana's 206 strikeouts in 2008 set a Mets record for left-handers.

Santana was hurting throughout September, but he demanded to take the ball.

"He told me that the only way he was not going to finish the season was if they took him to the hospital in an ambulance," agent Chris Leible said. "He went on his own two feet."

In his previous start, Santana threw a career-high 125 pitches in beating the Cubs.

Santana was on top of his game and was rarely in trouble, except for in the fifth inning. Cody Ross singled to lead off the inning and Jeremy Hermida walked with one out. Pitcher Ricky Nolasco sacrificed the runners to second and third base, but Santana intentionally walked Hanley Ramirez and worked out of the inning by getting John Baker on a lineout to right field.

At a Glance

WP: Santana (16–7)

Key stat: Santana CG 3-hitter, 9 Ks

Santana threw 104 pitches through eight innings but he came out to start the ninth.

The Met fans erupted in cheers once Santana darted out of the dugout to pitch the ninth. They then serenaded him with chants of "Jo-han, Jo-han!" as Jorge Cantu stepped into the batter's box to open the final frame.

When Endy Chavez settled under a shot by Cody Ross to deep left to strand Josh Willingham at second base for the final out, catcher Ramon Castro hugged Santana near the mound.

Asked if he wondered whether the shot by Ross would clear the wall for a game-tying homer, Santana said succinctly: "No. We had Endy over there."

Santana's surgery went well and he was back on the mound for the 2009 opening game in Cincinnati.

Mets Close 44-Year Run at Shea with Memorable Ceremony

After Hall of Famer Tom Seaver threw the ceremonial final pitch, Mike Piazza walked to the mound and arm-in-arm, the two great Mets walked toward center field to officially close Shea Stadium.

Shea Stadium housed some memorable games during its 44-year run, and now the Mets were saying goodbye.

Ryan Church became the answer to a trivia question when he flied out to Florida's Cameron Maybin in center field to postmark him as the final batter in the history of the ballpark. The Mets ended their tenure at Shea by dropping a 4–2 decision to the Marlins in front of 56,059 fans.

Following the game, the Mets honored their history at Shea by bringing back the names from the past. Players were introduced as they came in from beyond the outfield walls in right- and left-center field. The list included Len Dykstra, Wally Backman, Jerry Koosman and Ed Charles.

Keith Hernandez, Ron Darling and Darryl Strawberry received the loudest ovations and one of the more emotional intros occurred when Dwight Gooden reappeared at Shea after a long absence.

Gooden received a thunderous ovation from the fans and as he entered the field. He reached out to grab some of them along the railing as he walked by.

Last but not least were Seaver and Piazza.

Seaver let go of the "last pitch" to be thrown at Shea. It bounced in the dirt but no matter, the ceremony was complete.

Maine Looks Like a Champ with 14 Ks

John Maine came within four outs of a no-hitter and struck out a career-high 14 batters in blanking the Florida Marlins 13–0 before 54,675 at Shea Stadium.

With two outs in the eighth inning, Marlins catcher Paul Hoover (who was in the game because starting catcher Miguel Olivo was ejected in the fifth inning) spoiled the no-hit bid with an infield single.

Mets third baseman David Wright had no play on the little dribbler.

"I don't think he could've rolled it any better," Wright said.

"David's so far back. It's just one of those things," Maine said. "It's unfortunate."

At that point, the 26-year-old right-hander had thrown 115 pitches. With the one-sided score, Mets manager Willie Randolph decided to pull him.

The game featured a brawl that was ignited between Mets shortstop Jose Reyes and Olivo. In the fifth inning, second baseman Luis Castillo walked toward the mound, bat in hand, after he was brushed back by Marlins pitcher Harvey Garcia.

At a Glance

WP: Maine (15–10)

HR: Milledge 2 (6,7), Castro (11)

Key stat: Maine 7 ⅔ IP, 1 H, 14 Ks; Milledge 3-for-5, 3 runs, 3 RBIs; Wright 3-for-4, 3 runs

Both benches and bullpens emptied as both clubs were simply milling around home plate.

After a brief delay, play resumed. Castillo walked and Marlins manager Fredi Gonzalez came out to make a double switch.

Reyes, who was on third base, was jawing with Olivo, who was standing on the mound during the pitching change. Reyes said he was kidding with Olivo, but it turned into something more serious. Suddenly, Olivo charged Reyes and took a swing at him.

Third base coach Sandy Alomar held off Olivo, and Florida third baseman Miguel Cabrera grabbed Reyes as both teams poured onto the field.

Olivo was ejected and replaced by Hoover. Reyes remained in the game.

The Mets acquired Maine from the Baltimore Orioles in January 2006 for pitcher Kris Benson. Maine's best year was 2007, when he went 15–10 with a 3.91 ERA.

'Ya Gotta Believe' After a Win and Rain in Doubleheader

One of the most bizarre "pennant" races in National League history came to a close, a day after the regular-season schedule was originally slated to end.

Bad weather in Chicago forced the Mets and Cubs to finish their seasons with back-to-back doubleheaders.

The first of those two was played on Sunday, Sept. 30, which was supposed to be the final day of the regular season. The Mets lost the first game 1–0 but they clinched a tie for the National League East Division title with a 9–2 victory in the nightcap.

So all they needed was to win one game to clinch their second National League East Division title. But they were not only battling the Cubs—weather was once again a factor.

The game began at 11:20 AM before 1,913 die-hard fans at Wrigley Field, and the Mets grabbed a 1–0 lead in the second inning on a Cleon Jones home run into the bleachers in right-center field.

> ### At a Glance
> **WP:** Seaver (19-10)
>
> **HR:** Jones (11)
>
> **Key stat:** Staub 4-for-5, 2 runs; McGraw 3 shutout innings in relief; Grote 2-for-4, 2 RBIs; Staub 4-for-5, RBI

Jerry Grote's two-run single in the fourth inning made it 3–0.

Tom Seaver, who was reportedly pitching with a tender right shoulder, gutted it out for six innings. Despite giving up four runs on 11 hits, Seaver did not walk a batter, so he was able to limit the damage.

After Rick Monday's two-run homer in the seventh inning, Mets manager Yogi Berra lifted Seaver in favor of Tug McGraw, who coined the phrase, "Ya Gotta Believe," which became a rallying cry down the stretch.

The fiery closer finished the game with three scoreless innings but not without some drama in the bottom of the ninth.

Cubs catcher Ken Rudolph led off with a single. One out later, pinch-hitter Glenn Beckert hit a soft liner toward first base, where first baseman John Milner grabbed the ball and stepped on first base to complete the game-ending double play.

Rusty Staub led the offense with four hits and felt good about what the club had accomplished. "A couple of months ago we were out of it and then we really put it together," he said.

Berra was famous for being on hand for some of baseball's greatest moments, but he seemed to appreciate this division championship the most.

"I'm glad it's over," Berra said. "I never gave up and neither did the players. We had to go over five clubs to get here, and that makes you proud."

The Mets had to wait for the official word that the second game was not going to be played because of the weather. Once that came down, the real celebrating began.

There were 11 holdovers from the 1969 World Championship team including Seaver, who refused to get into any comparisons with that team.

"Nothing will ever be like 1969," Seaver said. "We were all so young then. Anyhow, we've only taken one step of the three. We still have to win a playoff and World Series to match 1969. But in a way, this was more earned."

October 1, 1985

Mets Beat Cardinals as Strawberry Beats the Clock with a Shot

Darryl Strawberry hit one of the longest home runs in Mets history when he blasted a monster shot in the top of the 11th inning that hit the Longines clock in right-center field at Busch Stadium to give the Mets a 1–0 win over the St. Louis Cardinals.

A crowd of 46,026 watched Ron Darling duel Cards starter John Tudor to a scoreless draw through nine innings. Tudor pitched the 10th inning and then Ken Dayley relieved him to start the 11th.

After the Cards' southpaw struck out Keith Hernandez and Gary Carter, Strawberry unloaded on a 1–1 pitch that traveled an estimated 440 feet and struck the clock, which read 10:44 PM Central.

"It was a mistake pitch," Strawberry said after the game. "A hanging curve. You want to be up there in that situation, you want to help..."

Reed's Best Game Ever Includes 3 Hits, 12 Ks

Rick Reed picked a good time to throw the best game he ever pitched in a Mets uniform.

The 35-year-old right-hander dominated the Pittsburgh Pirates to the tune of a 7–0, three-hit shutout that featured a career-high 12 strikeouts before a crowd of 36,878 at Shea Stadium.

Reed's outstanding effort enabled the Mets to control their own destiny in the NL wild-card race because the Cincinnati Reds lost in Milwaukee.

Going into the final day of the regular season, the Mets were tied with the Reds. The Mets could assure themselves of at least one more game if they could win the season finale on Sunday (see: Oct. 3, 1999).

Pittsburgh starter Francisco Cordova kept the Pirates in it with five scoreless innings, but the Mets broke through in the sixth.

A pair of errors helped the Mets score twice for a 2–0 lead.

In the bottom of the eighth inning, the Mets had runners on second and third base with no one out and Reed due up. Matt Franco was in the on-deck circle to bat for Melvin Mora, but the crowd thought he would bat for Reed, so they booed manager Bobby Valentine.

Reed was sent up to hit and, using fellow pitcher Masato Yoshii's bat, he stroked a two-run single for a 4–0 lead and the crowd went berserk.

Mike Piazza capped off the scoring with his 40th home run.

> ## At a Glance
> **WP:** Reed (11–5)
> **HR:** Piazza (40)
> **Key stat:** Reed 9 IP, 3 H, 12 Ks

Reed went out to the mound for the ninth inning amidst a thundering ovation. Adrian Brown singled to lead off the inning, but Reed induced Al Martin to bounce into a double play. Abraham Nunez was caught looking for Reed's 12th strikeout and the Mets had a huge win.

Valentine appreciated what he saw from his starting pitcher.

"I don't know if he was behind five hitters all night," Valentine said.

Mets Take Care of Pirates to Force One-Game Playoff

One of the most bizarre and rewarding days in Mets history ended nearly 12 hours after it began.

On Sunday, 50,111 were on hand when the first pitch of the Mets' crucial game against the Pittsburgh Pirates was thrown at 1:40 PM. The day would not be over until approximately 12:30 AM Monday morning, when the Cincinnati Reds finally beat the Brewers in Milwaukee.

As the teams entered the final, scheduled day of the regular season, the Mets and Reds were tied in the National League wild-card race.

Their good fortune in the standings was miraculous in itself, because the Mets were two games behind the Reds with three to play.

"Three days ago the entire world said we were dead," Matt Franco said. "Now, at worst, we're in a one-game playoff."

On the final weekend of the regular season, the Mets hosted the Pittsburgh Pirates at Shea Stadium, while the Reds played the Brewers in Milwaukee.

The Mets won the first two games against the Pirates, while the Reds were losing twice in Milwaukee.

So the race came down to Sunday, the final day, as the teams were tied entering play.

At a Glance

WP: Benitez (4-3)
Key stat: Young 2-for-4, RBI

If both teams won or lost, there would be a one-game playoff to determine the wild-card winner. If there were one winner, that team would go on to the National League Division Series against Arizona.

The Mets, who faced a "must-win" situation, independent of what went on in Milwaukee, beat the Pirates 2–1 on a "walk-off" wild pitch.

The teams were tied 1–1 in the bottom of the ninth inning and the Mets had the bases loaded with one out.

With Mike Piazza at the plate, Pirates pitcher Brad Clontz uncorked a wild pitch that allowed Melvin Mora to scamper home with the winning run.

The Mets stormed out of the dugout to congratulate each other at home plate but the job was not finished yet. The Mets had to wait to see the final result of the game in Milwaukee. If the Reds won, the Mets would fly to Cincinnati for a one-game playoff the next night. If Cincy lost, the Mets would fly to Arizona to open the NLDS against the Diamondbacks.

Either way, Al Leiter was going to pitch the next game.

"I was starting the next game, either the next night or in two days," Leiter said during an interview.

While the Mets' game ended in dramatic fashion, the Reds' game in Milwaukee had not started and was being delayed by rain.

As the Mets prepared to go to the airport to get on a plane for "parts unknown," the Reds game finally began at 9:50 PM Eastern.

Players, personnel from the front office, broadcasters and even the beat reporters had their future plans put on hold until they knew the final score in Milwaukee.

"Seven hours and we still don't know," longtime Mets broadcaster Gary Cohen said. "We flew to Cincinnati before we knew the result."

The Mets flew to the "Queen City" with the thought that if they were to play the Reds, they would be well rested because it was going to be played on Monday night. If not, they would fly to Arizona to open the NLDS on Tuesday.

There would be a game (see: Oct. 4, 1999) in Cincinnati.

The Reds took a 5–0 lead in the third inning and never looked back. Two hours and 36 minutes after the first pitch in Milwaukee, the Reds finished a 7–1 win that set up a one-game playoff the next night against the Mets.

Leiter Lights Up Reds in One-Game Playoff

Al Leiter had his finest moment as a Met as he tossed a complete game two-hitter to lead the Mets to a 5–0 win over the Cincinnati Reds in a one-game playoff at Cinergy Field. The victory lifted the Mets to their fifth postseason appearance and their first in 11 years.

Leiter pitched in big games before—he started Game 7 of the 1997 World Series for Florida—so it wasn't as if this was the first time.

"I was comfortable, I was confident, but I was nervous," Leiter said during an interview.

Leiter was superb, even though there was a point where he was trying to find his game.

"First two innings, I was wild with command," he said. "After the third inning, I started to get the feeling that they were a little anxious. I knew I had something special going when they started swinging at a lot of my sliders and hitting them way foul."

The 33-year-old lefty had all of his pitches working as he dazzled the Reds with a sharp-breaking curveball and a "biting" slider that had late movement.

The Mets' bats clicked right away to provide Leiter with a 2–0 lead before he even took the mound.

Future Hall of Famer Rickey Henderson led off with a single to left. Edgardo Alfonzo followed with a long home run to center field off starter and loser Steve Parris. Suddenly, the Mets had seized some early momentum.

Robin Ventura's bases-loaded walk in the third inning made it 3–0.

Henderson homered against reliever Denny Neagle to lead off the fifth inning and Alfonzo's RBI double gave the Mets a 5–0 lead in the sixth inning.

Leiter made it stand up and his dominance silenced the crowd of 54,621.

Mets	AB	R	H	RBI
Henderson lf	5	2	2	1
Mora lf	0	0	0	0
Alfonzo 2b	4	2	2	3
Olerud 1b	5	0	2	0
Piazza c	2	0	0	0
Ventura 3b	3	0	1	1
Hamilton cf	4	0	1	0
Cedeno rf	4	0	1	0
Ordonez ss	3	1	0	0
Leiter p	3	0	0	0
Totals	33	5	9	5

Reds	AB	R	H	RBI
Reese 2b	3	0	1	0
Larkin ss	3	0	0	0
Casey 1b	4	0	0	0
Vaughn lf	3	0	0	0
Young rf	4	0	0	0
Hammonds cf	3	0	1	0
Taubensee c	2	0	0	0
Boone 3b	3	0	0	0
Parris p	0	0	0	0
Neagle p	1	0	0	0
Stynes ph	1	0	0	0
Graves p	0	0	0	0
Lewis ph	1	0	0	0
Reyes p	0	0	0	0
Totals	28	0	2	0

NYM	2	0	1	0	1	1	0	0	0	-	5	9	0
CIN	0	0	0	0	0	0	0	0	0	-	0	2	0

Mets	IP	H	R	ER	BB	SO
Leiter W (13-12)	9	2	0	0	4	7
Totals	9	2	0	0	4	7

Reds	IP	H	R	ER	BB	SO
Parris L (11-4)	2.2	3	3	3	3	1
Neagle	2.1	2	1	1	3	2
Graves	3	2	1	1	2	2
Reyes	1	2	0	0	0	0
Totals	9	9	5	5	8	5

DP—New York; Cincinnati 2. 2B—New York Olerud, Alfonzo; Cincinnati Reese. HR—New York Alfonzo (27), Henderson (12). SF—New York Leiter. LOB—New York 10; Cincinnati 5. Attendance: 54,621.

Despite walking Pokey Reese to lead off the first inning, Leiter retired the next three hitters without much trouble to keep Cincy off the board.

Leiter retired 13 straight hitters until he walked Ed Taubensee to lead off the eighth inning. Aaron Boone hit into a double play and pinch-hitter Mark Lewis grounded out to shortstop to finish the inning.

Even with the big lead, Leiter was determined to finish the game.

"I really wanted to experience the game on the field as one of the nine players participating in the celebration," he said. "The few times I experienced it, I was always running from the dugout or somewhere else. It's a nice thrill."

Mike Piazza had some postseason experience with the Dodgers, so he knew that playing October baseball is special.

"You've got to enjoy this because very few players have this opportunity," Piazza said. "I've been in a few and we haven't done so great."

This was not only a significant win for the franchise, but it was also special for one particular member of the club. Longtime reliever John Franco had never pitched in the postseason and now he was going for the first time.

"Now I don't have to answer the questions anymore," the Brooklyn-born left-hander said. "Timing is everything in this game."

POSTSEASON

First baseman Donn Clendenon received the ultimate honor when he was named MVP of the Mets' first World Series in 1969. Clendenon hit two home runs against the St. Louis Cardinals on Sept. 24, 1969, to give the Mets their first National League East pennant.

Mets Win First World Championship

When future Mets manager Dave Johnson's fly ball was caught by Cleon Jones at 3:17 PM Eastern, the New York Mets completed a journey that began as a 100–1 longshot to become World Champions.

The Mets beat the "mighty" Baltimore Orioles 5–3 in Game 5 of the 1969 World Series for their fourth straight win and a four-games-to-one victory in the "Fall Classic."

The Mets came from behind as they trailed 3–0 in the sixth inning, but after a controversial hit-by-pitch on Jones, Donn Clendenon slammed a two-run homer off Orioles lefty Dave McNally to make it a one-run game. Home-plate umpire Lou DiMuro originally ruled that the ball did not hit Jones in the foot, but Mets manager Gil Hodges argued that it did and he pointed to the shoe polish on the ball as proof. DiMuro bought it and awarded first base to Jones.

The Mets tied the game when "light-hitting" Al Weis led off the seventh inning with a home run off McNally.

In the bottom of the eighth inning, Ron Swoboda's RBI double snapped a 3–3 tie and he scored on an error by Orioles pitcher Eddie Watt.

The 57,397 fans at Shea were going bonkers in the ninth inning. Future Hall of Famer Frank Robinson walked to lead off the inning, but was forced at second. Brooks Robinson, another future Hall of Famer, flied out to Swoboda in right for the second out.

After Jones caught the final, historic out, fans swarmed onto the field and tore it to pieces. Good thing there were no more games left to play.

'It Gets Through Buckner ... The Mets Win It!'

With two outs and nobody on in the bottom of the 10th inning, the Mets trailed the Boston Red Sox 5–3 in Game 6 of the 1986 World Series. They also trailed three games to two, so their season was literally down to its final out.

Bob Ojeda started Game 3 and Game 6 in the 1986 World Series. He came away a winner in the first outing and left with no decision in the second.

October 25, 1986
World Series Game 6
Mets 6, Red Sox 5 (10 innings)

Gary Carter singled to left to keep the game alive.

Pinch-hitter Kevin Mitchell lined a single to left-center and the Mets had some hope with the tying runs on base.

Ray Knight stroked a single to center to score Carter to make it a 5–4 game and send the tying run to third.

The crowd was announced as 55,078 but at this point, the noise made it seem like double that amount of people in the stands.

The Red Sox went to the bullpen for Bob Stanley and he threw a wild pitch that allowed Mitchell to score the tying run. Knight moved into scoring position as the winning run.

The speedy Mookie Wilson was the next batter and one of the most famous plays in World Series history was about to occur. Wilson hit a slow grounder toward first baseman Bill Buckner.

Hall of Fame broadcaster Vin Scully was working the game on television for NBC Sports. His call told the story of what happened next: "So the winning run is at second base, with two outs, three and two to Mookie Wilson. A little roller, up along first, behind the bag. It gets through Buckner! Here comes Knight and the Mets win it."

Mets Win National League Pennant in Thriller

The Mets won the National League pennant for the third time in franchise history when they beat the Houston Astros 7–6 in a 16-inning classic at the Houston Astrodome. The Mets won the National League Championship Series four games to two.

This was not only one of the greatest postseason games in Mets history. This was one of the great all-time postseason games.

The Mets scored three runs in the top of the 16th to snap a 4–4 tie and they would need all those runs because Houston rallied one more time. The Astros scored twice in their half of the inning, but closer Jesse Orosco finally ended this epic game when he struck out Kevin Bass with the tying and winning runs on base.

"I told Jesse I'd call for other pitches, but just keep shaking me off to confuse him," catcher Gary Carter said. "Just throw the slider."

The Mets trailed 3–0 entering the ninth inning against starter and "Mets killer" Bob Knepper, but Len Dykstra's leadoff triple keyed a three-run rally that tied the game.

"Lenny got the big hit to get us going," Carter said. "You could see the guys in the dugout saying to themselves, hey, we can hit this guy."

Manager Dave Johnson's team took a 4–3 lead in the top of the 14th on Wally Backman's RBI single, but Houston would not lie down as Billy Hatcher tied the game with a solo home run off Orosco that hit the foul pole down the left-field line.

After it was over, Johnson appreciated his first pennant as a manager.

"As a player, you're happy when you win the pennant," he said.

Johnson, who won pennants as a player with the Baltimore Orioles, added, "When you're the manager, to have players shake my hand, to hug me or kiss me. I've never had that experience before. What a series!"

Carter's Single Puts Mets in Control of NLCS

A pitching matchup of the "old" against the "new" ended on a walk-off RBI single by Gary Carter that gave the Mets an exciting 2–1 victory in 12 innings over the Houston Astros.

The win gave the Mets a three-games-to-two lead in the best-of-seven National League Championship Series.

Former Met and Astros starter Nolan Ryan went head-to-head with the Mets ace Dwight Gooden in a classic postseason pitching duel.

Ryan set down the first 13 batters and was protecting a 1–0 lead when Darryl Strawberry lined a ball off the right-field foul pole for a home run and a tie game.

The former Met and future Hall of Famer had no-hit stuff that day, and allowed only two hits in nine innings of work. With Gooden allowing only one run in 10 innings pitched, Strawberry's home run took on added importance.

It became a battle of bullpen closers as Houston's Charlie Kerfeld and New York's Jesse Orosco kept the respective teams at bay.

With one out in the 12th inning, Wally Backman reached on an infield single off the glove of third baseman Denny Walling.

Kerfeld tried to pick the runner off at first base, but threw it away for an error, allowing Backman to reach second.

Keith Hernandez was intentionally walked because the next batter, Gary Carter, was hitting .050 (1-for-21) in the series.

"I'm 1-for-21 and it's frustrating for me," Carter said. "I'm not an .050 hitter. I knew it was just a matter of time."

Carter worked the count to 3–0, but Kerfeld came back with two strikes to make it a full count. Carter then ripped a 3–2 pitch past the mound and second base and into center field.

Backman rounded third and scored the winning run as the Mets' dugout emptied in joy.

Mets Win Second World Championship

When Boston's Marty Barrett struck out to end an incredible series, Mets closer Jesse Orosco threw his glove high into the air in celebration.

The Mets were World Series champions for the second time in franchise history after they knocked off the Red Sox 8–5 in Game 7 at Shea Stadium.

Mookie Wilson (1) is greeted at home plate by Lee Mazzilli as Gary Carter (8) looks on in the sixth inning after Keith Hernandez's two-run single in Game 7 of the 1986 World Series. The Mets went on to beat the Boston Red Sox 8-5 to win the championship.

October 27, 1986
World Series Game 7
Mets 8, Red Sox 5

A crowd of 55,032 was hoping to see the Mets take some momentum from the miraculous comeback of Game 6 into this seventh game. Instead, they saw the Red Sox grab a 3–0 lead in the second inning.

Dwight Evans and Rich Gedman slammed back-to-back home runs and future Hall of Famer Wade Boggs added a RBI single off starter Ron Darling.

Sid Fernandez relieved in the fourth inning and gave the Mets a needed lift out of the bullpen with 2 $^1/_3$ scoreless innings to keep the game close.

The Mets tied the game in the sixth inning. Keith Hernandez's two-run single and an RBI force-out tied the game 3–3.

Ray Knight led off the seventh inning with a home run to give the Mets a 4–3 lead. Rafael Santana singled in a run and Hernandez's sacrifice fly made it 6–3.

Boston cut it to 6–5 in the eighth inning on a two-run double by Dwight Evans, but the Mets struck again in the home half.

Darryl Strawberry clubbed a monstrous home run to lead off the inning and Orosco singled in a run to make it an 8–5 game.

Orosco breezed through the ninth inning as the crowd was on its feet in anticipation of victory.

Barrett struck out and the coronation began.

The Mets rallied from losing the first two games at home to beat the Red Sox in seven games.

"We were destined to win," Darling said.

"We had to win four-out-of-five going to Boston one week ago," Hernandez said, "but the ability to bounce back from adversity marks this club."

Pratt's Walk-Off Homer Sends Mets to NLCS

Arizona center fielder Steve Finley drifted back on Todd Pratt's long fly ball. Finley ran out of room and made a desperate attempt to keep the ball from going over the wall to end the game and the series. Finley made a leaping attempt and when he landed without the ball, Pratt and the Mets knew they had won.

Pratt's walk-off home run in the bottom of the 10th inning off Arizona's Matt Mantei gave the Mets a 4–3 victory over the Arizona Diamondbacks that clinched the series in Game 4 of the National League Division Series.

Al Leiter gave the Mets seven solid innings, but with two outs in the eighth, Arizona mounted a rally by putting two runners on base against the left-hander.

Armando Benitez relieved Leiter and promptly gave up a two-run double to Jay Bell as Arizona took a 3–2 lead.

Luis Gonzalez was intentionally walked and Matt Willliams lined a single to left, but left fielder Melvin Mora made a perfect throw to Pratt at the plate to nab Bell and end the inning.

Pratt said, "I saw him rounding third and Melvin releasing the ball at the same time and I was just saying, please be on line."

The Mets came right back thanks to Arizona right fielder Tony Womack, who dropped a fly ball to put runners on second and third base with no one out.

Roger Cedeno's sacrifice fly tied the game to set up Pratt's heroics.

"I know I'm not Mike Piazza," Pratt, the backup catcher, said. "But for one swing I was."

When Pratt faced hard throwers like Mantei, he would usually choke up on the bat, but this time, he did not.

"I'm swinging," Pratt said. "I need to get out in front of this one, and he actually threw it to where my favorite pitch is, a little up and out over the plate."

Ventura's 'Grand Slam Single' Forces Game Six

Robin Ventura hit a "grand slam single" in the bottom of the 15th inning to lead the Mets to a 4–3 win over the Atlanta Braves in Game 6 of the National League Championship Series.

With the bases loaded and one out, Ventura drove a pitch from Kevin McGlinchy over the wall in right-center field for what should have been a walk-off grand slam. After rounding first, Ventura's teammates ran on the field and surrounded the "hero," who never reached second or touched the other bases.

According to the scoring rules of Major League Baseball, since he didn't touch second, third or home and the winning run already scored, Ventura was credited with a single, instead of a home run.

The Mets took a 2–0 lead in the first inning on a two-run homer by John Olerud off Greg Maddux.

Atlanta tied the game in the fourth inning on an RBI double by Chipper Jones and an RBI single by Brian Jordan.

It remained tied for the next 10 innings, but the Braves had a chance in the top of the 13th. With two outs and a runner on first base, Chipper Jones lined a ball to right-center field. Keith Lockhart tried to score, but right fielder Melvin Mora threw him out at home.

In the top of the 15th, the Braves took a 3–2 lead on Keith Lockhart's RBI triple and it appeared as if Atlanta was on their way to the World Series.

The Mets would not quit.

Shawon Dunston began the winning rally with a single to center after an incredible at-bat. He saw 12 pitches and had six fouls with a 3–2 count.

After Dunston stole second base, pinch-hitter Matt Franco walked.

Edgardo Alfonzo's sacrifice bunt moved the runners to second and third base. Olerud was intentionally walked to load the bases and Roger Cedeno ran for Franco.

The strategy backfired on the Braves when McGlinchy walked Todd Pratt on four pitches with the bases loaded to tie the game 3–3.

Historically, Ventura was very successful with the bases loaded and the veteran third baseman knew they had the 22-year-old McGlinchy on the ropes.

"It's different when the bases are loaded and the guy has already walked a guy," Ventura said. "He really can't fool around and throw a bunch of pitches in the dirt."

Ventura ran the count to 2–1 and then lifted a deep fly to right-center field. Once the ball left the bat, the outcome was never in doubt because, at the very least, the drive was deep enough to score Cedeno from third base.

But the ball kept traveling and it went over the wall for what was initially believed to be a walk-off grand slam.

As Ventura went around first base, he was met by a mob of his teammates who did not let him touch the other bases.

Official scorer Red Foley properly credited Ventura with an RBI single as the Mets kept their season alive for one more game.

Franco Strikes Out Bonds to End a Classic

Mets reliever John Franco struck out three-time National League MVP Barry Bonds in the bottom of the 10th inning with the tying run on base to preserve a thrilling 5–4 win over the San Francisco Giants at Pacific Bell Park. The victory evened the National League Division Series at a game apiece.

The Mets were two outs away from tying the series when Giants first baseman J.T. Snow clubbed a game-tying, three-run home run off closer Armando Benitez.

It was a stunning blow, but the Mets showed their character by staging a two-out rally in the ensuing inning. With two outs and no one on, pinch-hitter Darryl Hamilton doubled into the gap in right-center field.

Jay Payton followed with an RBI single off losing pitcher Felix Rodriguez to give the Mets a one-run lead.

Franco entered with a runner on base and no one out in the 10th. A sacrifice bunt sent Armando Rios to second base, but he tried to take third on Bill Mueller's grounder to short and was thrown out for the second out.

Bonds was 3-for-16 in the series before facing Franco in the 10th, but with 49 regular-season home runs, it made for quite a finish.

The slugger looked at a called third strike from Franco and the Mets had a gutty postseason win.

"This is probably the biggest moment of my career," Franco said. "It's the biggest save of my career."

Agbayani Walk-Off Gives Mets 2-1 Edge

Benny Agbayani slammed a walk-off, one-out, home run in the bottom of the 13th inning to give the Mets a 3–2 win over the San Francisco Giants and a two-games-to-one lead in the best-of-five National League Division Series.

The Hawaiian-born Agbayani was an after-thought in spring training, but he made himself a valuable commodity because of the faith vested in him by manager Bobby Valentine.

"Bobby Valentine told me things have a way of working out," Agbayani said. "I understand that. Now I do."

The Giants took a 2–0 lead in the fourth inning, but the Mets chipped back with a run in the sixth on Timo Perez's RBI single and then tied the game on Edgardo Alfonzo's RBI double in the eighth.

Rick Reed started and gave up two runs in six innings, but five relievers got the job done with scoreless ball over the final seven innings.

After tying the game, the Mets had runners in scoring position for the next four innings in a row but could not score. The Giants had opportunities as well but could not cash in as they left 16 runners on base.

After Robin Ventura grounded out, Agbayani unloaded on a 1–0 fastball from losing pitcher Aaron Fultz and drove it over the left-field wall for the dramatic victory.

Agbayani received the traditional greeting at home plate, led by utility man Joe McEwing.

"You throw all the money out because it means nothing," McEwing said. "This is why we start playing when we're kids, to get to this point, to have a chance to win the World Series. It's so awesome that every pitch means something. Every pitch counts."

Jones Pitches 1-Hitter to Push Mets into NLCS

Bobby J. Jones tossed a one-hit shutout to lead the Mets to a 4–0 victory over the San Francisco Giants in Game 4 of the National League Division Series at Shea Stadium.

The win put the Mets into the 2000 National League Championship Series against the St. Louis Cardinals, but it was the veteran right-hander's performance that was the "talk of the town."

Catcher Mike Piazza said Jones took advantage of a Giants lineup that seemed to be trying too hard after they fell behind in the first inning.

The Mets took a 2–0 lead on a two-run homer by Robin Ventura off losing pitcher Mark Gardner.

Jones set down the first 12 Giants hitters and was in total command.

Jeff Kent led off the fifth inning and lined a ball just foul over the left-field wall, but he doubled to left (the ball grazed Ventura's glove) for what turned out to be the only hit for the Giants.

After the double, Jones issued two walks and loaded the bases. With two outs, the Giants, who were short on pitchers, decided to let Gardner hit and he popped out to end the inning.

The Giants would not get another sniff as Jones sat down the final 12 hitters, including Barry Bonds, who lined out to center to end the game.

Jones felt he had the best command of his pitches that he ever had. Mets manager Bobby Valentine agreed, but added, "People look at the speed gun, he's only throwing 84, 86 miles an hour, but its how he complements that with his curveball, change-up and a slider that torments hitters. He's why we're here."

Mets Claim Their Fourth National League Pennant

Mike Hampton went the distance on a three-hit shutout as the Mets won the fourth National League pennant in franchise history with a 7–0 win over the St. Louis Cardinals at Shea Stadium.

Mike Hampton pitched a complete-game three-hitter over the St. Louis Cardinals to lift the Mets to their fourth National League pennant in 2000.

October 16, 2000

National League Championship Series Game 5
Mets 7, Cardinals 0

When Mets center fielder Timo Perez caught a fly ball off the bat of pinch-hitter Rick Wilkins, the Mets had wrapped up the National League Championship Series 4–1 and were on their way to the fourth World Series in Mets history.

The Mets jumped on losing pitcher Pat Hentgen for three runs in the first inning. Run-scoring singles by Edgardo Alfonzo and Robin Ventura plated two runs and the Mets added a third on a ground-out.

In the fourth inning, Shea Stadium and a sellout crowd of 55,695 rocked when Todd Zeile cleared the bases with a double for a 6–0 lead.

The Mets completed the scoring in the seventh inning as they scored a run on a wild pitch by Rick Ankiel.

Hampton was rolling along as he walked only one and struck out eight in going the distance.

There was an incident in the eighth inning as tempers flared when Jay Payton was hit in the face by a pitch from Dave Veres. The center fielder charged the mound as both benches emptied.

After the game, Payton, who was cut and had some discoloring around his eye, had the satisfaction of being on the team that's going to the World Series.

"We're going to the World Series," Payton said. "I'd take a shot to the head every year to get to the World Series."

Mets Take NLCS Lead in Brawl-Filled Contest

Rusty Staub hit two home runs as the Mets topped the Cincinnati Reds 9–2 in Game 3 of the National League Championship Series at Shea Stadium. The game was marred by a brawl between Pete Rose of the Reds and Bud Harrelson of the Mets.

The incident occurred in the top of the fifth inning. With Rose on first base, Joe Morgan hit a grounder to first. Rose went in hard at second base to break up the double play, but Harrelson took umbrage with that and the two started a fight near second base.

"I thought he hit me with his elbow on the left side of the head intentionally," Harrelson said. "It was strictly a spontaneous thing."

During his at-bat, Rose was brushed back by a Jerry Koosman pitch, which may have sparked the furor initially.

"I don't know if he was throwing at me," Rose said. "But he'd (Koosman) had good control all day before that."

Rose felt as if he had done nothing wrong.

"I just slid in there the way I always do, to break up a double play," Rose said. "He called me a name and I grabbed him."

Both benches and bullpens emptied as another fight broke out between Pedro Borbon of the Reds and Buzz Capra of the Mets.

"He (Borbon) blindsided me on the right cheek," Capra said.

A little bit of humor ensued when Borbon left the field mistakenly wearing a Mets cap instead of his Reds hat.

When he realized that he was wearing the hat of the "enemy," he took it off, bit the cap and tossed it away to the delight of the 53,697 fans at Shea.

Those same fans caused another problem in the bottom of the fifth inning when the Reds took the field. Rose, who was in left field, was bombarded with flying objects (including whiskey bottles) from the left-field stands that prompted Reds manager Sparky Anderson to remove his team from the field.

A forfeit was a real possibility if the crowd did not calm down.

With that scenario in mind, Mets manager Yogi Berra led a contingent that included Tom Seaver, Willie Mays, Cleon Jones and Rusty Staub out to left field to implore the fans to behave themselves so the game could be resumed.

October 8, 1973
National League Championship Series Game 3
Mets 9, Reds 2

It was Mays' first appearance since he announced his retirement (see: Sept. 20, 1973) and with his arms outstretched, he pleaded for calm.

The five-man peace committee marched back to the dugout, the debris was cleared and the game resumed.

No one was tossed and the crowd kept up their anger with their voices and not their throwing arms.

In order to ensure that calm would prevail, the New York Police Department stationed officers along the foul line and in the stands in left field.

When the Reds left Shea via chartered bus, they had a police escort for the trip back to Manhattan while several hundred fans shouted and booed.

The Mets already had a 9–2 lead when the melee broke out.

Staub got things going in the first inning by smacking a 2–2 pitch with two outs for a solo home run off losing pitcher Ross Grimsley.

Staub hit a three-run homer in the second inning to key a five-run rally. The Mets took a 6–0 lead and were on their way to another playoff victory.

ACKNOWLEDGMENTS

There are so many people to thank who contributed in one way or another to the making of this book.

Let me start with my lovely wife, Kathy, who I've been with for more than 30 years. Of course, I have to thank my two sons, Danny and Jake, my sister, Carol Shore, and her husband, Barry. My wonderful nieces, Wendy and Sharon Shore, and their families, and of course, Melanie Shore.

The New York Mets organization, which has always treated me as a professional and has afforded me the privilege of covering the team as a reporter for the past 30 years.

To the New York Mets Media Relations Department, led by Jay Horwitz, who began his Mets tenure in 1980, the same year that I started in the business of covering baseball. Many thanks to Ethan Wilson, Billy Harner, Shannon Forde, Nicole Chayet, and the entire Media Relations staff.

To Bill Shannon, who has been my mentor and who believed in me enough to put his own reputation on the line in supporting my desire to become an "official scorer."

To my fellow scorers, including Jordan Sprechman, David Freeman, and Billy Altman.

To the friends I've made while covering the team. Mets public address announcer Alex Anthony, broadcasters Howie Rose, Wayne Hagin, Ed Coleman, and Gary Cohen, along with "the immortal" Chris Majkowski.

This book would not have become a reality without the players. Al Leiter, Ken Singleton, Ron Darling, Keith Hernandez, Pedro Martinez, and Dave Campbell have always been helpful. Thanks for your time and your friendship.

A special thanks to Tom Seaver, who was very gracious in giving me a few minutes of his time. Of course, he gets many mentions in the book.

Former Mets manager Willie Randolph, my first and longtime friend from the playing field, and Billy Sample, the former Yankee who has become a good friend over the years.

Kevin Kernan, Peter Botte, Bill Madden, Murray Chass, Dave Anderson, John Feinstein are all professionals with whom I've had the pleasure of interacting over the years.

Thanks to former Mets beat reporters Marty Noble and Jack O'Connell, who helped me with some historical notes from their own personal experiences.

My buddies at the Elias Sports Bureau, starting with John Labombarda, Bob Waterman (my "right hand man" at Citi Field), Bob Rosen, and all my Elias softball teammates.

Bryan Herrity, Scott Orgera, and Jeff Melnik, who work with me at Mets and Yankee games; Larry Fleisher, Russ Cohen, who is my hockey compatriot and a big Mets fan, Eric Mirlis, Rich Mancuso, and Mitch Mele, who may teach me a thing or two about umpiring.

Steve Cohen, Nick Pavlatos, Steve Torre, Chris Russo, Dino Costa, Glenn Younnes. Zig Fracassi, Andrew Bogusch, and all my colleagues at Sirius/XM Satellite Radio. Some of the ideas for this book may have been created in the "newsroom."

Radio friends Steve Somers and Bob Heussler of WFAN. Bob's passion for the Mets helped me with getting some perspective of the team's history. Steve has always been a friend.

Jay Nadler, Corey Friedman, Gregg Trachtenberg, Mark Feinman, Lew Rose, Rick Goldfarb, Eddie Gorman, Gary Simon, Gary Axelbank, Dean Hoffman, Jay Brustman, Colm and Sascha Cahill, Andres Wirkmaa, and Lew and Judy Stiefel are all good friends from outside the business.

My teammates, past and present, from Bullets basketball and all my softball friends from the Bronx. Thanks for letting me be part of the team.

Speaking of the past, Franklin Cruz and Wilfredo Sotolongo were two of my baseball teammates at Lehman College in the 1970s. We've recently hooked up again and I'm thankful for that.

Ken Samelson, who got me started in the business of writing books.

My best friends in radio, Rich Coutinho and Mike Mancuso. From being around Rich, I've developed an appreciation for the Mets and their history. Mike is a huge Mets fan but doesn't show it like Rich does. Thanks guys.

A very special and heartfelt thanks to David Wright, who honored me by authoring the Foreword.

I'd be remiss if I didn't thank Mitch Rogatz, Tom Bast, and Adam Motin of Triumph Books. Enjoy working with you gentlemen and thank you for your faith in me.

Always thinking of my late mother and father, Ruth and Sidney Karpin.

I acknowledge those who helped me along the way and continue to extend their support.

REFERENCES

BOOKS

Bjarkman, Peter C. *The New York Mets Encyclopedia*. Champaign, Ill.: Sports Publishing, Inc., 2000.

Lang, Jack, and Peter Simon. *The New York Mets: 25 Years of Baseball Magic*. New York: H. Holt, 1987.

The New York Mets 2010 Media Guide.

WEB SITES

Baseball Reference (www.baseball-reference.com)

ProQuest-New York Times Historical (www.proquest.com)

Retrosheet (www.retrosheet.com)

Wikipedia (www.wikipedia.com)